ROUTLEDGE LIBRARY EDITIONS:
POLITICAL PROTEST

Volume 12

LIBERTY AND ORDER

LIBERTY AND ORDER
Public Order Policing in a Capital City

P.A.J. WADDINGTON

Routledge
Taylor & Francis Group

LONDON AND NEW YORK

First published in 1994 by UCL Press

This edition first published in 2022
by Routledge
2 Park Square, Milton Park, Abingdon, Oxon OX14 4RN

and by Routledge
605 Third Avenue, New York, NY 10158

Routledge is an imprint of the Taylor & Francis Group, an informa business

© 1994 P. A. J. Waddington

British Library Cataloguing in Publication Data
A catalogue record for this book is available from the British Library

ISBN: 978-1-03-203038-8 (Set)
ISBN: 978-1-00-319086-8 (Set) (ebk)
ISBN: 978-1-03-204271-8 (Volume 12) (hbk)
ISBN: 978-1-03-204275-6 (Volume 12) (pbk)
ISBN: 978-1-00-319123-0 (Volume 12) (ebk)

DOI: 10.4324/9781003191230

Publisher's Note
The publisher has gone to great lengths to ensure the quality of this reprint but points out that some imperfections in the original copies may be apparent.

Disclaimer
The publisher has made every effort to trace copyright holders and would welcome correspondence from those they have been unable to trace.

Liberty and order
Public order policing in a capital city

P. A. J. Waddington
University of Reading

UCL
PRESS

First published in 1994 by UCL Press
UCL Press Limited
University College London
Gower Street
London WC1E 6BT

The name of University College London (UCL) is a registered
trade mark used by UCL Press with the consent of the owner.

ISBN:
1-85728-226-4 HB
1-85728-227-2 PB

British Library Cataloguing-in-Publication Data
A CIP catalogue record for this book is available from the British Library.

Library of Congress Cataloging-in-Publication Data
Waddington. P. A. J.
    Liberty and order : public order policing in a capital city/
P. A. J. Waddington.
        p.   cm.
    Includes bibliographical references and index.
    ISBN 1-85728-226-4. — ISBN 1-85728-227-2 (pbk.)
    1. Law enforcement—England—London. 2. Great Britain.
Metropolitan Police Office. 3. Police—England—London. 4. Human
rights England—London. 5. Riots—England—London.
6. Demonstrations—England—London.   7. Rites and ceremonies—
England—London.   I. Title
HV8196.L6W33 1994
363.2'09421—dc20   94-33893
                                                            CIP

Typeset in Times.
Printed and bound by
Biddles Ltd, Guildford and King's Lynn, England.

To Sir Peter Imbert and Alan Smith
with gratitude and affection

Contents

Contents

Acknowledgements

This research would not have been possible without the support of the Nuffield Foundation and Leverhulme Trust. For the period from September 1990 to December 1991 the Nuffield Foundation reimbursed travelling expenses incurred in my frequent visits to London to attend meetings and observe demonstrations. From the following January to December the Leverhulme Trust awarded a grant that not only covered travelling expenditure, but also allowed me a year's study leave to undertake observations on a full-time basis. I am enormously indebted to both these charities for allowing this research to go ahead.

I am no less indebted to my colleagues at the Department of Sociology, University of Reading, without whose tolerance and forbearance I would not have been able to reschedule my other commitments so as to observe public order operations during the particularly fascinating period of the Gulf war.

It goes without saying that without the support of the Metropolitan Police this research would simply not have been possible. I cannot thank Sir Peter Imbert enough for the trust and confidence he has been prepared to vest in me over more than a decade. Obviously, it helps when the "boss" authorizes research, but there are many others in any organization who could easily have frustrated this research by passivity and minimal co-operation. Throughout the Metropolitan Police I never once felt that there was any semblance of resistance to my presence. This is truly remarkable when one considers the sensitivity of many of the public order operations that I observed in the immediate aftermath of the anti poll tax riot. This willingness to accept the scrutiny of an external observer is, I am sure, a telling index of the confidence that officers of all ranks had in themselves and their colleagues.

Throughout this research I have intruded into the professional lives of too many officers to thank individually. I can thank them only as a whole for their generosity and co-operation and hope that this book does them the justice they deserve. There are some on whom I relied so heavily that it would be discourteous not to thank them individually. The staff of the Public Order Branch were always welcoming, friendly, helpful and generous. I relied enormously on Peter Bean during the initial phase of my research. Without his help I am sure that I would not have negotiated the thickets of bureaucracy so effectively. Kevin Delaney both amused and informed me, and, subsequently, Mike Davies showed me the same backing as his predecessor. Alex Ross proved a great support. Martin, Dave, Jack, Gordon, Michael, John, Marie, Susan, Jenny, Rod and Shane all contributed to making my life easier at the expense of making their own more difficult. Graham Bartlett not only went to great lengths to assist my research, but contributed by providing a critique of some early writings that was both academically and professionally informed. The staff of the Special Events Office at 8 Area Headquarters were no less generous in their helpfulness and hospitality. Deputy Assistant Commissioner Tony Speed and Commander Tom Laidlaw (and later John Purnell) were unstinting in their support of my research. I came to rely on Eddy (and his predecessor John), Kevin, Bruce, Elaine and Dave for all manner of assistance from coffee on cold winter afternoons to advice and guidance. Senior officers from 8 Area accepted my presence with far more good humour than could reasonably have been expected: to John Ricketts, Trevor, Malcolm, Mike, Gerry, Alan, George, Dick, both Franks and both Steves, I give my sincere thanks. I was an equal burden to the officers who commanded the Notting Hill Carnival, and they too were unsparing in their hospitality and co-operation. I would like to thank Deputy Assistant Commissioner Alan Fry and Commander Ian Quinn for allowing me to intrude into the first carnival for which they were responsible (and which must have presented itself as an awesome responsibility). I must also thank especially those officers whom I accompanied during the carnival – Jim and Dennis – for their help and co-operation.

Apart from the police, I would like to take this opportunity to thank the many protest organizers and others involved in the events I observed for also accepting my intrusion with more good grace than I had any reason to expect. I wish to thank especially Peter Tatchell of "OutRage!" for his assistance in writing the chapter on that group's campaign and Nell Myers of the National Union of Mineworkers, who commented on the chapter on negotiations.

Finally, I must thank all the staff of the Metropolitan Police Catering Service for keeping me more than well supplied with food and drink. I will never again look upon black pudding without thinking of them!

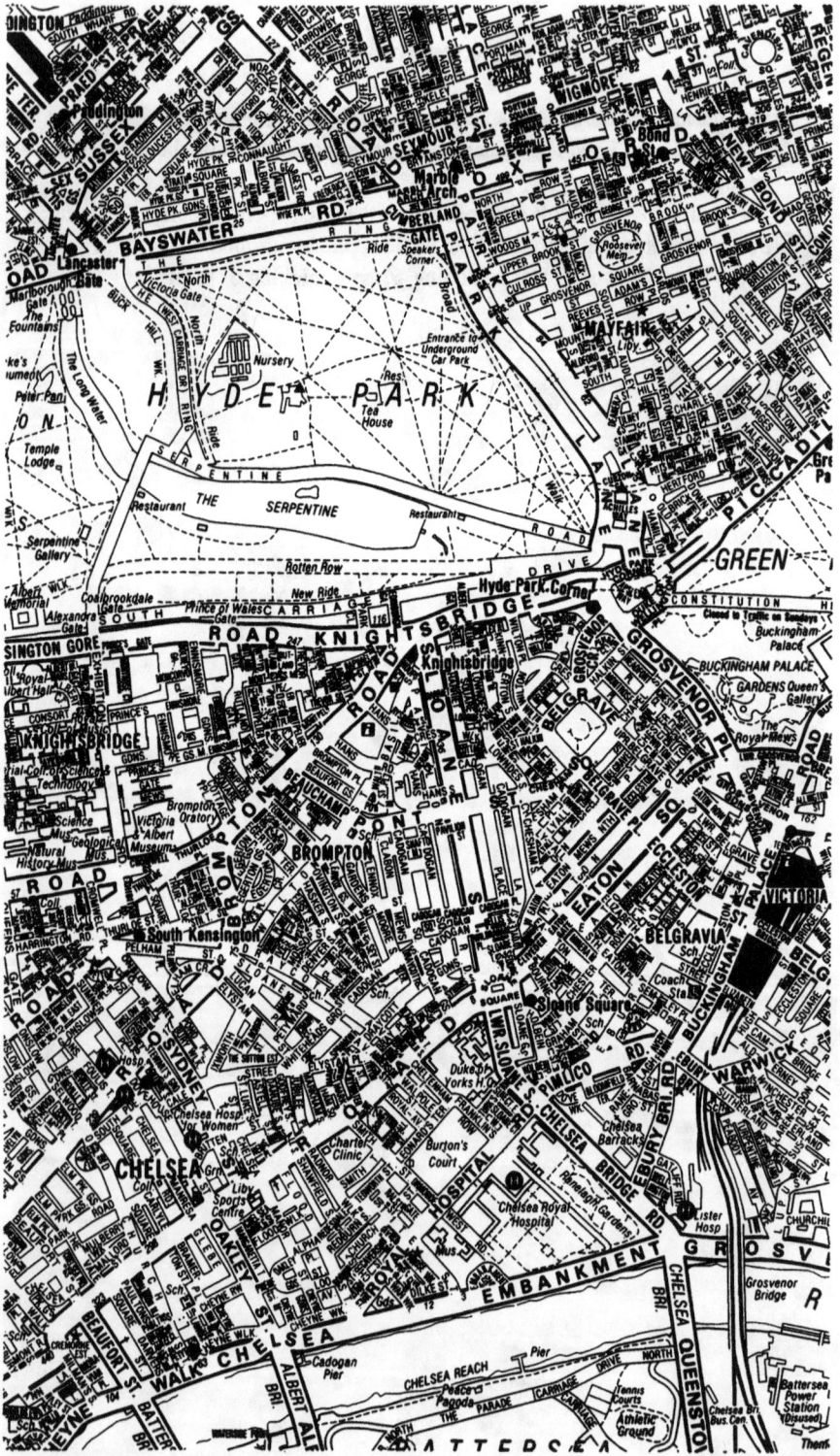

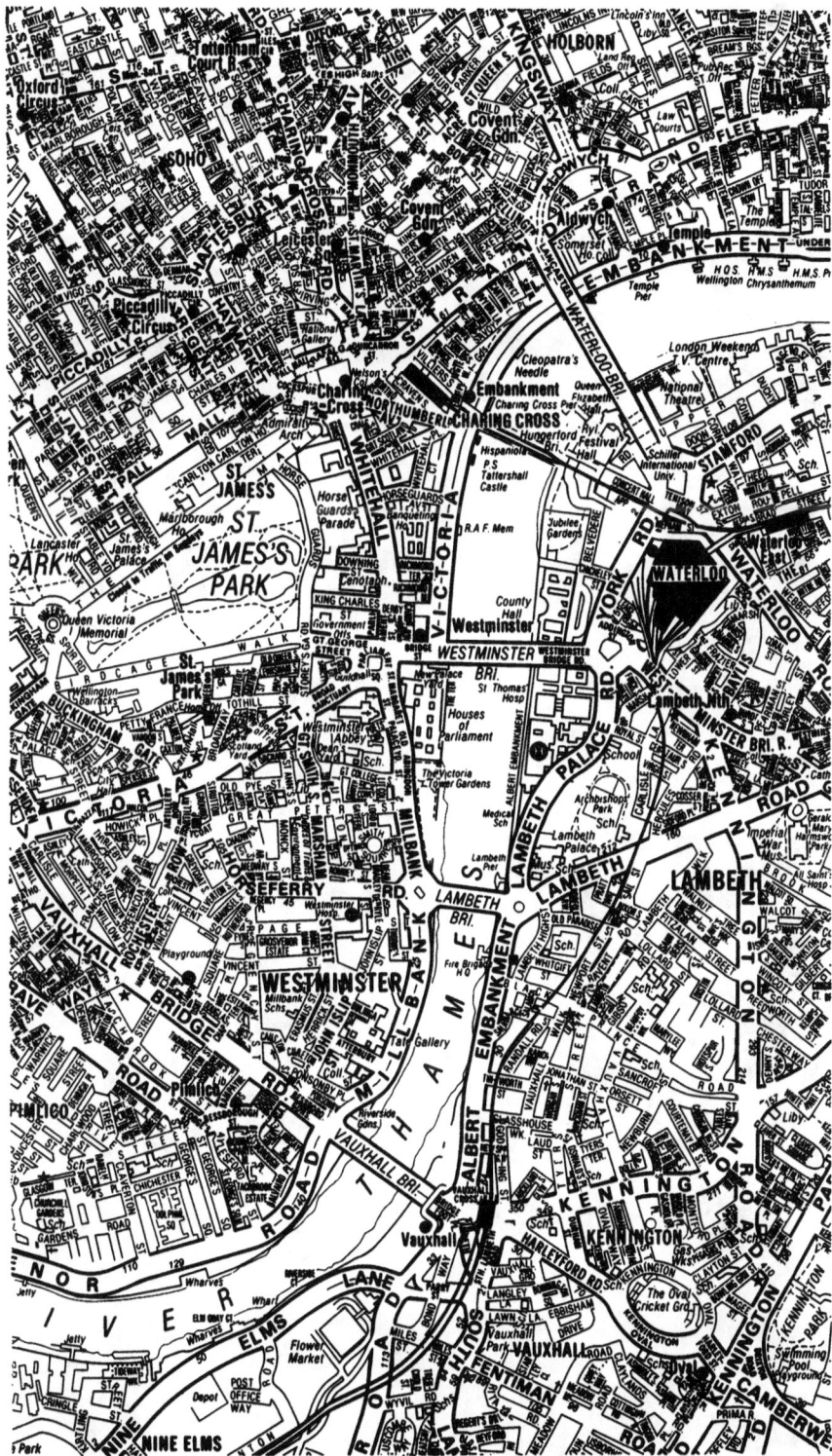

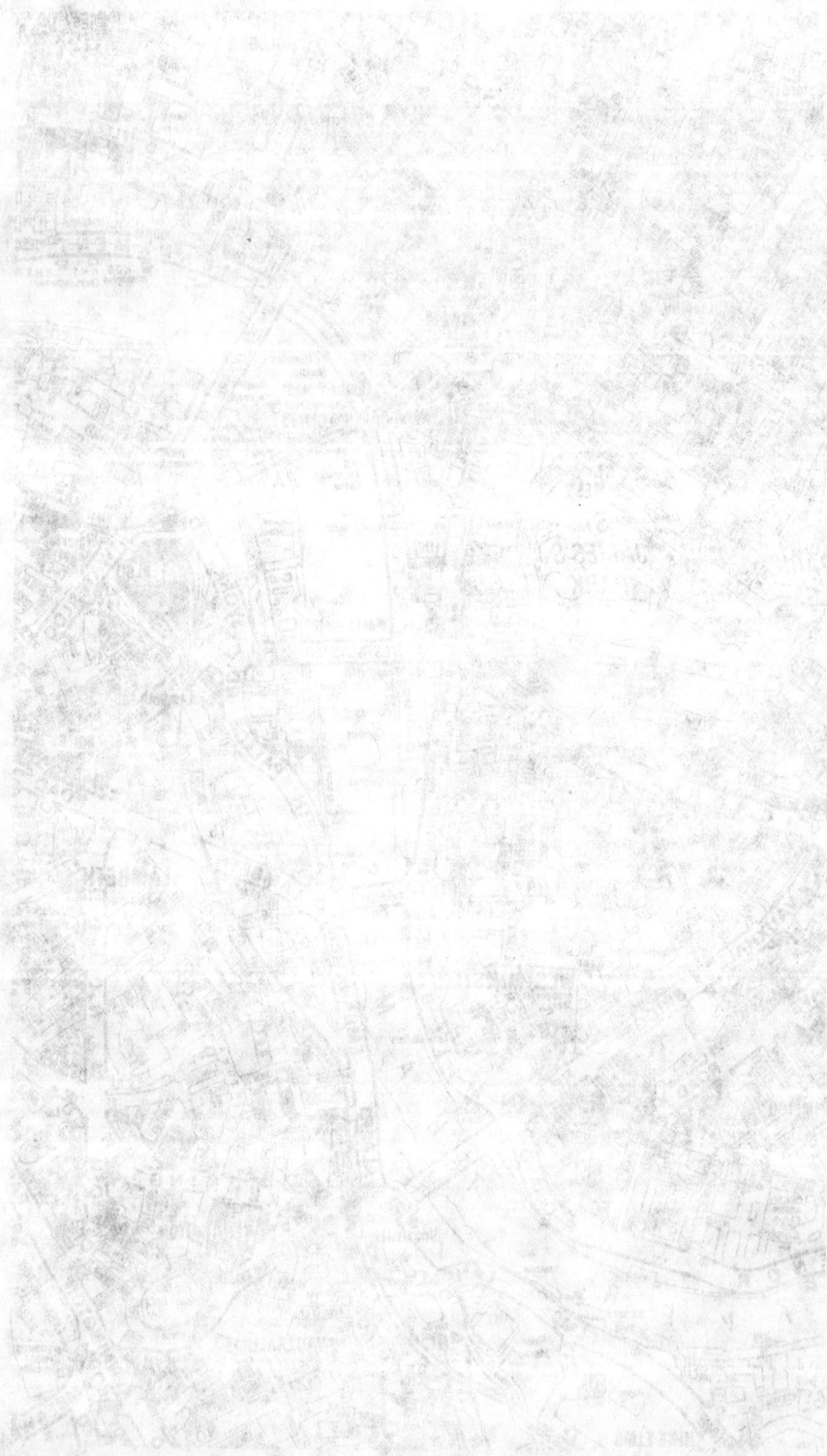

CHAPTER 1

Taking rioting, protesting and policing seriously

Introduction

In the Philippines, East Germany and other former Soviet bloc countries of eastern Europe, peaceful protestors confronted the military might of authoritarian regimes and defeated them. When counter-revolution threatened democratic reform in Russia itself, "people power" became the saviour of democracy. But "people power" does not invariably succeed: in Tiananmen Square it was literally crushed by the forces of totalitarian authoritarianism. Nor is "people power" the inevitable servant of democratic values. In South Africa, violent protest by the extreme right has aimed to obstruct democratic reform. Throughout re-unified Germany, protesting crowds have resurrected the spectre of Nazism, illuminated in the glow of burning refugee hostels.

These are just some of the many faces of public protest. They illustrate the fundamental moral and political dilemmas that it poses. Mass action can be the defender or destroyer of democracy. Official repression can extinguish freedom and liberty or defend the weak and vulnerable. Liberal democracies must steer a precarious path between these opposing evils. In liberal democracies, those who repeatedly find themselves treading that path are the police. They in effect decide, within the law, the boundaries of freedom of protest. Protestors who overstep that boundary are liable to arrest, and assemblies that break the law may be dispersed. These are onerous responsibilities, but how they are exercised has remained largely obscured from public view. When protest turns conspicuously to violence, scenes of police battling with rioters are widely broadcast by the news media, but how representative of normality are such scenes? How do police deal with routine protests that may never reach the attention of the news media? Are freedom and liberty subverted or safeguarded? Are there reasons to fear for the health of democracy? These are the questions to which this book is addressed.

In this chapter, the wider context in which these questions arise will be discussed. Since it is rioting that has brought the issues of the policing of public order to academic attention, it is with this that we will begin. What are the causes of the riots that convulsed the ghettos of American cities in the 1960s and British inner-cities in the 1980s? What continuity, if any, do such riots have with more obvious forms of protest? What is the nature of protest and what are its implications for policing? What issues have given rise to protest throughout liberal democracies and how were they expressed in London during the early 1990s?

Taking riots seriously

The riots that engulfed major American cities during the 1960s, echoed in British inner-cities two decades later, propelled policing on to both the political and academic research agendas. The Kerner (1968) and Scarman (1981) reports authoritatively placed much of the responsibility for out-breaks of disorder upon insensitive and racist policing. Police reform, designed to re-legitimate policing amongst ethnic minorities, became a major plank of government policy on both sides of the Atlantic. Spurred by the shock waves that these episodes of rioting had on public life, policing also became an object of intense academic interest. Naturally, a focus of that academic interest lay in the causation and policing of riots.

Riot-as-protest

The academic debate that followed was remarkably consistent on both sides of the Atlantic and centred on the repudiation of the so-called "riff-raff" theory of rioting. This view, owing its intellectual origins to the nineteenth-century French theorist Gustav LeBon (1896), attributes outbreaks of rioting to irrationality – crowds liberate the beast that lurks in the breast of human-kind. It was readily apparent that many official commentators adhered to much the same view as LeBon, dismissing the riots as orgies of lawlessness (McCone 1965). Critics of this view also detected echoes of LeBon in theories that attributed the riots to the psychology of rioters. Theories of

2

"de-individuation" (Zimbardo 1970), imitative learning (Berkowitz 1973), frustration–aggression (Feierabend & Feierabend 1966, 1969, 1973) and relative deprivation (Gurr 1968a, 1968b, 1968c, 1969, 1970) were all repudiated because the motives they imputed to rioters did not conform to the rioters' own perception of their actions. Rioters who felt they were expressing their rage at racial discrimination and police brutality and harassment were told that they were expressing some ulterior motive. Likewise, theories that traced the origins of riots to social and economic conditions that rioters did not comprehend were also rejected. Davies' "J-curve" theory (Davies 1962, 1969) suggested that outbreaks of disorder tend to occur when a period of gradual improvement is interrupted by a downturn. This implies that rioters are playthings of forces beyond their control. Perhaps the most prominent theory of collective behaviour – Smelser's "value added" theory (Smelser 1962) – was doubly repudiated. It traces outbreaks of collective behaviour to "strain" in the functioning of the social structure, compounding that by attributing riotous motivations to "generalized beliefs" that may be exaggerated and distorted (Currie & Skolnick 1972 but see also Smelser 1972).

The alternative, which came to acquire the status of an orthodoxy, was that rioters had to be taken seriously. Their motives had to be taken at face value: they *were* expressing profound grievances against racism and police brutality. In the United States this was articulated most coherently by Skolnick (1969), Fogelson (1970, 1971) and Hahn & Feagin (1973), and in Britain by Kettle & Hodges (1982) and Benyon (1984, 1987). It was implicitly and authoritatively endorsed by official commissions of inquiry (Kerner 1968, Scarman 1981). And it had enormous implications for policing. If rioters were to be taken seriously, then their allegations of police racism, harassment and brutality could not be dismissed. Indeed, much scholarly attention focused not upon the riots themselves, but upon the deprivations and discrimination suffered by black people in American city ghettos and British inner-cities (see, for example, Cowell et al. 1982).

The political imperative for taking rioters seriously is clear: it counters the attempt by the political establishment to dismiss rioting as merely a lawless outburst and thus to discredit the grievances of ethnic minorities. Insisting that rioting is a form of political protest dignifies it and demands that the grievances of rioters be addressed. In the political context, as Turner (1969) argues, the acceptance of violence as protest rather than as crime is crucial if demands to remedy grievances are to receive attention. Protest has the status of a communicative act, even when it is violent.

3

> Looting is not primarily a means of acquiring property, as it is nor-
> mally viewed in disaster situations; breaking store windows and
> burning buildings is not merely a perverted form of amusement or
> immoral vengeance like the usual vandalism and arson; threats of
> violence and injury to persons are not simply criminal actions. All
> are expressions of outrage against injustice of sufficient magnitude
> and duration to render the resort to such exceptional means of com-
> munication understandable to the observer. (Turner 1969: 186)

Thus imbued, demands for redress of grievances can legitimately be press-
ed, for the aggrieved rioter is as much a victim of injustice as a perpetrator
of violence (Lipsky & Olson 1973).

Although the theory of riot-as-protest was undoubtedly highly influential
as a political theory and programme of reform, its theoretical adequacy was
much more doubtful. I have argued at length elsewhere (P. Waddington
1991, ch. 7) that the theory is better regarded as a means of attributing
blame and responsibility rather than explaining the aetiology of riot. A central problem in assessing the explanatory utility of this notion lies precisely
in identifying the views of rioters that are to be taken seriously. As Berk
(1972) points out, there are enormous methodological difficulties in study-
ing riots and he chastises researchers for making assertions in the absence
of necessary data. Because those who live in areas afflicted by riots suffer
deprivations and discrimination that would justify their rioting does not
mean that, at the time of the riot, deprivation and discrimination were
uppermost in their minds.

It is plausible to suppose that some riots are expressions of grievances,
whereas others are not. Gary Marx (1972) suggests distinguishing between
"issue-oriented" and "issueless" riots, so as to differentiate riots-as-protest
from other collective outbursts. Unwittingly, however, Marx succeeds in
accentuating the methodological difficulties identified by Berk (1972), for
how are we to establish whether any given instance of disorder was "issue
oriented" or "issueless"? Following Marx, David Waddington argues:

> Whereas the disorder associated with violent demonstrations, riots
> or industrial confrontation tends to focus on the defence or asser-
> tion of "rights" which are perceived as being violated or denied,
> football hooliganism is an issueless form of activity, pursued pri-
> marily for pleasure and excitement, and to achieve the status and
> respect of one's peers. (1992: 138)

The problem with this lies in adjudicating which of these motivations prompt disorder. David Waddington elsewhere (D. Waddington et al. 1989) maintains that a clash between police and young men accused of spitting on passers-by in a shopping mall *was* "issue oriented" because "territory is at stake". If such a claim to territory is to qualify as "issue oriented" then why should football hooligans be deemed "issueless"? Is attacking rival fans, as did supporters of Liverpool FC in the Heysel stadium, resulting in 38 deaths, "for pleasure and excitement" or to assert the "right" of Liverpool supporters exclusively to occupy a section of the terraces? Such attributions are inevitably contestable and are often contested as part of the process of political inquiry that follows significant disorder, but academic researchers are rarely in a position to confirm any attribution because they lack the necessary data.

Black ghetto and inner-city rioters were dignified as "issue oriented" for well-intentioned but transparently *political* reasons. However, participation in these riots may have had a more prosaic academic explanation. McPhail & Miller (1973) suggest that participation in rioting may have simply been a consequence of availability. Most riots in America and Britain occurred on warm summer weekend evenings near the intersections of major roads where people tended to congregate. McPhail's secondary analysis of a plethora of research studies on participation in riots concludes:

> There is no compelling reason to accept the inference that persons are more impetuous because of their youth, more daring because of their gender, more disenchanted because of their race, or less rational because of their educational level. An equally plausible interpretation of these data is that such persons are simply more available for participation by virtue of the large amount of unscheduled or uncommitted time which results from being young, black, male, and without educational credentials in the urban ghettos of contemporary U.S. society. (McPhail 1971: 1069)

Nor is there any compelling reason for believing that any common motivation lay behind the many and diverse actions of individuals during the course of a riot. As McPhail (1991) has convincingly argued, to do so is, perversely, to accept the assumption of LeBon and his intellectual heirs that the crowd is a single entity. Rioting may have emergent properties of social organization, but there is no reason to suppose that that organization arises from common motivation.

The implication of taking rioters seriously is that riot is just a species of the genus protest. Eisinger (1973) insists, however, that riot and peaceful protest are both conceptually and empirically distinct. It is true that ghetto and inner-city rioters, like protestors, tend to be "relatively power-less people" and that protest is one of those "collective manifestations" that are "disruptive in nature". However, the crucial distinction, according to Eisinger, is that peaceful protest is an instrumental act in which pro-testors weigh the costs and benefits of their actions. "Violent actors in con-trast have essentially thrown cost considerations to the winds" (p. 13) and are engaged in an expressive, rather than instrumental, form of activity. Moreover, he finds that the social, economic and political correlates of riot and peaceful protest, even by black ghetto dwellers, do not correspond, suggesting that they are quite distinct forms of activity.

Perhaps conceptual confusion owes much to the indiscriminate use of the term "riot" itself. There are circumstances when demonstrations, pickets and other forms of overt protest turn violent, but these are quite distinct from the "community disorders" that convulsed American ghettos and British inner-cities. They arise in the context of a scheduled event organ-ized for the purpose of protest (McPhail & Miller 1973). Protestors articu-late their grievances quite explicitly through their banners and orchestrated slogans. Here violence may be used quite instrumentally to achieve the goal of the protestors, for example the closure of strike-bound premises. However, this does not apply to "community disorders" whose rationality, purpose and instrumentality rely on inference to a degree that becomes almost entirely speculative. While actors on the political stage (who may include academic researchers) may contest the motives to be attributed to participants in such "community disorders", academic researchers seeking an explanation for riot will be in no privileged position to determine what those motives actually were.

Taking protest seriously

Taking overt acts of protest seriously poses few of the problems that accompany taking rioters seriously. Few inferences need to be drawn about the purpose of protestors, compared with the motivations of rioters. Protestors hold marches, demonstrations, rallies, lobbies, pickets, sit-ins and so forth, consciously designed to bring about some form of social

6

change. These usually occur in the context of a protest movement, or what is more commonly called a "social movement".

There is, however, a version of the "riff-raff" theory that applies even to such overt acts of protest. It dismisses any genuine sense of grievance that protestors may express and attributes participation in social movements to the personal deficiencies of the protestors or their isolated and marginal position in society. This is the view that protestors are "rent-a-mob", for whom the object of protest is merely an excuse to express their inchoate frustrations and anxieties. Such reasoning was common during the 1960s as a means of diminishing the grievances articulated by student radicals throughout the Western world. The same approach is used to demean supporters of right-wing movements, such as McCarthyism, who are assumed not to be genuinely anxious to rid society of communist subversives, but merely to be expressing their "status anxiety" (Trow 1970).

It is easier to refute "riff-raff" theories of protest than to reject equivalent theories of riot, because organization is a defining feature of protest activity. Protestors tend not to be the isolated and marginal members of society that the "riff-raff" theory would imply. Protestors tend to be well integrated into social networks that serve as the basis for the mobilization of support. This is as true of right-wing movements as it is of civil rights and other groups. Contrary to earlier suggestions, supporters of Senator McCarthy were not alienated and isolated victims of "status anxiety" but well-integrated conservatives who had a profound fear of communism (Polsby 1960, Rogin 1967, McEvoy 1971). Here too there is reason to distinguish protest activity from "community disorder", for the deprived tend to lack the resources that facilitate protest. Snyder & Tilly (1972) found that in France the occurrence of disorder was not correlated with periods of maximum hardship when peasants were forced off the land and into the cities. Disorder occurred in cities, they contend, because the city offers a milieu conducive to mobilization and protest reflected national political conflicts.

In opposition to the "riff-raff" theory of protest, there has arisen over the past 20 years a theoretical framework that does take protest seriously. This theoretical framework is known as "resource mobilization theory" (McCarthy & Zald 1977), for it asserts that the reason social movements arise when and where they do, take a particular form and follow a given life cycle is largely explained by their organizational features. It is how a movement mobilizes the available resources that distinguishes success from

7

failure. Since most social movements suffer a severe lack of resources, this theoretical assumption is more than a statement of the obvious.

The first, and possibly most challenging, contention of the theory is that social movements do not arise spontaneously, but must be effectively organized. As Killian (1984) has admitted, this is a conclusion that earlier researchers on the American civil rights movement avoided for political reasons, since it might have been thought to vindicate right-wing accusations that bus and lunch-counter sit-ins occurred at the instigation of "agitators". Revisionist accounts of the civil rights movement (McAdam 1982) point out that Rosa Parks was not simply an old black woman whose feet hurt so badly she felt compelled to sit in a seat reserved for whites and not move when instructed to do so – an event that prompted the Montgomery bus boycott. She was instead a long-time civil rights activist who belonged to a network that could support her and the movement, albeit that her particular act of defiance was not premeditated (Killian 1984).

The priority given to organization as the crucial variable has led some resource mobilization theorists to doubt whether there is *any* connection between grievances and protest. McCarthy & Zald (1977) cite Turner & Killian (1972) as claiming that "there is always enough discontent in any society to supply the grass-roots support for a movement if the movement is effectively organized". They continue that for "some purposes we go even further: grievances and discontent may be defined, created, and manipulated by issue entrepreneurs and organizations" (p. 1215).

This is not to say that the external environment does not affect social movements. Eisinger suggests that "structures of political opportunity" can be exploited by well-organized social movements (Eisinger 1973: 11; see also Jenkins & Perrow 1977, Kitschelt 1986). Tarrow (1989) argues that, in conditions of serious cleavage in the political structure, protest movements tend to multiply, creating a "protest cycle". New movements using unorthodox methods of protest tend to arise and capture public attention. Subsequently, established movements respond, as do the political authorities, institutionalizing protest within conventional channels or suppressing it.

Resource mobilization theory also diverges from the riot-as-protest approach in another, for our purposes, crucial respect. It pays almost no attention to the police. In so far as the police are included amongst the *dramatis personae* of protest episodes, they are restricted to an occasional walk-on part, usually swinging clubs. It is the aim of the remainder of this section of the chapter to demonstrate that this is a serious omission. If resource mobilization theory is correct, then we can expect that protest will

8

pose a number of acute policing problems. Just as it is necessary that we take protest seriously in order to understand it, so too it is essential that we take policing seriously in order to understand its response to protest.

The policing of protest

The resource that is potentially most readily available and useful to a social movement is people who can be employed to express opposition or make vocal demands. Hence, protest is a political resource that can be used by otherwise powerless groups (Lipsky 1968, 1970).

Licensing protest

How protest is used is clearly of crucial significance to our understanding of how it might be controlled. Lipsky argues that the power of protest does not lie in directly compelling those in power to concede to the demands of protestors. (If a gun could so easily be held to the head of the powerful, they could hardly be regarded as powerful at all.) Protest is designed to rally wider support. This need to influence others imposes limits upon the activities in which protestors engage and requires the skilful handling of the media so that the correct image is presented. His detailed analysis of the New York rent strike (Lipsky 1970) shows how skilfully public opinion can be managed to bring pressure to bear on the political authorities.

Protestors are also dependent upon those in political power for the ultimate achievement of their goals. Unless the powerful relent, the relatively powerless protestors will not achieve their aims. Protestors are most dependent on the political authorities for hearing them at all. As Eisinger notes:

> Those who pursue protest as an ongoing tactic must in effect gain license from the authorities in the system to do so. That is to say, protest will probably not be used in contemporary American cities where it is suppressed by violence. Violent reactions by the authorities will likely stimulate violence by the potential protest population or will cause withdrawal from aggressively demonstrative politics. Official tolerance, signified by the unwillingness or even inability to suppress protest by force, may serve as the functional equivalent of license to protest. Such license represents an opportunity in the whole structure of opportunities: protest offers a chance to gain a hearing in public councils. The openness of the system, in other words, is conducive to protest. (1973: 27)

Although many agents of the political authorities may be involved in "licensing" protest, the police are to the forefront. If protest is to be "suppressed by violence", then it is the police who will act as the prime agents of suppression. Yet the conditions under which tolerance or suppression predominates are largely ignored. The implication seems to be that the police are simply instruments of the political leadership, but this is an untested assumption. The police may have their own interests to pursue in licensing or not licensing protest.

Police suppression of protest has a direct effect on resource mobilization, for it is one of the more controversial assumptions of resource mobilization theory that protestors are rational to the point of assessing the costs and benefits of participation. This has a number of implications that do not concern us, but clearly the threat or actuality of police suppression is likely to be regarded as a cost of participation to most protestors. Whether the police impose this cost has, therefore, a direct impact on the likely success of the protest movement.

Violence as a protest tactic

Protest can, of course, take a wide variety of forms. Polite protest may entail nothing more than writing letters to elected representatives. The kind of protest that will involve the police entails some measure of disruption. According to Eisinger (1973), a delicate line must be trodden by powerless groups, who must indicate a threat of violence sufficient to motivate potential allies to exert pressure for "something to be done" about the issue, but not so much that they alienate support and legitimate repression. On the other hand, Tilly (1973) and Gamson (1975) both observe that the historical record in France and the United States, respectively, confirms that violence and disorder often succeed and may be pursued as a rational strategy by dissident groups (see also Frey et al. 1992, Sherman & Wallace 1991). What may be a viable tactic for protestors is, of course, a problem for the police, whose task it is to prevent violence and quell it if it occurs.

"Rent-a-crowd" and agitators

The "riff-raff" theory of social movements regards protest as the product of trouble-making agitators. Resource mobilization theory implies that there may be more than a grain of truth in these allegations. Activists with strong ideological commitment tend to comprise the core membership. Membership of different social movements tends to overlap, with people active in more than one. Movements themselves tend to have fraternal links, ready to support each other over specific issues. Gerhards & Rucht (1992) found this network was important in mobilizing integrated action to protest at the visit of President Reagan to Berlin in 1987 and the holding of the annual meeting of the International Monetary Fund in that same city a year later. From a resource mobilization point of view, one of the principal difficulties for a protest movement is to secure the commitment of dedicated protestors and also to recruit more widely from less dedicated people, either of whom may tire of the cause and shift their allegiance to another.

From the point of view of the police there may be advantages, as well as disadvantages, in dealing repeatedly with the same individuals as members of different groups. Their behaviour may become increasingly predictable, the more experience the police have of their protests. They may be easier to infiltrate. The police may come to develop an amicable working relationship with them. On the other hand, mutual hostility might be exacerbated as police come into repeated conflict with the same coterie of "agitators".

Overlapping membership of protest movements and specific groups does not imply that the protest community is an amorphous homogeneity. The social movement sector, as it is sometimes called, consists usually of various factions adopting differing strategies in pursuit of divergent goals, some of whom will be moderate and others more militant (Henriques 1991). Factions that fail to attract large numbers of supporters can compensate by making themselves prominent through militant action. In this way, groups on the fringe of a movement may, quite rationally, seek to sway their more moderate and widely supported counterparts. For example, the militant ecological protest group "Earth First!" has engaged in various militant "stunts", from unfurling a drape across the face of a dam to give the appearance of a crack to "spiking" trees with nails so as to pose a threat of injury to loggers. These "stunts" are designed to raise public awareness of ecological issues that can be, and have been, exploited by mainstream ecological pressure groups (Lange 1990, Short 1991).

The different rôles played by various factions are important in the development of the "protest cycle" (Tarrow 1989), such as those witnessed in Italy during the 1960s and early 1970s. First, groups whom Tarrow calls "the early risers" tend to initiate protest cycles by seizing upon new issues and novel forms of protest and organization. They are likely to catch both the authorities and established social movements, such as trade unions, off guard. It tends to take a little time before the authorities learn how to counter the "early risers" and for established social movements to incorporate them. Secondly, protest groups in one sector seek support from counterparts in different sectors of society by convincing them that they share a common struggle. Thus, in Italy militant students joined picket-lines not only to support strikers, but to solicit support from industrial workers for student demands. From the authorities' point of view, of course, this represented the infiltration of moderate movements by extremists and threatened to spread disaffection. Thirdly, these militant groups tend to compete amongst each other for the support of the mainstream. Since they find it difficult to compete in terms of membership, they often do so in terms of militancy. As the protest cycle comes to a conclusion, militant groups must strive all the harder to recruit adherents and influence the mainstream. Hence militancy increases and may, in extreme cases, lead to terrorism of the sort pursued by the Red Brigades in Italy.

The use of violence as a tactic by extremists poses a dilemma for the police: on the one hand, the presence of militant factions within a moderate protest movement may pose a direct threat of violence, but, on the other, coercive measures designed to counter such a threat may be counterproductive if they alienate mainstream protestors. This is a dilemma that the police must resolve, and it is clear that they do not only swing clubs and fire tear-gas, they also abstain from the use of violence on some occasions. Lofland (1985) describes *inter alia* how the state police tolerated frequent invasions of a state governor's parlour, but does not explain why they did so. Thus, just as the threat or use of violence is a delicate tactical issue for protest groups, so too is the threat or use of coercion by the state.

Intellectuals and authority

One of the resources available to a protest movement is the manner in which a grievance is presented, or "framed" (Tarrow 1989). Support for a conservation group protesting about industrial development in an area of natural beauty could be framed in purely local terms, which would minimize the available constituency, or as a global threat to the environment, in which case support would likely come from much further afield. Gerhards & Rucht (1992) have illustrated the importance of framing issues for mobilization of protests in Berlin against the visits of President Reagan and the IMF. They identify "master frames" promulgated by protest groups that were able to unite protestors from diverse ideological standpoints under a common umbrella.

The ideological work entailed in devising such frames draws attention to an aspect of protest that has been a persistent focus of attention since Crane

Brinton's pioneering research on revolution (Brinton 1965) – the rôle of intellectuals. Parkin (1968) drew attention to the crucial rôle played by prominent intellectuals and those in the creative arts, education and the ministry in the Campaign for Nuclear Disarmament (CND) during the 1950s and 1960s. Pinard and Hamilton (1989) identify a distinct culture of intellectuals that encourages sympathy for "neoliberal, neonationalist and women's movements" (p. 100) in Canada, the United States, France, Germany, Belgium and throughout Great Britain.

The rôle of intellectuals poses a number of potential problems for the policing of protest movements. First, the "frame" in which intellectuals couch grievances and demands is likely to de-legitimize the established political and social order that the police are duty-bound to defend. Secondly, its uncompromising and comprehensive (Bittner 1963) radicalism may represent a threat to how political activity is normally conceived, perhaps encouraging the police to overestimate the militancy of the protest. Blain (1989) points to how the rhetoric of "victimage" is employed by movement activists to incite themselves and others to take action. In this discourse, the activist is pitted in a "war" against "villainous powers" who must be defeated for the good of humankind. This is the process of "agitation" (Bittner 1951) that the authorities fear most. Thirdly, in maintaining order, the police are vulnerable to the accusation that they defend injustice. Fourthly, the culture to which Pinard and Hamilton refer would seem fundamentally antipathetic to the police. The police are a uniformed disciplined organization who, as specialists in the use of force, are likely to be tainted by authoritarianism and brutality in the eyes of such intellectuals. Finally, intellectuals will be articulate in their own and others' defence and are likely to "know their rights". They conform perfectly to what American cops are wont to describe as "assholes" (Van Maanen 1978) who are particularly troublesome to deal with. In sum, dealing with intellectuals represents a challenge to the authority and power of the police.

The questionable authority of the police in the eyes of intellectuals and their followers does not only create difficulties for police officers, it may also be instrumental in causing confrontation and violence. Sykes & Brent (1983) conducted systematic observation of encounters between police and citizens during the course of routine police work. They concluded that most encounters were characterized by co-operation; confrontation was relatively rare. Co-operation arises from the compatibility of action and reaction, such as when a question is followed by an answer. When a question is followed by an inappropriate response, such as a question – "What's

13

going on here?", "Who wants to know?" – the encounter rapidly degen-
erates into a confrontation. Since it is the police who take charge of any
encounter and tend, therefore, to initiate each exchange (they ask the questions, for example) it is the variability of the citizen's response that predicts
the outcome. Sykes & Brent speculate, on the basis of this analysis, that
policing protest demonstrations is a recipe for confrontation because protestors are unlikely to respond in appropriate ways to police-initiated
exchanges. Analysis of the rôle of the intellectual supports their contention.

Protest as a policing problem
Thus, for the police, protest represents a threat to public order. First, it is
designed to be disruptive, in order to attract the attention of bystanders.
Secondly, violence may be a viable tactic used by protestors. Thirdly, factions may find it expedient for a variety of reasons to use militant tactics,
which may catch the police off guard. Fourthly, protestors will often be
supported by intellectuals who not only articulate demands but de-legitimize
police action.

To conclude this part of the discussion, I have argued that, if we "take
protest seriously" as a rational activity, then we are obliged to take the
policing of protest equally seriously. However, policing has been largely
ignored.

The context of protest

About what issues did people protest in London during the period of these
observations? To what general themes did these issues belong? What kinds
of social movements were actively engaged in protest? What types of people were they who protested? The methodological appendix lists all the
observations of police operations in connection with the various protest
movements. This section will briefly describe the context of protest, pointing to the most salient features of the protest movements as they presented
themselves to the police in London during the early 1990s.

Equality
The traditional stimulant of protest has been inequality that has provoked
those suffering some deprivation or disadvantage to seek a remedy. This
constitutes what are now regarded as the old or traditional social movements: working-class people, motivated by socialist ideals, seeking eco-

nomic, political and social equality. Historically, it has been the political left that has constituted the usual adversaries of the police in public order situations from mass demonstrations to strikes (Critchley 1970).

Industrial disputes

The traditional battleground on which the police and working class met was the picket-line (Geary 1985, Wiles 1985, Scraton 1985, R. Morgan 1987, Kahn et al. 1983, Weinberger 1991). The British "battleground" was always much less bloody than that in the United States (Taft & Ross 1979) and elsewhere throughout the industrializing countries of the nineteenth century, but it was bloody enough. In recent years, police and strikers have again met in a series of bloody confrontations, most conspicuously during the year-long miners' strike of 1984–5 when riot police frequently battled with pickets (Fine & Millar 1985, D. Waddington et al. 1989). Although relations between former strikers and their local police have been restored to a remarkable extent (D. Waddington et al. 1991), this has been achieved by local people and their local police conspiring to blame confrontation on those officers drafted in from elsewhere. In this demonology the Metropolitan Police have enjoyed a position of some prominence.

It was against this background that the announcement by the government of the closure of 31 collieries and the resulting protests on behalf of miners should be read. Within days of the announcement the National Union of Mineworkers (NUM) staged a lobby of Parliament and a protest march of 50 000 demonstrators around Hyde Park (see pp. 70–75). The following Sunday the Trades Union Congress (TUC) mobilized 150 000 marchers to protest in the pouring rain by marching through central London. Both marches were conducted without disorder, despite attempts by some radical factions to lead an illegal breakaway march to Parliament Square from the official NUM march.

Taxation

A source of protest whose origins stretch back to the Middle Ages is taxation. The decision by Mrs Thatcher's government to reform local taxation and impose a flat-rate charge (the so-called poll tax) proved highly controversial and eventually led, along with other factors, to her resignation as prime minister and the repeal of the tax by the incoming Major government. The poll tax prompted demonstrations that were associated with violent disorder and culminated in one of the worst riots of recent times and probably *the* worst to take place in central London for over a century (see pp. 52–3). This riot was to cast a shadow over the policing of public order for the entire period of this research and was a background against which all other events should be interpreted.

Heirs to the 1960s

The literature on social movements has been preoccupied in recent years by the distinction between "new" and, by implication, "old" social movements. New social movements arose out of the 1960s. They are predominantly middle class and concerned less with rectifying a grievance felt by the protestors themselves than with the pursuit of universal ideals. They are also movements that have spawned innovative methods of social protest, such as the "sit-ins" of the student protest of the 1960s. Issues of equality represent "old" social movements; issues of rights, sexual politics and, perhaps most clearly of all, peace represent "new" social movements. What was common to all those movements was the involvement of youth, especially students.

Students

As Tarrow (1989) notes, the rebellious 1960s defined many of the issues and styles of protest that continue to reverberate today. This was a period characterized by the civil rights movement in the southern states of America and campus riots throughout the Western world (Gurr 1969, Voirst 1979, Spiegel 1972, Tarrow 1993). In 1964, the University of California's Berkeley campus was convulsed by a series of confrontations that not only lasted a year but prompted the wider student rebellion (Heirich 1976). Although issues were often couched in terms of "free speech", the "primary root cause" was disaffection with the Vietnam war (Smith 1972). The end of the decade was to be marked by the killing of four undergraduates at Kent State university when they protested at the bombing of Cambodia (Lewis 1972).

What characterized the 1960s was the involvement of predominantly middle-class young people in rebellion against the political establishment (Fisk 1970, Jupp 1970). The effects of this youthful rebellion were felt throughout Europe as students protested in Germany, Italy (Tarrow 1989) and, most conspicuously of all, in France during May 1968 (Hanley & Kerr 1989, Tarrow 1993). Although confrontation was not on the same scale of intensity as elsewhere, confrontations between students and those in authority were experienced in the United Kingdom (Clutterbuck 1973). In March and October 1968 mass demonstrations against the Vietnam war

16

were held outside the American embassy in London amid scenes of serious disorder (Halloran et al. 1970). Taking their lead from the civil rights movement in the United States, students organized a movement to extend full civil rights to the Catholic minority in Northern Ireland, which resulted in violent confrontations with the police and culminated in the "troubles" that claimed 3000 lives during the next 25 years.

Although student activism has subsided from the heights of the 1960s, students continue to be amongst the most active protestors both as members of the National Union of Students and as participants in other protest groups. What the police in London regarded as the demonstration "season" corresponded with the academic year, for once students turned their attention to examinations after Easter and then dispersed during the long summer vacation the opportunities for mobilizing mass demonstrations were greatly restricted. During the period of this research, four protest marches were organized by student organizations, three of which opposed government policies on higher education. These came in the immediate aftermath of a violent confrontation in 1989 between police and students on Westminster Bridge, immediately adjacent to the Palace of Westminster (more commonly known as the Houses of Parliament). Although vindicated by an official inquiry into the violence, conducted under the auspices of the Police Complaints Authority, senior police officers continued to regard student demonstrations with the utmost caution in the wake of this confrontation.

Civil rights

The civil rights movement in America is indelibly associated with the 1960s (Voirst 1979). From its origins in bus boycotts and lunch-counter sit-ins in the southern states (Oberschall 1989, McAdam 1982), it spread to include voter registration drives and thence to the famous march on Washington in 1963. It is inseparable from the persona and rousing rhetoric of Martin Luther King and his insistence on non-violence in the face of Ku Klux Klan violence and police tear-gas, snarling dogs and birdshot.

Opposing racism

Although campaign groups have existed in Britain to defend and further the civil rights of the black minority, there has never been a counterpart to the American civil rights movement (Lewis 1970). There was, during the period of these observations, an attempt to mobilize the Afro-Caribbean community under the "National Forum for All African Organizations in Europe", which staged a sparsely attended march in mid-July 1992.

17

However, the issue of race relations has arisen most frequently in the context of confrontations between neo-fascist right-wing organizations and their opponents – confrontations that became all the more ominous in view of the growth of right-wing movements throughout Europe (Bréchon & Mitra 1992). These took various forms during the period of this research. In southeast London there were several marches in connection with alleged racially motivated murders. The National Front (one of the right-wing groups) staged a march in the immediate aftermath, and near the site, of such a murder, which was violently opposed. Thereafter there were two anti-racist marches in the same area to protest at the presence of the headquarters of the British National Party (BNP) (the other right-wing organization) in the area.

Meanwhile, in the East End of London the BNP held two election meetings in a local authority hall in Bethnal Green. The first was in connection with the 1992 general election and the second was a local authority by-election. Both of these were opposed by anti-fascist groups. These events had particular poignancy for the police, if for no one else, because during the 1979 general election campaign a similar election meeting by the right-wing National Front led to severe disorder outside Southall town hall in which it was held during which a protestor, Blair Peach, was struck on the head, apparently by police officers dispersing a crowd of missile-throwers, and died of his injuries (Dummett 1980a, 1980b). This was followed by a lengthy inquiry and considerable negative publicity for the Special Patrol Group (a unit of public order specialists), which contributed to the eventual demise of the Group.

In addition, each year during the afternoon of Remembrance Sunday the National Front marches to the Cenotaph in Whitehall ostensibly to pay homage to the war dead. This event was usually associated with disorder as the march was opposed by anti-fascist groups.

Notting Hill Carnival

The principal event associated with the Afro-Caribbean community is the annual Notting Hill Carnival, which is reputedly the largest street festival in Europe. It is also the largest single public order operation routinely mounted by the Metropolitan Police.

The carnival originated in an attempt to transplant to this London neighbourhood a Trinidadian tradition (but common elsewhere). In the mid-1960s the practice grew of holding such a festival in this area of high Afro-Caribbean settlement, which had suffered race riots in 1958. It now lasts

18

throughout the long weekend of the public holiday at the end of August and has been attended by up to an estimated 1 million people. Floats carrying steel bands and attended by dancers in exotic costume are the most public face of the carnival (Edgar 1988). However, in an area comprising several blocks, people throng through streets in which alcoholic and other drinks and a variety of foods are sold. Dotted throughout this area are "sound systems" – banks of loudspeakers blasting out reggae music – around which carnival-goers gather to listen and dance.

The carnival has had another and, for the police, a less agreeable face. According to Cohen (1980), the carnival always had political overtones as an offshoot of groups campaigning against landlords who exploited recently arrived immigrants from the Caribbean. After a series of internal rifts within the local community, the original Trinidadian origins of the carnival were transcended in the early 1970s by a more aggressive assertion of black identity. This "resistance through ritual" (Keith 1993; see also Gutzmore 1982, Pryce 1985) affirmed a more confrontational stance towards racial discrimination and deprivation through adherence to "Black Power" ideology transmitted through the militant lyrics of reggae music. The police were a prime target of this "resistance" for they had come into conflict with the local black population following drug raids on the "Mangrove" community centre (Pryce 1985). All of which testifies to the essentially *political* significance of the carnival.

From the police perspective, the carnival increasingly became associated with street crime and the sale and consumption of illegal drugs. Police attempts to prevent crime and arrest offenders have caused confrontations in the past. In 1976, 300 police officers were injured in a pitched battle, which, for young black people, was celebrated as a defeat for the police (Pryce 1985). It convinced the Metropolitan Police of the need to equip officers with reinforced plastic shields (Waddington 1991) and raised the policing of the carnival to the status of a major operation. Since 1976 there have been sporadic outbreaks of disorder, with further riots in 1987 and 1989.

Since the late 1980s the carnival has undergone something of a transformation under the aegis of Notting Hill Carnival Enterprises Limited (NCEL). The aim now is to make the carnival a financially independent commercial success that attracts a wide spectrum of visitors. The police aim is to ensure a safe and crime-free carnival by acting in collaboration with, not in opposition to, the new carnival organizers. Even so, the carnival continues to be a barometer of police race relations and is regarded as the most sensitive public order operation that the Metropolitan Police mount. It commands enormous police resources – at the time of these observations it involved around 9000 officers.

Civil rights in Ireland

The American civil rights movement inspired others to demand civil rights for minority groups. It prompted such a movement amongst Northern Ireland's Catholic minority, which saw violent confrontations throughout 1968, culminating in British troops taking almost full responsibility for internal security in response to the terrorism of the Provisional IRA (PIRA). Terrorism and public disorder continue to blight not only Northern Ireland but the mainland of Britain and London in particular. The period of this research coincided with a PIRA bombing campaign, which had obvious significance for routine policing, especially in central London where most protest took place.

The political violence of Northern Ireland also has a direct impact on protest in London. Each January a march is held to commemorate the killing of 13 people by British paratroopers on "Bloody Sunday" 1972. This attracts groups like the Troops Out of Ireland movement and is regularly opposed by right-wing counter-demonstrators. The 20th anniversary of Bloody Sunday in 1992 had particular significance, especially in the context of the terrorist bombing campaign.

Sexual politics

In the 30 years since the civil rights movement began, the concept of minorities has been extended to embrace all manner of minority groups. One arena of particular contention has been that of sex and sexual orientation. The feminist movement is, perhaps, the archetype of the "new social movements" consisting of middle-class sympathizers whose mission is as much to change social consciousness as it is to change government policy. The feminist movement was not active in public protest during the period of observation, but the issue of sexual politics was very much on the agenda.

As in the United States, particularly since the election of President Clinton, there has been a strong movement in favour of extending civil rights to gay men and lesbians. Like many groups, this comprises a range of protest groups pursuing different tactics. "Stonewall" adopts an assimilationist position for homosexuals and seeks to persuade through respectable lobbying (Carter 1992). Its leading members include such establishment figures as the actor Sir Ian McKellen, who held discussions with the prime minister, John Major, about homosexual law reform. At the opposite end of the spectrum are the militant gay rights group "OutRage!" and the AIDS awareness campaigners "ACT-UP" (the former more prominent during this period than the latter). "OutRage!" has adopted the tactics - developed by "ACT-UP" in the United States - of staging "stunts" that have "often deliberately trespassed the bounds of good taste - throwing condoms, necking in public places, speaking explicitly and positively about anal sex, 'camping it up' for the television cameras" (*Newsweek*, quoted in Gamson 1989), the aim of which, according to commentators (Gamson 1989), is to create a sense of community amongst the gay population. Spokespeople for "OutRage!" (Tatchell 1992a, 1994) claim that they are confronting homo-phobic bigots with their own bigotry, seeking to "embarrass, ridicule and shock" them into quiescence. "OutRage!" aligns itself with the left, joining the campaign for a Bill of Rights that will grant liberty to all minorities (Tatchell 1990, 1992b).

Between the extremes of "Stonewall" and "OutRage!" are a number of conventional campaigning organizations. Amongst these is the relatively new Lesbian and Gay Coalition. This came to prominence in mobilizing opposition to Clause 28 of the Local Government Act 1988 (Carter 1992), which imposed the requirement that sex education must not present homo-sexuality as normal, and to Section 25 of the Criminal Justice Act 1990, which imposed more stringent penalties for such offences as importuning and which was believed to be aimed at the gay community. Moreover, each year in the middle of summer a march and festival are staged by "Gay Pride": 30 000 or more gay men and lesbians march through central London and then hold a festival in a large park in south London. It is accompanied by tableaux on lorries depicting such scenes as "gay weddings".

Connected with the gay rights movement has been the AIDS awareness campaign (Watney 1990). Many of the gay rights groups and their protests described above included an AIDS awareness aspect. During this research the principal organization devoted to AIDS alone was "Reach Out and Touch with Flowers", which held an annual march terminating in Trafal-gar Square.

Peace

The other defining feature of the 1960s was the peace movement. This had two distinct, but interrelated, foci of interest: protesting against nuclear weapons (Driver 1964, Byrne 1991, MacDougall 1991, Marullo 1991,

Mattausch 1991, Meyer & Kleidman 1991) and opposition to the Vietnam war (Rabel 1992). Neither of these was a live issue by the early 1990s. The Vietnam war had thankfully been terminated long before and the collapse of the Soviet Union had, at least for the time being, drawn the sting from opposition to nuclear weapons (Klandermans 1991a). However, the peace issue continued to have both a specific and general influence on the context of protest.

War and peace were catapulted back on to the political agenda in August 1990 when Iraq invaded Kuwait. As the Gulf war became increasingly imminent and then came to fruition, so protest against the war grew more intense. The Campaign to Stop War in the Gulf was formed, principally around a nucleus provided by the Campaign for Nuclear Disarmament. Marches, numbering over 40 000 at their height, were held in London with increasing frequency as war approached. On the night that the United Nations ultimatum to Iraq expired, again a couple of nights later when the bombing of Iraq commenced and then once more a month later when the land war began, there were impromptu illegal demonstrations outside Parliament and acts of civil disobedience.

Foreign nationalism

All the protest movements outlined above were aimed at influencing domestic British politics. Throughout this period there were also several protest marches and demonstrations by various émigré or immigrant groups relating to events in their native countries. Some of these were annual events marking anniversaries, usually of assassinations, murders and massacres. Various Islamic groups protested against the governments of Sudan, Iraq, Iran, amongst others. Christians from Pakistan protested at the treatment of their co-religionists in their homeland. Sikhs and Kashmiris marched in protest to the Indian High Commission demanding independence for the Punjab and Kashmir respectively. In the aftermath of the Gulf war, Kurdish nationalists demanded a Kurdistan state.

The policing context

The events described in this book took place against an organizational background that may not be known to many readers. This section will briefly describe how the policing of public order is organized by the London Metropolitan Police.

Policing in London is divided into eight semi-autonomous areas, seven of which (Areas 1–7) radiate like segments of an orange. The eighth area is much smaller than the rest and serves central London, excluding the City of London, which has its own separate police force. New Scotland Yard houses departments whose functions transgress the boundaries of individual areas. One such function is public order, for protests and other public order operations may extend across boundaries, as when marches start in one area and terminate in another. Some public order operations are so manpower intensive that personnel must be supplied from throughout the force. Other public order operations may need specialist services such as closed-circuit television monitoring, which can best be organized centrally. In addition, if an event is regarded as likely to be disorderly, then Scotland Yard will take a close interest. If any of these contingencies arise, then planning for the event will probably be taken on by the Public Order Branch.

Another central public order function is provided by the Public Order Training Centre, where officers are instructed in public order tactics. The instructors at this centre were also occasionally deployed in an operational capacity. They often acted as advisers to commanding officers, accompanying them during the operation and also occasionally providing physical protection. A group of instructors was also sometimes deployed as a specialist squad on occasions when violence and disorder were anticipated. On these occasions they might act as a specialist arrest squad or as a squad of riot-control police. Finally, members of the centre were asked to stage "table-top" exercises for senior officers planning major public order operations. Their task was to imagine various contingencies that might arise and pose them to command teams to respond to in "real time".

Events that do not merit the attention of the Public Order Branch are planned at either area or divisional level. Each of the areas differs in how it routinely manages public order operations. In 8 Area, which plays host to most such events, including ceremonials, they are organized at area headquarters in the "Special Events Office". This is divided into ceremonial and public order sections, jointly under the supervision of an inspector. He is responsible to the superintendent, chief superintendent (operations) and commander (operations), who, in turn, are accountable to the Deputy Assistant Commissioner responsible for the area. In outer London areas, public order duties are normally handled by the "Ops Office", rather than by officers dedicated to public order alone. One major exception is that the policing of the Notting Hill Carnival is administered by dedicated staff at 6

Area headquarters. An inspector and constable, supplemented as carnival approached by another constable, are responsible for organizing this massive event.

Summary

Contemporary theories of protest insist that protestors should be taken seriously. This is problematic when applied to "community disorder", but profitable when applied to overt political, social or economic protest. Whereas, however, accounts of "community disorder" pay close attention to policing and its rôle in provoking disorder, theories of protest have singularly ignored the police, despite their evident importance. This book will examine the rôle of the police in relation to protest and other public order operations.

The context of protest throughout the period of observations reflected the broad span of concerns that have been the object of protest throughout the Western world for a generation. There were traditional types of protests concerning the fate of miners facing redundancy and opposition to the poll tax. There were also manifestations of themes now associated with the "new social movements": civil rights, including the rights of gay men and lesbians; and war and peace, especially opposition to the Gulf war. In addition, there were protests by foreign nationals or immigrant groups about conditions in their respective homelands.

CHAPTER 2

Law and the authoritarian state

Introduction

If rioting has dominated our view of political protest, the state's response to riot has had an even more profound impact on our perception of public order policing. The term has become almost synonymous with police in riot gear battling with rioters. This vision of policing lends credibility to the more fundamental and profoundly worrying allegation that Britain is becoming increasingly authoritarian.

Policing the riots

The inner-city riots wrought an obvious change in the appearance and tactics of the police (for details, see P. Waddington 1991). In 1976, following disorder at the Notting Hill Carnival, the police developed a long plastic shield for protection against missile attack (see p. 19). Following the inner-city riots of 1980 and 1981, the police supplemented these shields with visored crash-helmets and flame-retardant overalls. As the 1980s passed, so further revisions in tactics and equipment led to the adoption of short round shields and long truncheons, and the more aggressive use of "snatch squads". Although not yet used on the streets, the police were also equipped with armoured Land Rovers and plastic baton rounds (colloquially known as "rubber bullets") and CS gas. These developments were interpreted by many commentators as the "strong state" "tooling up" to suppress dissent from wherever it arose (Ackroyd et al. 1977, Manwaring-White 1983,

BSSRS 1985, Cousin et al. 1985, Scraton 1987a, 1987b, Brewer et al. 1988, McCabe et al. 1988, Northam 1988, Stephens 1988).

Police in public order operations are deployed in squads rather than as individuals exercising the traditional discretion of the constable. Police Support Units (PSUs) comprise one inspector, three sergeants and 18 constables – PSUs are referred to in the Metropolitan Police as "serials". Some officers belong to specially trained public order squads. These are amongst the most controversial aspects of public order policing. In the Metropolitan Police they were initially known as the Special Patrol Group (SPG), who came to prominence through their deployment in saturating crime-ridden areas in which they conducted a policy of "stop and search". This provoked considerable criticism from black civil rights groups, who accused the SPG of harassment. Following the killing of Blair Peach apparently by SPG officers during disorder outside Southall town hall during the 1979 general election (see p. 18) their public order rôle was reduced and the squad eventually disbanded. They were then replaced by District Support Units, but they too acquired an unsavoury reputation after an incident in which officers from one such unit severely beat three black youths and then conspired together to maintain a "wall of silence". Shortly afterwards and following force reorganization, these units were replaced by Territorial Support Groups (TSG), who perform much the same public order rôle as their predecessors.

In addition, the command of public order has been made increasingly paramilitary. The most senior commander is designated as "Gold", and his function is to determine the overall strategy and make "slow-time" decisions. "Silver" is the forward ground commander, who is responsible for the tactical implementation of "Gold's" strategy and takes "quick-time" decisions. The "Silver" commander is aided by "Bronze" commanders, who usually have responsibility for territorial sectors and the serials operating therein. "Gold Control" is normally remote from the scene of the public order operation, possibly in the Special Operations Room at New Scotland Yard, which is equipped with closed-circuit television and computers to record messages and the deployment of serials. Particular concern was aroused during the 1984–5 miners' strike by the discovery that the National Reporting Centre (since then renamed the Mutual Aid Co-ordination Centre) operated nationally from New Scotland Yard, deploying officers from forces supplying mutual aid to those requesting it. It was alleged that this also became the conduit through which national policy was covertly disseminated (Kettle 1985).

26

The adoption of paramilitary tactics for dealing with disorder is regarded, by critics, not as a limited response to particular public order contingencies, but as portending a changed relationship between police and public, especially the disadvantaged and the powerless (Jefferson 1987, 1990, 1993). Northam (1988) alleges that these developments amount to the abandonment of the tradition of "policing by consent" and its replacement with a style of policing imported from Hong Kong and essentially colonial.

The notion that "community disorders" were "riot-as-protest" had profound implications for the policing of public disorder, since taking rioters seriously discredited police attempts at riot-control. The police were seen not as neutral enforcers of the law and maintainers of the peace, but as parties to a conflict. They were engaged in a battle of moral equals. This had a significant impact beyond the context of the riots themselves, at least in Britain. The acquisition of riot-control equipment and tactics following the riots was regarded by many academic commentators as inappropriate on two grounds. First, it was thought to be an irrelevant response to rioters' grievances: if community disorders were riot-as-protest, then the prevention of future riots lay not in suppression but in remedial action designed to address the grievances of rioters. Worse still, the development of a riot-control capability might encourage the very aggressive aspects of policing that were deemed to have led to the riots in the first place. Secondly, the assumed continuity between protest and riot was paralleled by the supposed continuity between the forceful suppression of riot and the equally forceful suppression of other forms of protest. Thus, when violence erupted on the picket-lines during the miners' strike of 1984–5 and elsewhere, the sight of riot-clad police battling with strikers was interpreted as revealing a unity of experience, and hence of interest, between black youth and strikers (Geary 1985, Gordon 1985). Policing the inner-city riots had transformed policing, and henceforth all protestors were thought likely to suffer at the hands of a "paramilitarized" police (Scraton 1987b, D. Waddington et al. 1987, 1989, Jefferson 1990).

These developments occurred not in isolation but against a background of confrontational government policies towards immigrants, ethnic minorities resident in Britain, welfare claimants and the trade unions and the pursuit of market-led economic policies designed to inject competition into British industry but inevitably resulting in the virtual collapse of much of the industrial base of the economy. Moreover, as East–West tension increased throughout the 1980s and Britain played host to Cruise missiles, defence policies were opposed by a new generation of anti-nuclear protestors, typified by the Greenham Common Peace Women, who remained encamped around the most prominent cruise missile base. Not only did all this bring the police into increasing confrontation with pickets and others opposed to these developments, but the police were virtually the only part of the public sector immune to financial cutbacks. The relatively privileged position of the police invited the accusation, frequently made by their critics during the 1980s, that they were "Maggie's private army".

The growth of the authoritarian state

These developments are regarded by many commentators as merely the most overt and alarming manifestations of a more fundamental change in British society. It is alleged that Britain has become increasingly authoritarian. The policies of the Thatcher government contributed to the conditions that led to the inner-city riots and the authoritarian response to those riots that continues to threaten liberty.

While most commentators equate this growth in authoritarianism with the Thatcher government, Hall (1979) foresaw that Britain was "drifting into a law and order society" even before Mrs Thatcher's reign and attributes it to socio-economic processes of more enduring significance than the temporary occupant of prime ministerial office. Its origins lay, Hall argues, in the crisis of the capitalist economy. Building upon themes established in *Policing the Crisis* (Hall et al. 1978), Hall's argument is that the modern British state faces a crisis of legitimacy because of the economy's chronic inability to fulfil the material aspirations of its citizens. Faced with increasingly violent challenges to the capitalist hegemony, both Labour and Conservative governments have resorted to increasingly coercive means to stifle dissent. Thus, the paramilitary muscle of the police was underpinned by a framework of law that was essentially coercive in intent. It is to that law that we now turn.

Police powers

Two pieces of legislation encapsulate the alleged shift towards authoritarianism seen during the 1980s – the Police and Criminal Evidence Act 1984 and the Public Order Act 1986 (referred to here as the 1986 Act for brevity). These Acts were accused by their critics of being gross infringements of civil liberties that extended police powers without adequately safeguarding the rights of citizens. Both Acts were presented by government ministers as being tough on "law and order", and one could be forgiven for imagining that the 1986 Act was a direct response to the inner-city disorders and picket-line violence of the 1980s.

The Public Order Act 1986, an outline

The Act is divided into four sections. In the first, the common law offences of riot, rout, unlawful assembly and affray were replaced and s.5 of the Public Order Act 1936 was revised and an entirely new offence of "disorderly behaviour" was created. Five new offences were enacted:

- *Riot*: "Where 12 or more persons who are present together use or threaten unlawful violence for a common purpose and the conduct of them (taken together) is such as would cause a person of reasonable firmness present at the scene to fear for his personal safety, each of those persons using violence for the common purpose is guilty of riot."
- *Affray* is essentially fighting in a manner that would cause fear "to persons of reasonable firmness present at the scene".
- *Violent disorder* is the first of two offences that replaced the common law offence of "unlawful assembly". It makes it an offence for three or more people to use or threaten "unlawful violence" in a manner sufficient to "cause a person of reasonable firmness present at the scene to fear for his personal safety".
- *Threatening behaviour* completes the pair of replacements of "unlawful assembly". It makes it an offence to use "threatening, abusive or insulting words or behaviour" either with intent to cause another to fear that violence will be used against them or where it will provoke violence from that other person, or where others are likely to believe that violence will be used or provoked.
- *Disorderly conduct* is a new offence designed to outlaw acts of hooliganism. It entails the use of "threatening, abusive or insulting words or behaviour" in the presence of others who are "likely to be caused harassment, alarm or distress".

For the purposes of the first three offences the "person of reasonable firmness" is hypothetical only. No one need actually be present; it is simply a means of assessing the degree of violence threatened or used. In the last two offences people must actually be present, but they need not give evidence as to their fear or "harassment, alarm or distress".

In the second part of the Act, controls over the holding of marches were extended and new statutory restrictions were introduced to regulate static assemblies. The 1986 Act requires that organizers of marches or processions must (subject to certain limited exceptions) give six clear days' notice to the police, identifying themselves and the time, date and route of the march. The government intended that this notification should initiate a process of negotiation between the police and the organizer. The police are empowered, either in advance or at the scene, to impose conditions on the march if it is reasonably believed that the march will result in serious disorder, serious damage to property, "serious disruption to the life of the community", or is intended to be intimidatory. The police can also apply (in London to the Home Secretary and elsewhere to the relevant district council) for the march to be banned if it is reasonably believed that it will result in serious disorder that cannot be prevented by the imposition of conditions. Conditions, on grounds similar to those that apply to marches, can be imposed on static assemblies of 20 or more people, but there is no requirement that notice be given of such an assembly, nor can they be banned.

The third part of the Act deals with offences in connection with racial hatred. Its provisions are neatly summarized by Smith:

> The Act creates six offences all of which involve the use of language or material that is "threatening, abusive or insulting" . . .
> These are the use of words or behaviour, or the display of inflammatory written material, the publication or distribution of racially inflammatory written material, publicly performing a play containing such material, broadcasting or including inflammatory material in a cable programme service and possessing with a view to publishing or distributing it. (1987a: 150)

Part four of the Act introduces exclusion orders for those convicted of offences of football hooliganism. Part five deals with miscellaneous matters, most notably contamination of food and other goods, and creates a new criminal offence of trespass, evidently aimed at the "Peace Convoy" and similar groups of "travellers".

It is the first three sections of the 1986 Act that concern us most, especially those aspects that have a direct bearing on protest activity.

The civil libertarian critique

Of what does the 1986 Act stand accused by its critics? There is, in fact, a remarkably consistent civil libertarian critique from which individual commentators derogate only at the margins (see, for example, Hewitt 1982, Wallington 1984, Staunton 1985, Thornton 1985, Greater London Council 1985, 1986, Driscoll 1987, McCabe and Wallington 1988, Uglow 1988, Robertson 1989, Ewing & Gearty 1990). In general, this critique accuses the Act of greatly and needlessly extending police powers without adequately protecting the rights of citizens, to the detriment of police-public relations. Specifically:

- it consists of vaguely defined offences that leave enormous discretion in the hands of the police that can be used to harass marginal groups;
- it extends the regulation of marches and introduces entirely new controls over static assemblies that represent a threat to picketing and other demonstrations;
- the exercise of these powers is not subject to effective judicial or political oversight or accountability; and
- it fails to deal rigorously enough with racism.

In sum, it is accused of criminalizing the entirely peaceful exercise of democratic rights. Without the protection of a Bill of Rights, its critics argue, protest will be allowed only on terms dictated by the police.

Thus, it would seem that the 1986 Act fully vindicates Hall's thesis (Hall 1979); it has certainly become a commonplace of academic commentary on policing that this legislation marks a way-station on the road to authoritarianism. Scraton (1987b) regards the passage of the 1986 Act as a clear indication that Britain is an authoritarian state. Hillyard & Percy-Smith (1988) also regard it as an integral part of the creation of a "coercive state". Brewer et al. (1988) describe the Act as a "quantum leap" in police powers. David Waddington and his colleagues (D. Waddington et al. 1987, D. Waddington 1992) argue that the Act will undermine negotiations between police and crowds, encouraging confrontation. Jefferson (1990) and Fielding (1991) complain of the increased discretion afforded to police officers by the Act. Cashmore & McLaughlin (1991) regard the 1986 Act as part and parcel of the paramilitary response to the inner-city riots, and Benyon (1987) too regards the Act as a suppressive response to recent disorder.

An authoritarian threat to liberty?

The notion that the Act significantly increased police powers and amounts to a step along the road to authoritarianism has escaped serious academic scrutiny. The predictably hyperbolic denunciations of the Act by its opponents voiced during its passage through Parliament cannot be accepted uncritically. A less impassioned appraisal is needed. It is one thing to argue that legislation is not to the liking of civil libertarians, it is quite another to accept that it represents an extension of police powers and is an increase in state authoritarianism. Civil libertarian critics equate these two claims, but there are good reasons to suppose that, although there is arguably more law following the passage of the 1986 Act, it does not empower the police to circumscribe civil liberties any more than was previously the case.

Chronology of reform

Before comparing the law before and after the passage of the Act, one point needs clarification. The antecedents of the 1986 Act lie not in the events of the 1980s, but in the experience of the 1970s, especially confrontations between right-wing groups and their opponents. The incoming Thatcher government announced a review of public order law in 1979, following the disorders that had accompanied the preceding general election.

The government's announcement initiated an inquiry by the Home Affairs Committee (1980), the publication of a government Green Paper (Home Office 1980), a working paper and report from the Law Commission (1982, 1983), and a government White Paper (Home Office/Scottish Office 1985). While some aspects of the Bill incorporated concerns that *were* current during the 1980s, such as measures against football hooligans and "travellers", the general outline of the Act was apparent from the outset of this process.

The 1986 Act and the existing law

The authoritarian state thesis is a theory of social change: it asserts that the state has become *more* authoritarian in recent years. Crucially at issue here is the relationship between the 1986 Act and the law that preceded it. Implicit in the view of critics of the 1986 Act is the belief that the preceding law was more circumscribed than that which replaced it. On the contrary, the common law and relevant statutes conferred, and continue to confer, immensely wide, vaguely defined and discretionary powers upon the police. The 1986 Act may have done nothing to narrow those powers, most of which remained unrepealed. It may also have created new offences and police powers. But new offences and powers that merely duplicate those that already exist do not extend the scope of the laws however much they add to the weight of law books. In short, it is my contention that there has been little or no change in the legal powers of the police.

Any attempt to compare the 1986 Act with the existing law is hampered by the rather confused state of the common law and the plethora of statutes that may have a bearing on public order. As the Law Commission (1983) found, any attempt even to define such central common law concepts as "riot" and "unlawful assembly" were bedeviled by diverse and often conflicting precedents. What is clear, however, is that the central plank of public order law prior to the 1986 Act was the concept of "breach of the peace". The common law duty of a constable to maintain the peace was, and remains, accompanied by vague and extensive powers allowing all manner of police interference with the otherwise lawful conduct of fellow citizens. Constables can issue, as they had long been able to issue, instructions that, if resisted, would occasion prosecution for obstructing or assaulting a constable in the exercise of his duty.

These various legal powers have long endowed the police with enormously wide discretion in effect to regulate the exercise of democratic freedoms. The extent to which they did, and continue to do, so is illustrated by considering what is "the peace" that should not be breached and what a person must do in order to "breach" it. The peace is an ill-defined state of tranquillity (see *R.* v. *Caird and others*) that is almost bound to be breached by any act of protest, for, as Eisinger (1973) notes, even peaceful protest is by definition disruptive and even potentially violent. Under common law it does not matter whether the peace is threatened by lawful or unlawful conduct, actively or passively, with or without peaceful intent. In *O'Kelly* v. *Harvey*, it was held that those who enforced the law had a "paramount duty . . . to preserve the peace even if, as the court assumed, the meeting concerned was not unlawful" (cited in Law Commission 1983). Even if non-violent protestors were thought likely passively to resist workmen, then the police should intervene to prevent an anticipated breach of the peace (*R.* v. *Chief Constable of Devon and Cornwall, ex parte Central Electricity Generating Board*). Perhaps most surprisingly, under common law the peace can be breached in private as well as public places (*Thomas* v. *Sawkins*).

The capacity of the law to interfere with what is said has also long existed. Blasphemy and seditious libel directly interfered with the liberties of rabble-rousers, and legislation against inciting racial or religious hatred (Leopold 1977), including provisions in the 1986 Act, represent the contemporary manifestations of these established restraints. But it was in seeking to avoid confrontations between protestors voicing offensive views and those whom they offended that the greatest scope for interference with freedom of speech has been created. Pastor Wise's anti-Catholic tirade led to his lawful arrest (*Wise* v. *Dunning*); provocatively wearing an orange lily was also lawfully prevented (*Humphries* v. *O'Connor*); and even the expression of anti-Semitic sentiments to an audience whom the courts acknowledged had come specially to be offended and to cause trouble was unlawful (*Jordon* v. *Burgoyne*). There is some confusion in case law surrounding this issue arising from the leading case of *Beatty* v. *Gillbanks*. Here it was held that the Salvation Army could not be prevented from marching because their opponents, the so-called Skeleton Army, would use violence against them. Smith distils the "spirit" of the decision thus:

> a man should not be held to commit an unlawful act when he does an act that is otherwise lawful merely because those who oppose him respond with violence or the threat of it. (1987a: 176)

On the one hand, *Beatty* v. *Gillbanks* may be regarded as a modest and isolated blow for freedom, but on the other it creates sufficient uncertainty to offer the police room for manoeuvre should they choose to use it.

Nor must the police await the outbreak of disorder before interfering with the exercise of what seem to be basic democratic freedoms. Mrs Duncan was arrested ostensibly because she refused to move away from a centre for the unemployed from which quarter the police *feared* disorder might erupt (*Duncan* v. *Jones*). More recently, the courts held that the police policy of stopping picketing miners some distance from the coal mines they intended to picket was lawful, since the officers *apprehended* a breach of the peace that was yet to materialize (*Moss* v. *McLaughlin*). It is against this background that the powers in the 1986 Act need to be considered.

On the face of it, the Act circumscribes the right to protest by the obligation on protestors to give the police six days' notice of a march. However, prior notification was already established in 95 boroughs and 12 counties through local Acts of Parliament. This obligation substituted a single national requirement for a plethora of various local requirements.

Again, on the face of it, the police have acquired more extensive powers to impose conditions on marches and entirely new powers to impose conditions on assemblies. In reality, the police could always exercise those powers in furtherance of their duty to prevent a breach of the peace. Furthermore, any assembly on the public highway is almost bound to cause an obstruction under the Highways Act 1980 (and had been so under preceding legislation) and if held uninvited on private land would amount to a trespass and therefore become vulnerable to a civil injunction. This would take a little time to arrange, but affords a proprietor considerable protection against a continuing campaign (Wallington 1976). Equally, an assembly could constitute a "public nuisance", which is curiously both a criminal offence and a civil tort that allows the imposition of an injunction (*Hubbard* v. *Pitt*). In short, according to English law the highway (including footpaths) is for "passing and re-passing" and not for the holding of assemblies. That position remains unaltered by the 1986 Act.

Critics have expressed concern that the police would use their new powers under the 1986 Act to prevent intimidation so as in effect to thwart picketing. However, the courts had held as long ago as 1961 (*Piddington* v. *Bates*) that the police could limit pickets to just two per entrance to prevent a breach of the peace. As Ewing & Gearty concede, under common law:

> The police are thus empowered arbitrarily to limit numbers and to form cordons to allow lorries and workers through to work. The requirement that there be a real possibility of a breach of the peace before they act is rarely subject to close judicial scrutiny. (1990: 93)

The fact is that any assembly that satisfied any of the grounds for imposing conditions on static assemblies under the 1986 Act would, in all likelihood, have continued to be unlawful under common law. Indeed, in the only reported case to emerge so far (*Police* v. *Reid*), the magistrate's court took a more restrictive view of intimidation under the 1986 Act than has been taken in the past with regard to cases brought under breach of the peace.

In some respects the 1986 Act limits the scope of the police to take action. The Law Commission, having reviewed the common law public order offences, suggested a continuation of reliance on breach of the peace (1982), but subsequently was persuaded instead to anchor those offences more firmly in the concepts of violence and damage to property. It also restricted the definition of "threatening behaviour" and "disorderly conduct" to behaviour that was "threatening, abusive or insulting", rather than merely a breach of the peace. This was intended to raise the threshold at which the law might be breached, since following *Brutus* v. *Cozens* it is held that this formulation distinguishes unlawful conduct from that which is merely annoying or irritating.

It could be argued that the offence of "disorderly conduct" extends the powers of the police into controlling vaguely defined "unacceptable behaviour" (Ewing & Gearty 1990). However, a person wearing a T-shirt that others might find offensive would be, and always would have been, liable to be told to cover or remove it so as to prevent a breach of the peace (*Humphries* v. *O'Connor*). Refusal to comply would have amounted, and would still amount, to obstruction of a constable in the execution of his duty, just as refusal to comply with an instruction to desist under s.5 of the 1986 Act would constitute an offence.

Blows for freedom

It has already been noted that the 1986 Act redefined the common law offences in ways designed to restrict the enormous ambit of the notion of "breach of the peace". In other respects, too, the Act amended the law in ways consistent with the protection of civil liberties. There was little change to the conditions under which marches may be banned, save that it was to be no longer merely the "opinion" of the chief officer that serious disorder would arise but his "reasonable belief". Smith (1987a) argues that this alteration in phraseology makes the decision to ban more vulnerable to review by the courts, albeit that he is sceptical as to whether the courts will second-guess the judgement of the officer on the spot.

The Act also repealed several obsolete statutes, namely the Tumultuous Petitioning Act 1661, s.23 of the Seditious Meetings Act 1817, and s.1 of the Shipping Offences Act 1793. Although these Acts may have "fallen completely into desuetude" (Smith 1987a: 24), they did exist on the statute book. The revival of the Conspiracy and Protection of Property Act 1875 during the miners' strike, after a period when it too went largely unused, shows the scope that might be afforded to the agents of an authoritarian state by such legislation. Moreover, the debate about the reform of public order law revolves not around how the law would actually be enforced, but in what it *may* allow. The existing law contained offences of an "archaic nature and remarkable breadth" (Law Commission 1982: 163) that were repealed by the 1986 Act, limiting thereby the potential scope of public order law – not the action of an increasingly authoritarian state.

It should also be noted that during the period when Britain was supposedly "drifting into a law and order society" other, potentially oppressive legislation was also repealed. Perhaps the most significant example of this was the Riot Act itself, repealed in 1967. On the other hand, the Education Act 1986 struck a small blow for freedom of speech by imposing a duty on universities and other institutions of higher education to preserve freedom of speech, arguably the first positive affirmation of such a right in British law (Smith 1987b).

Exercising rights at the discretion of the police

Existing common law and statute empowered the police to exercise extensive control over the expression of democratic rights. As Ewing and Gearty accurately observe:

> The practical consequence of the range of laws we have described was that, by 1979, the freedom to engage in peaceful protest in this country was traditionally dependent not on the law but rather on the benevolent exercise of discretion by those in power. (1990: 94)

In sum, there appears to be little to support the contention of civil libertarians and other critics of the 1986 Act. It did not materially reduce civil liberties because the common law and existing statutes left precious little scope for any further reduction in civil liberties. If the police wished to impede the exercise of democratic rights, they have always enjoyed enormous legal powers with which to do so. If Britain was an authoritarian society after the passage of the 1986 Act, it was no more so than before. This, of course, is cold comfort to civil libertarians, but it does place recent changes in context.

Using legal powers

Although it is arguable whether the powers contained in the 1986 Act represented a further erosion of civil liberties, we can be much more certain about how the Act has been used. In short, its most controversial provisions have hardly been used at all. Up to the conclusion of this research, the Metropolitan Police had banned no marches and imposed conditions on only four. This is against a background of around 150 marches notified each year. The picture is similar amongst most of the other 42 police forces in England and Wales. They were asked for details, for the years 1987–92, of the number of marches notified, and the occasions upon which marches were either banned or had conditions imposed upon them. A total of 36 replies were received. Eight forces replied that they did not collate such information and were unable to give figures. Another nine also did not keep full records, but indicated that bans had certainly not been imposed and conditions, if imposed at all, were rare. A further 11 replied that there were no notified marches in their respective areas, and hence no bans or conditions. Finally, eight forces had records of notified marches. Amongst these none had imposed bans and, apart from the West Midlands Police, there were a total of 12 occasions when conditions were imposed. In the West Midlands, the imposition of conditions was much more frequent than elsewhere, suggesting a policy of using the powers contained in the Act more freely than in other forces.

However, the general picture is clear, albeit that the details are fuzzy. Since the imposition of conditions is the responsibility of the Chief Constable or his deputy and banning a march requires that application be made to the district council, it is virtually inconceivable that forces would be unaware of the occasions when either course of action was taken. Thus, it seems safe to conclude that these powers are used sparingly, particularly by the Metropolitan Police, who bear by far the heaviest burden of policing such events.

Arrests

It seems that arrest for minor public order offences under the 1986 Act is as common in routine policing as was arrest under s.5 of the 1936 Act. However, in the context of political protest, arrest for any offence is uncommon. For the 82 operations observed and for which information is available in the files, 45 had no recorded arrests, a further 16 contained no information on arrests (suggesting that none were made), 7 operations recorded between 1 and 5, and 5 operations had between 6 and 10 arrests. Only 9 operations recorded over 10 arrests. These included 339 arrested during the anti poll tax riot, and 105 arrested during disorder that followed the second anti poll tax march. Two of the remaining 7 operations were in connection with confrontations between neo-fascists and their opponents. Three others involved passive sit-down protests in which no violence occurred. One of the highest arrest figures – 157 – was recorded, not during a political protest at all, but at the 1991–2 New Year's Eve celebration in Trafalgar Square and throughout the West End, and these were predominantly for drunkenness. In other words, the predominant pattern is for few arrests to be made and violence to be even rarer. It is, perhaps, worth noting that 50 000 supporters of the NUM and 150 000 TUC demonstrators protested against the pit closures without a single arrest being made.

This is not because arrests could not in fact have been lawfully made on many of these occasions. On the contrary, on some occasions the police would have been lawfully entitled to make wholesale arrests, but they consciously chose not to do so. There were many instances, some of which will be described in the remainder of this book, when police could have arrested individuals, but abstained. As will be seen later (see pp. 176–8), many participants at the annual "Gay Pride" march and festival acted in an ostentatiously provocative manner, but senior officers deliberately erected procedural impediments to discourage their subordinates from making arrests.

Conclusions

In sum, although the 1986 Act did not expand the capacity of the police to interfere with citizens' civil rights, the police do not lack legal powers to do so. The common law and a plethora of other statutes have long given the police enormous scope for such interference. Yet this scope is not exploited. The police have not imposed legal restrictions – through the imposition of bans or conditions – and the police observed in the course of this research showed a strong disinclination to arrest protestors, even when they had ample legal justification. In short, they abstained from using their paramilitary muscle and legal power.

Yet the period covered by this research included all three anti poll tax demonstrations, protests against the Gulf war, the general election campaign of 1992, a campaign for gay rights, trade union demonstrations against the closure of coal mines and other contentious issues. In other words, this was a period when an authoritarian state would clearly be tempted to flex its muscles against the government's opponents, but those muscles were not flexed. What is the reason for this reticence? Why do the police not use their legal and paramilitary might more readily? The answer to these questions is to be found not in the "law in books" but in the "law in action".

CHAPTER 3

Avoiding trouble: the public order context

Introduction

The "authoritarian state thesis" fails to explain the policing of political protest because it subscribes to an impoverished conceptualization of policing itself. It assumes that, because a legal or coercive capacity exists, that capacity will be used to the full. It is a view of policing rightly ridiculed by Robert Reiner (1985) as the "law of inevitable increment". It is as inapplicable to public order policing as it is to policing in general. Patrolling police officers massively *under-enforce* the law, and so do their public order counterparts. If we take the policing of political protest as seriously as resource mobilization theory takes political protest itself, then we must seek to understand the aims of police officers, the obstacles they face and the resources they are able to utilize. This requires us to contextualize the policing of political protest within the wider ambit of policing in general and public order policing in particular. Thus, in this chapter we will consider how the policing of political protest fits into the wider picture of the policing of public order, including the policing of ceremonial events and celebrations, specifically the policing of New Year's Eve in Trafalgar Square.

"Trouble" in the police context

In his history of the British prison officer, Thomas (1972) argues that the actual, possibly undisclosed, goals of an organization can be reliably inferred from what constitutes organizational disasters to be avoided. On this basis, he suggests that the actual goals of the prison service are, and have always been, the containment and control of prisoners. The aim of rehabilitation was always, he argues, a pretence serving only to confuse.

Thomas's "disaster criterion" can be thought of as the institutional expression of what Chatterton (1979) describes as the "trouble" that those in an organization seek to avoid by exerting maximum control over their immediate occupational environment. Chatterton argues, from a participant observation of routine police work, that police officers conceive of two kinds of trouble, "on-the-job" and "in-the-job". On-the-job trouble arises from the routine problems that police confront on the street: quelling minor disorder, dealing with challenges to authority, making arrests, and so forth. In doing this the police officer will employ all manner of expedients, mainly informal and possibly of dubious legality. In-the-job trouble arises from the lower ranks' relationships with their superiors, both within and outside the police force, including the courts. Officers seek to avoid "grief" by managing information about what they do in the "low visibility" (Goldstein 1960) conditions of the street. This is most commonly achieved by non-disclosure, but sometimes it may be necessary to "tell a good story" in order to prevent some discomfiting "comeback". "Covering your back" is a perennial preoccupation of police officers of all ranks.

An application of Chatterton's conceptualization is to be found in his analysis of how assault charges are dealt with by police officers (Chatterton 1983). Contrary to the apparent hierarchy of progressively more severe assault charges corresponding to the amount of injury inflicted by an attacker, contained in the Offences Against the Person Act 1861, police view assaults along two orthogonal dimensions: the moral culpability of the attacker and the vulnerability of the officer to "comeback". Thus, if an attacker is not deemed by the police to be morally culpable and the injury is not serious, then little or no action will be taken and the incident will be dismissed as a "common assault" not requiring police action. On the other hand, in comparable circumstances, but when the attacker is deemed to be culpable, then the police will prefer a charge of "assault occasioning actual bodily harm". Should the victim suffer injury serious enough to receive hospital treatment, then the officer's vulnerability to "comeback", arising from medical staff knowing of the incident, is exacerbated. Avoiding on-the-job trouble requires the officer to "cover his back". Thus, the non-culpable attacker may be charged with simple "wounding", whereas the culpable attacker might be charged with the more serious "wounding with intent to cause grievous bodily harm". In sum, practical police work entails dealing with on-the-job trouble whilst avoiding in-the-job trouble by maintaining as much control over the situation as possible and "covering one's back" as a precaution.

It is often supposed by police researchers that this approach to the management of trouble is just one manifestation of the malign sub-culture of the lower ranks. The antipathy that is often expressed by the lower ranks for their superiors is taken at face value as indicating a pervasive difference of approach between "street cops" and "management cops" (Reuss-Ianni & Ianni 1983, Holdaway 1983, Punch 1985). However, the circumstances in which lower and higher ranks routinely work are quite different and it would be strange if those differences were not reflected in the respective approaches taken towards work. "Management cops" do not routinely face the type of on-the-job trouble that confronts their subordinates, nor do they habitually work in conditions of "low visibility". However, commanding a public order operation re-acquaints senior officers with some of the realities of policing, albeit that it could hardly be called "low visibility" decision-making.

Public order operations pose their own forms of on-the-job trouble, namely ensuring that an event – from a protest demonstration to a joyful celebration – takes place with maximum safety and minimum disruption to others. Equally, there are endless opportunities for in-the-job trouble arising from the threat of having to account for one's action to superiors at New Scotland Yard or, *in extremis*, to an independent inquiry. The avoidance of these twin sources of "trouble" may prove contradictory: allowing, say, demonstrators to march along a certain route may lead to complaints from those inconvenienced thereby, whilst not allowing a march along a particular route may lead to complaints from the marchers and even a riot. Confrontation is normally regarded as something to be avoided almost at all costs. It is instructive to note that confronting a crowd was described in police argot as "dying in a ditch", because of the dire implications for both in- and on-the-job trouble. However, there are occasions when, and places where, to "die in a ditch" was regarded as unavoidable, lest even more trouble was created.

Just as the humble patrolling constable seeks to avoid "trouble" by gaining as much control over the situation as possible, so too do senior officers commanding public order operations. Routine conversations regarding public order operations are peppered with references to "losing" this or that. What is lost is control, be it control of the traffic or of the behaviour of the crowd. The imperative, therefore, is to extend maximum control over every aspect of the public order operation, but to do so without suffering the "grief" of in-the-job trouble.

Trouble and public order context

Applying this analysis to public order operations generally reveals three types, in which different levels of police intervention are considered permissible. Contrary to the assumptions of the "authoritarian state thesis", political protest is typically the occasion *least* likely to elicit a forceful response from the police.

The three types are defined by the principal preoccupation of the police: security from terrorist attack was the abiding concern of ceremonials; public safety was the top priority for New Year's Eve celebrations in Trafalgar Square; and the maintenance of order was the major concern of political protest.

Security and ceremonials

In terms of the sheer scale of any disaster that might confront the police, undoubtedly the worst would be a terrorist attack on a royal ceremonial. This represents the ultimate in both on-the-job and in-the-job trouble. The on-the-job trouble that could be anticipated would be dealing with many dead and injured people and animals. The in-the-job trouble that would result is also potentially horrendous: there would certainly be an inquiry, probably a public inquiry, in which police competence might be called into question.

On-the-job trouble is exacerbated by the fact that ceremonials breach all the usual security rules. They are highly predictable: Remembrance Sunday, Trooping the Colour, the State Opening of Parliament and Beating Retreat all occur at precisely known times, at fixed locations. Terrorists can plan an attack well in advance, achieving maximum publicity and demonstrating in the most dramatic fashion the inability of the British government to safeguard even the Head of State. Moreover, the presence of large numbers of military personnel, regarded as "legitimate targets" by terrorist groups, and whose movements are equally predictable, make ceremonials particularly attractive terrorist targets.

In the Metropolitan Police's Special Operations Control Room at Scotland Yard watching the television screens relaying the annual service of Remembrance for the war dead from Whitehall, the senior officer

43

commanding the event confided that he began to breathe much more easily once the royal family and senior politicians had left the Cenotaph. When I asked what he would do if, heaven forbid, mortars were to land in the midst of the ceremony, he replied that he would implement the various contingency plans that have been formulated and then, when the situation had returned to normal, would write his letter of resignation and return home to tend his garden. It was confidently anticipated by senior officers in central London that a successful terrorist attack on a royal ceremonial would necessitate a scapegoat to be found, and the officer in overall command would be of suitable seniority.

However, there is a paradox, for, although a successful attack on a royal ceremonial was the ultimate disaster to be avoided, the police did not approach such occasions with the foreboding that might have been expected. On the contrary, it was regarded as something of a "nice day out". When, during the Gulf war, senior officers in central London were looking for senior officers from elsewhere in the capital to take command of the various marches and demonstrations that the war prompted, they sometimes offered the opportunity to participate in royal ceremonials as a reward or inducement. Certainly, the social atmosphere amongst senior officers at the event was not one of foreboding. The Commissioner and various Assistant Commissioners were to be seen at these occasions riding along in their ceremonial uniforms, resplendent in plumed hats – hardly dressed for battle. How can this be?

The answer is to be found in the opportunities there are for the police to exert control over ceremonial events. It is here that the police flex their muscles and the velvet glove is removed. First, the operation itself was highly predictable – an "off-the-shelf job" that had been implemented many times previously in much the same way. After each operation there was a debriefing so that the lessons learned could be applied to the future. Since the operation was not the creation of the senior officers that implemented it, there was an element of corporate responsibility if things went "pear shaped". As one senior officer expressed it: "The shit will fly well above my level." Furthermore, such operations were invariably large scale, involving several senior officers in command of designated sectors who shared responsibility for planning and preparation. Because the operation was highly predictable, detailed arrangements could be made to ensure that police officers engaged on the operation understood their function. They were thoroughly briefed and given intelligence assessments regarding likely terrorist activity. For some ceremonials, films had been specially made of how military ceremonial escorts would deploy in the event of an attack and how police should support them.

Second, the events themselves were timed to the minute, thus allowing any unusual or potentially alarming event or incident to be instantly recognized. Thus, at one Trooping the Colour the chief superintendent whom I was accompanying was chatting to an even more senior officer when there was a tremendous explosion from the direction of Buckingham Palace. I was startled, but my companions casually glanced at their watches and announced that it was the first of the gun salutes from Green Park.

Third, in view of the security threat to ceremonial occasions, the police were officially allowed – indeed encouraged – to take control of the area in which the ceremonial took place for weeks prior to its occurrence. There was little restriction on intelligence-gathering, since this was a continuing feature of anti-terrorism operations. The area was physically searched, literally inch by inch, by specialist search teams. Manholes and other street furniture were sealed and "the ground" handed over by the security patrols to the officers policing the occasion. Roads were closed and even pedal cycles were forbidden on the ceremonial route. Rooftops were patrolled and anti-sniper protection provided by marksmen. Armed patrols provided security around the perimeter, supported by helicopter surveillance. Locations from which mortars and similar munitions could have been fired had been identified before the event and parking suspended in the vulnerable streets and special attention paid to them. It was on these occasions that the full paramilitary potential of modern policing was deployed.

The spectating public were carefully screened so as to exclude anyone who, or anything that, might have posed a threat to either the security or the dignity of the occasion. Anyone wishing to get close to the ceremony was required to pass through metal detection arches and be subjected to a personal search. Suspects known to have a preoccupation with royalty were identified on briefing sheets handed to all officers and were liable to be temporarily detained if seen in the area. Cameras scanned the crowds looking for anyone behaving suspiciously. There was a heavy presence of police lining the route of any procession each of whom "adopted" a section of the crowd, establishing a relationship with them so as to note their mood and whether anyone was behaving suspiciously.

Not only is every effort made to eliminate terrorist attack, acts of protest that would diminish the dignity of the occasion are rigorously prevented. A person carrying a tin-whistle that might have been blown during the two-minute silence at the Cenotaph on Remembrance Sunday was ejected from the crowd. People thought to be preparing pacifist protests during Trooping the Colour were stopped and searched, and then escorted from the area. As will be seen later (see pp. 183-5), a peaceful protest by gay rights activists during the State Opening of Parliament led to their immediate arrest. In exercising legal powers and legally dubious powers of temporary detention and exclusion from the ceremonial route, the police were given virtual *carte blanche*. In other words, the "ground is taken" well before the event and police exercise comprehensive control over the entire area and the people within it.

The public themselves not only consented to this, they participated more or less actively. People did as they were bidden largely without complaint and police perceived spectators as "friendly", "pro-police" and willingly compliant. There was little "hassle" from spectators on such occasions. What hassle there was came not from the ordinary public but from participants, such as royalty and MPs, who are notoriously difficult to deal with (see pp. 120-23).

All of this left the senior officers in charge feeling relatively "comfortable". They knew that it was a well-planned operation, over which they had extensive control, where nothing unpredictable was likely to occur. As for a terrorist attack, they hoped to deter or detect it before it came to fruition, but they were ultimately fatalistic about such a possibility, since they believed that there was little more that could be done to prevent it. In sum, the ultimate in-the-job trouble posed by ceremonials is largely negated by the almost untrammelled control allowed to prevent on-the-job trouble.

Safety and celebration

If royal ceremonials can be regarded as a "nice day out", New Year's Eve in Trafalgar Square was viewed with something approaching unmitigated horror. It typified the problems of ensuring public safety: that is, preventing serious accidental injury arising from the uncontrolled movement and behaviour of a mass of people, such as the stampede that led to the deaths of 95 football fans at the Hillsborough stadium in 1989 (Taylor 1989).

The Hillsborough tragedy had, according to senior police officers, wrought a transformation in the way that all public order events were approached. Public safety was a much higher priority than in the past. It was a consideration that impinged on virtually every type of public order event, but was most prominent in unorganized festivities held in public places deemed to be ill suited to such events. The classic illustration of such an event was the New Year's Eve celebrations throughout the West

End of London, but especially in Trafalgar Square. Another was the "Pavarotti in the Park" concert (see pp. 97–101), but because it was held on private land it did not quite represent the same threat.

The potential for on-the-job trouble at New Year's Eve was regarded as enormous – "a disaster waiting to happen". The composition of the crowd was thought to epitomize irrationality and irresponsibility. A high proportion of revellers were believed to be drunk and liable to do "silly things" such as "making waves" by pushing others, climbing unsafe structures such as flimsy ornamental street furniture and then diving headlong into the crowd, relying on others amongst the crowd to catch them. The sheer size of the crowd was such that tremendous pressures built up, particularly in certain pockets, with the concomitant dangers of crushing. As people flowed into the Square in the final minutes before midnight and then reversed that flow shortly afterwards as they left, swirling motions occurred in the crowd like irresistible whirlpools. All this occurred within a physical space not designed for this kind of gathering. Unlike a purpose-built stadium, there were no crush barriers, numbers could not be limited and the structure was not tested and awarded a safety certificate. On the contrary, the Square was seen as containing numerous hazards: buildings that lined its perimeter had more or less flimsy ornamental railings and walls, beyond which lay light wells some three or four metres deep into which people might have fallen; street furniture was not designed to withstand the pressures or the abuse to which they were subjected by revellers and had in the past collapsed, causing injury to members of the crowd; the stairs at the north end of the Square presented a danger to people entering or leaving.

The police response to this "disaster waiting to happen" was to assume almost as much control as they did at ceremonials. In doing so, the police exploited what is simultaneously regarded as one of the chief problems they face – the absence of an organizing body. In effect the Metropolitan Police organized the celebration almost without restriction. They co-ordinated the various outside agencies, such as Westminster City Council, the Department of National Heritage, London Underground and Buses, the British Transport Police and Royal Parks Police, St John Ambulance Brigade and London Ambulance Service, and the London Fire Brigade. The operation was controlled from the Special Operations Room at Scotland Yard where these various agencies had their representatives.

By the time it crossed the minds of the first revellers to make their way to Trafalgar Square to celebrate the New Year, the police had already

47

"taken" the Square. In collaboration with the respective public authorities, the fountains had been drained and the sculptured centres enclosed in hoarding. Likewise, hoarding protected statues that adorn the Square to prevent climbing, because intoxicated climbers tend to fall, injuring themselves and those upon whom they land. Barriers had been placed so as to create unimpeded access for emergency vehicles and a casualty handling area had been erected around King Charles Island. The plinth at the base of Nelson's Column was encased in scaffolding, which supported a large "matrix" signboard, broadcasting police messages to the crowd. Barriers, constructed in box formations linked together to provide maximum strength, surrounded the base of Nelson's Column and stretched towards and around the Christmas Tree. On the northern edge of the Square, across the road from the National Gallery, there were more barriers preventing people pressing against the flimsy balustrade, which might have collapsed if the pressure became too great. Yet more barriers kept the crowd away from South Africa House. In Duncannon Street, the St John Ambulance Brigade had established their own casualty-handling provision. At each of the entrances to the Square, barriers stretched across the roads and there were signs explaining in all the major European languages that cans, bottles and aerosols were not permitted into the Square. Further away, the traffic division had implemented its diversion plan to direct traffic away from the Square and do what could be done to minimize congestion. In liaison with the transport utilities, entrances from the Square to the Charing Cross tube station had been closed and encased in hoarding to prevent revellers falling into the stairwell; buses had been re-routed and a police "no waiting" area enforced at the Aldwych so as to create a temporary bus station for late-night buses. The reveller who decided to celebrate the New Year in Trafalgar Square stepped into "police property" not public space.

Not only did police comprehensively "take the ground", they also imposed extraordinary control over the crowd. At the perimeter of the Square, cordons of officers searched everyone entering, removing bottles, cans and aerosols. Inside the Square, officers on observation points directed special squads of TSG officers to locations of suspected crime or disorder. In the past, the celebrations have become prey to "steaming gangs" and police had used cameras to obtain evidence of the offences, directing the TSG officers to intercept and arrest the gangs. Increasingly, however, the rôle of the TSG officers was to quell disorderly behaviour, which was defined as a threat to public safety. Indeed, police control over the event was so total that it was they who announced the New Year on the "matrix" signboard erected around the base of Nelson's Column, which announced "A Happy New Year from the Metropolitan Police". On one occasion observed, they made this announcement two minutes early because it was felt that the density of the crowd was becoming excessive and the police wanted people to leave the Square as early as possible.

The difficulties of planning such a complex operation are, like royal ceremonials, minimized by the fact that this operation was annually "taken down off the shelf", revised and implemented. The lessons of previous years were incorporated into future events and there was accumulated experience amongst senior officers who had commanded sectors during previous operations and who could be relied upon (see pp. 44-5).

Where this operation differed markedly from that of a royal ceremonial was in two crucial respects. First, the legal authority for these measures was frankly acknowledged by police to be dubious. No doubt, the police could argue that some common law power or authority derived from the Metropolitan Police Act allowed them to search revellers and confiscate cans, bottles and aerosols. Like the patrolling police officer who uses, rather than enforces, the law to maintain public order, police in the Square could rely on the likelihood that anyone who did resist police control was likely to be inebriated and, therefore, vulnerable to arrest. Since also the centre of the Square is technically private property, owned by the Department of National Heritage, the police could impose restrictions acting as agents of the government department. However, the police actually relied on the consensual value of ensuring public safety to secure compliance. Like the spectators at a royal ceremonial, the crowds who flocked into Trafalgar Square did not resist police controls. Unlike a ceremonial they did, in principle, have the choice.

Secondly, police control was limited by the sheer size of the crowd and the inability to control its movement. The density of the crowd was so great that not only were police unable to move freely inside the Square during the period of maximum danger – either side of midnight – but ordinary officers were forbidden from entering the Square singly or in pairs. Only the specialist TSG squads were permitted to move within the crowd. Police had plans for evacuating the Square, but frankly admitted that they had little confidence in their ability to implement them during the period of maximum density. The senior officers' nightmare was that, as the Square was cleared, bodies would be discovered. Police control was literally restricted to the periphery of the event, and the conditions most likely to cause a disaster – mass movement within the crowd – were beyond their capacity to prevent. As was openly said at a planning meeting, when senior officers new to the event were having the situation explained to them, the police "hold their breath and hope a disaster does not happen".

If a disaster did happen, it was envisaged that enormous in-the-job trouble would follow, as it did at Hillsborough with the Taylor Report (1989). To some considerable extent, the likelihood of in-the-job trouble was exacerbated by the fact that the police assumed control in the Square. For example, in an effort to minimize crushing and afford emergency access into the middle of the crowd, the police erected barriers. However, the ordinary police crowd-control barriers used were not designed for this purpose and some senior officers expressed concern that they could cause injuries if people were crushed against them. In that event, the police might have acquired a legal liability they otherwise would not have had.

Thus, police felt that they would be held responsible for a disaster over which, despite their best efforts, they had little control. When patrol officers confront comparable situations, they "guard their backs". There were signs that senior officers were beginning to "guard their backs" also, by spreading responsibility. As part of the Metropolitan Police's "Partnership" scheme, Westminster City Council, the Department of National Heritage and the Property Services Agency were consulted about how best to improve the safety arrangements on a long-term basis. Although these authorities between them own the Square and surrounding streets, they do not own all the buildings that line the perimeter. Indeed two of the most prominent buildings are embassies over which the British government was unwilling or unable to exert control. The respective governments represented by these embassies were thought to need convincing that they should spend considerable sums to minimize the dangers that might befall the citizens of their host country who insisted on acting irresponsibly. Informal approaches were made to discover how best to exert influence. In addition, the Deputy Assistant Commissioner responsible for 8 Area publicly expressed his concerns in an interview in *The Times* (18 January 1993) that had all the hallmarks of preparing a defence of "I told you so" should the worst occur.

What security and public safety operations have in common is the enormous scope of police control over the event and interference with the liberties of ordinary citizens. It is against this background that the policing of public protest needs to be contrasted.

Protest

The policing of demonstrations and marches can now be considered in its public order context. Police insisted that they were "blind" to the political overtones of protest activity, but this was only partly so. The same considerations applied to policing protest as to the other public order operations considered above. Where it differed was in the ability of the police to control trouble. For the police exercised tremendous caution in how they exerted control.

The opportunity for police to exert extensive control over ceremonial and public safety operations was, in the view of the police, facilitated by the attitude of the public who attended these events, which was to enjoy themselves and not to confront the police. Those who attended demonstrations and marches, by contrast, were perceived as motivated by quite different considerations. They attended to pursue a political aim, to voice grievances and express opposition. Police action that impeded the effectiveness of their protest was thought likely to be resisted and might spark disorder. Protestors were regarded as archetypical "challengers" (Holdaway 1983) or "assholes" (Van Maanen 1978), that is people who are difficult to control because they are vocally knowledgeable of their rights. They were seen as having influential supporters amongst journalists, campaigners and MPs, who would join in protesting about any police action that might have been construed as infringing freedom of speech (see pp. 121–5). Given also that protest marches and demonstrations were likely to attract what the police regarded as extremist factions intent on confronting police at the first opportunity; that the issues that stimulated a protest might be deeply felt; that bystanders or rival groups might be prompted to oppose the marchers or demonstrators; and that foreign nationals or immigrants were often perceived as culturally volatile; there was ample on-the-job trouble in policing such events.

Not only were demonstrators seen as being much more difficult to control than were spectators at ceremonials and revellers on New Year's Eve, the policing operation too was less well tuned. Although there were repetitive elements in many marches and demonstrations, such as the "standard route" from Hyde Park to Trafalgar Square via Piccadilly and the Haymarket, each operation tended to be a "one off". Many protesting groups were unknown to police, their grievances were unfamiliar, and they sometimes followed a previously unused route, all of which meant that police had not had the opportunity to learn from previous experience. Because of the sensitivities surrounding state interference with political protest, intelligence was usually very limited and often non-existent. It was widely believed that disorder was unpredictable. It was thought to be provoked either by militant extremists over whom the police could exert little or no influence, or by some random concatenation of circumstances that were inherently difficult to control.

The highly qualified powers of the police

The conditions of political protest would seem ripe for the use of the apparently formidable legal and paramilitary power at the disposal of the police. However, we have already seen (see pp. 37–9) that those powers are rarely used. What dissuades the police from resorting to their legal powers when there is such a clear incentive to exert maximum control? The answer is the avoidance of trouble: flexing the corporate muscle of the police was regarded by senior officers as a recipe for trouble.

Confrontation – recipe for disaster

Police normally eschewed confrontation, since it was a recipe for both on- and in-the-job trouble. It is tempting to imagine that extensive discretionary legal powers backed by police public order tactics, with their paramilitary command structures, would facilitate the arrest of wrongdoers and dispersal of an unruly crowd with clinical precision (P. Waddington 1991). Senior police officers entertained no such illusions. They knew that when serious disorder erupted it was almost impossible for them to control events. Rioters have the initiative, since the police are obliged to respond to whatever disorderly or criminal acts they commit. Officers quickly become scattered over a large territorial area. The command structure tends to break down and so too does the communications system.

This is what occurred during the anti poll tax riot. On 31 March 1990 in excess of 25 000 people marched in protest at the imposition of a new system of local taxation introduced by the Thatcher government – the "Community Charge", colloquially known as "the poll tax". They marched from Kennington Park, south of the River Thames, to Trafalgar Square. The march was routed along Whitehall, past the entrance to Downing Street. According to the internal police inquiry report (Metcalfe 1991), there were factions that proved difficult to control from the outset. They appeared to have been drinking heavily, refused to march in line and began knocking over bright yellow boxes connected by white tape that marked the route.

When the march began proceeding along Whitehall, some marchers began to gather opposite Downing Street, causing congestion as other marchers tried to pass by on their way to Trafalgar Square. As Whitehall became blocked, marchers still *en route* were redirected along the Embankment and Northumberland Avenue into Trafalgar Square where the scheduled rally was being held in what was described by the sector commander as a "carnival" atmosphere. However, the mood of the protestors in Whitehall was becoming increasingly violent and the police officers in ordinary uniform guarding the entrance to Downing Street came under attack and some suffered injuries.

Eventually, the decision was made to use officers in ordinary uniform to split the group of protestors and push half of them down Whitehall towards Parliament Square and the remaining half northwards towards Trafalgar Square. This manoeuvre met with increasingly vigorous resistance and mounted officers were deployed in support. As the group were forced towards the Square, fighting intensified and as this group neared the top of Whitehall they were joined by a rush of supporters from the Square itself. Fierce fighting between police and protestors ensued, and it was at this stage that officers in riot equipment were brought in to reinforce their colleagues. Disorder spread to the Square itself as the disorderly group were forced towards it and soon there was a fully fledged riot in progress, with mounted officers charging into the crowd, missiles thrown, and a nearly completed building seriously damaged by fire. Police eventually dispersed the rioters from the Square, but in so doing succeeded only in spreading the disorder throughout the West End. During the evening there were sporadic confrontations between rioters and police. Shops were looted and cars turned over and set alight, and general mayhem reigned for several hours before order was eventually restored. The extent of on-the-job trouble can be gauged from the official statistics: 502 major crimes and 1336 other crimes were reported, 408 arrests were made on the day and 123 subsequently, and 542 police officers were injured (Metcalfe 1991). The Metropolitan Police paid a total of £9 million in riot damages.

In other words, the decision to confront the relatively small group of admittedly violent and disorderly protestors gathered around Downing Street initiated a succession of events over which police had little control. During the evening, as small groups of rioters attacked property at different locations throughout the West End, the police could do little more than rush from one outbreak to the next. They were not in control of the situation. Indeed, senior officers were barely in control of their subordinates as personnel carriers raced around with their sirens blaring despite repeated instructions from the control room not to do so.

Such disorder not only brought on-the-job trouble, it also created enormous in-the-job trouble. When any disorder occurred, the officer in command of the operation was required to complete a report to the Assistant Commissioner Territorial Operations, which might then have formed the basis of a report from the Commissioner to the Home Secretary, depending on the seriousness of the disorder. There was also the possibility that an inquiry would be held, as it was after the anti poll tax riot, when a team of 13 officers spent virtually a year compiling a debrief report that was severely critical of certain aspects of the operation (Metcalfe 1991), or the "Flanders report" into the second anti poll tax march (Flanders 1991). Moreover, some junior officers threatened to take civil action against the Metropolitan Police, claiming that health and safety laws were violated with the result that they needlessly suffered injury. The senior officer in command of central London and of the policing of the anti poll tax protest was moved to another post shortly afterwards, whether as a result of the riot or not cannot be ascertained.

Although it was a conspicuous example of the "grief" that might follow serious disorder, the anti poll tax riot was not alone. The so-called "battle of Westminster Bridge", when an illegal breakaway contingent of the National Union of Students marched to Parliament (see p. 17), also led to an inquiry by an outside force and the payment of £40 000 damages to a student who claimed to have been injured by a horse during the dispersal operation. Police recalled with horror the killing of Blair Peach during disorders outside Southall town hall (see p. 18).

Taken together, these considerations influenced senior officers in favour of exercising their powers with the utmost caution.

Arrests

Proponents of the "authoritarian state thesis" and other critics point to the highly discretionary nature of public order law and assume that it grants the police *carte blanche* to do as they please. In fact, arrests were regarded by the police as the last resort, for they risked escalating on-the-job trouble by sparking a greater confrontation. In the action that led to the anti poll tax riot, it was only when injuries to officers guarding Downing Street reached an unacceptable level that the risk was taken of intervening to move the crowd away.

Arrests also risk in-the-job trouble, for police actions are open to scrutiny in any court action that follows. In the confused circumstances of disorder, the risk entailed in making an arrest is that evidence will be insufficient. Unlike arresting a drunk in a pub brawl, the arrest of a protestor during disorder is likely to take place in front of press and television cameras. The political nature of protest also means that the arrest and any charges that follow are likely to be contested. "Legal observers" may be present and make their own recordings of the arrest (see pp. 119–20). The protest group may well have the services of sympathetic lawyers to plead their case. Acquittals were thought not only to be common, but to occur in circumstances that invited criticism of the police, both individually and corporately.

Critics of public order law can point to the use to which bail conditions and bind-overs were put during the miners' strike to corroborate their contention that the law is discretionary (see Blake 1985, Christian 1985, East & Thomas 1985, McIlroy 1985). On the other hand, the collapse of major riot trials following the Bristol, St Paul's (Joshua & Wallace 1983), and Orgreave (Jackson 1986) riots illustrates the obstacles that can face the prosecution. Severe criticism from the Police Complaints Authority of police action during the "battle in the beanfield" (National Council of Civil Liberties 1986), the policing of Leon Brittan's visit to the University of Manchester Students' Union (Independent Inquiry Panel 1985) and the policing of the Times International dispute on 24 January 1987, which led to the charging of 27 police officers with various offences, all testify to the "grief" that can accrue from taking a confrontational approach.

Certainly, senior officers approached the prospect of making arrests with considerable caution. Where it was thought likely that arrests would be made, subordinates were issued with *aides-mémoire* reminding them of necessary procedures. For example, prior to the final anti poll tax march, inspectors in charge of serials were briefed by a detective superintendent about procedures to be followed when making arrests. This was because it was felt that in the past too many arrestees had been released without charge because of inadequate evidence from arresting officers and others had been acquitted at court for much the same reason. Public order law might appear to be highly discretionary when viewed from the outside, but to police officers it was regarded as perilous to make an arrest in the sometimes confused circumstances of disorder. For these reasons, senior officers tried to impose restrictions upon which officers were to make arrests should they become necessary. On large or problematic operations, TSG officers were given this responsibility, because they were regarded as "professionals", able to make arrests skilfully and thus avoid the unedifying spectacle of a "rugby scrum" of several officers struggling with a single prisoner.

Following the disorders that had occurred around the country as councils set their respective poll tax demands in early 1990 and the particular disorder that there had been outside Lambeth town hall when the council had first discussed the issue, the police in Brixton mounted a major operation to control any assembly that gathered outside the town hall when the council convened to set the poll tax on 29 March 1990 – two days before the anti poll tax riot. Anticipating that arrests would be made, instructors from the Public Order Training Centre were deployed as a specialist arrest team. There was, in fact, rather less disorder than feared, but several people were arrested during the course of the evening. Surveillance officers gathered evidence on suspects and then the arrest team moved in. On each occasion that I witnessed, the suspect was whisked away with such speed that there was hardly the opportunity for others in the crowd to react. This was, however, unusual; what senior officers feared was the sight of officers struggling on the ground with a suspect that they were unable to control.

Senior officers could exert only limited influence over their subordinates, who retained, under the doctrine of "constabulary independence", the discretion to make an arrest in a public order situation, as elsewhere. This sometimes created difficulties that, on some occasions, needed immediate intervention. One such occasion was during an anti-racist march through Welling, when police halted the marchers while they dispersed a group of neo-fascist opponents who had congregated further along the route of the march. However, when the police attempted to resume the march, the marchers refused to proceed. It appeared that one of their number had been arrested by an officer when he had attempted to break ranks and confront the neo-fascist opponents. The senior officer in charge of the march went to where the arrested person was being temporarily held in a police personnel carrier. It was important for him to obtain the release of the prisoner, but to do so in a way that did not undermine the authority of his subordinate, for that could also cause trouble. So he began by asking what the arrested man had been arrested for and was told that it was for a breach of the peace and that the officer intended to have him charged with obstructing police. The senior officer convinced the officer that the breach of the peace was now unlikely to recur since the neo-fascists had been dispersed. He also secured the officer's agreement to proceed on the charge of obstruction by way of summons, thus allowing *the officer* to release the arrested man and allow the march to continue. The man was escorted back to the march by the senior officer and greeted with a loud cheer. The marchers then continued with their protest.

Offensive weapons

The carrying of weapons has long been outlawed in Britain and might be thought to present few problems of enforcement. After all, the police have every incentive to disarm protestors with whom they might come into conflict. However, Sikhs traditionally carry swords as part of their protests. The Metropolitan Police have a formal policy of allowing Sikhs to carry five such swords at the head of properly arranged marches. Five, and only five, swords are allowed because this number has religious significance for Sikhs.

Offensive slogans vs. freedom of speech

On some marches, the wording of banners and placards and the slogans chanted were thought sufficiently offensive to warrant intervention. However, senior officers were acutely aware of the precarious line to be drawn between the acceptable and unacceptable exercise of freedom of speech.

During the Gulf war the police consulted their solicitors after complaints were received about some of the banners and placards being carried by protestors. It was decided that references to the military or leading politicians or named countries being "murderers", or advocating "killing" opponents, would be grounds for taking action. On one occasion only was official action taken against such a banner. A faction attending an anti Gulf war march arrived at the assembly carrying a banner accusing "Jews" of "murder" and advocating the killing of MPs and soldiers. The group were asked to furl the banner, but refused. Police then confiscated it and arrested one of the group who refused to move on. However, there were several occasions when such banners were displayed, but it was thought too confrontational to intervene. Intervention was much more likely to be informal: trying to dissuade protestors from carrying banners and placards bearing what police regarded as unacceptable slogans. Even so, the police were extremely reticent about intervening at all and even more reticent about taking official action.

If action was taken at all – and it should be emphasized that it was very rare – it was usually in response to the complaints of others. On only one occasion did I witness a complaint made directly from a bystander and that

57

occasioned immediate action. A group of Palestinian sympathizers were marching from Hyde Park to Trafalgar Square. Many of their banners were written in Arabic, but as they proceeded along Park Lane a bystander alleged that one of the banners referred to Israelis as "murderers". The senior officer asked the organizer of the march what the banner said, and when this wording was confirmed, the officer removed it, in the course of which there was a modest scuffle. For a few minutes the marchers refused to continue, but eventually they did so. However, some of the marchers then provoked the police by chanting in English that Israelis were "murderers". Those chanting these slogans over hand-held loudhailers (who were assumed to be the instigators) were warned that unless they ceased they would be arrested. The chants then ceased and no arrests were made.

Deciding not to ban

Even greater caution was shown in the exercise of the more controversial powers granted by the 1986 Act. This research afforded the opportunity to observe three occasions when a decision to ban or impose conditions arose. The two most notable occasions followed the anti poll tax riot in Trafalgar Square. The first of these was when the London branch of the All England Anti Poll Tax Federation notified police of their intention to march in south London in the autumn of 1990; the second was when the national organizer for the Federation announced that a march would be held in central London to celebrate the first anniversary of the anti poll tax riot.

On both occasions there was strong pressure on senior officers to ban the march. These pressures included external political pressure, and it was the perception of the senior officers involved that any application to the Home Office for a ban would be sympathetically considered. The Assistant Commissioner with delegated authority for making such decisions held meetings with senior staff on both occasions, when the issues were discussed. The reasons for opposing a ban were remarkably consistent on both occasions.

Less formidable than it seems

The underlying reason why banning orders were not sought for these marches was that the police regarded the legislation as much less formidable than do many of its opponents. They argued that the requirements that needed to be satisfied before a ban could have been imposed were so onerous that it was a practical impossibility. The sole ground for seeking a ban is the avoidance of "serious public disorder" that cannot be prevented by the imposition of conditions, having regard to the resources available to the police to counter any such disorder. Police in London argued that it was highly implausible for the Commissioner of the Metropolitan Police to claim that, with all the officers available to him, together with the imposition of conditions governing the route and conduct of the march, serious disorder could not be prevented or, at least, effectively contained. It would not only have been absurd, it would also have been humiliating for the Commissioner even to try, so trying was not a realistic option.

This may seem a strange view for the police to have taken. However, senior officers did not share the academic opinion that the courts will not second-guess police discretion. They assumed, on the contrary, that protestors would challenge the exercise of these powers in court and the outcome of a court case would be unpredictable. The 1986 Act was new legislation that had yet to receive interpretation by the courts. The police feared that, in interpreting a new Act, the courts would in effect establish a precedent and, if this went against the police, then it would hinder them for the indefinite future. This was a risk they were willing to take only in the most clear-cut circumstances, and things were rarely, if ever, so clear cut.

The imposition of conditions suffered many of the same drawbacks. What might seem, on the face of it, extensions of police powers were experienced by police officers as offering practical assistance only in very circumscribed conditions. The most controversial addition to the law was the ground for imposing conditions so as to avoid or minimize "serious disruption to the life of the community". Opponents imagine that this would consign protest to places and times where and when they would hardly be seen, thereby condemning protest to impotence. Yet the police in London have yet to impose conditions on this basis. For, fearing an adverse precedent if challenged, the police interpreted this clause to mean that the whole of the West End would need to be disrupted for hours, or its equivalent, before the courts would uphold its use. They anticipated that they would be challenged to justify imposing conditions on a protest march when events like the London Marathon in effect closed large parts of London for an extended period. They conceded that it would be difficult to rebut such a challenge.

An indication of the seriousness with which the police viewed the possibility of a legal challenge is the steps they took to ensure that they had sufficient evidence to back their decision. When the possibility of imposing conditions on the second anti poll tax march arose, photographers and video cameramen were dispatched to the area of maximum congestion and a helicopter flew along the route to gather evidence as to the likelihood of "causing serious disruption to the life of the community". However, the conclusion of this exercise was that the area was no more congested than many comparable alternative locations. To prevent a march passing through this area because of the congestion it caused would justify preventing any march from passing through any shopping street. That, they conceded, was not a reasonable interpretation of the law.

Police frequently drew attention to how they could "get away with" banning and imposing conditions only on the National Front. The National Front's strategy of appearing ostentatiously to comply with the law made them vulnerable to legal restrictions. Other groups were perceived as not only far more willing to challenge legal restrictions, but also as better equipped to do so. One of the intellectual resources available to liberal and left-wing social movements was thought to be access to sympathetic lawyers who would argue their case in court.

Thus, whilst critics suppose that the police will exercise their powers to the full, in reality the police were wary of doing so. They wished to avoid the possibility of being circumscribed for the indefinite future by precedents set by the courts. Of course, as the police become more familiar with the legislation and precedents are established, then they may become less wary and use the Act more readily.

More trouble than it is worth

Another reason why bans were not sought lies in tactical problems of enforcement. For the police, enforcement of a ban was more trouble than it was worth.

If the police had successfully banned either anti poll tax march, this would not, in itself, have prevented those who intended to march from assembling in the area through which it was proposed to process. There is no legal requirement to notify police of an assembly and so protestors could have assembled and then announced their intention to assemble elsewhere, "walking" rather than "marching" between the two. Indeed, banning the march might have created a *cause célèbre*, which might have inspired more supporters to attend, simply in order to oppose the ban. Indeed, there was information that the Trafalgar Square Defence Campaign were preparing to "occupy" Trafalgar Square on the occasion of the last anti poll tax march if the march was banned. The occupation of Trafalgar Square would not have been subject to the discipline of an organized march – assembling at a known time and in a known place and following a predictable route. Police feared that any such assembly would have been disorganized and potentially disorderly. It was conceivable that, if police prevented the occupation of the Square, protestors would have engaged in "guerrilla tactics" throughout the West End and so re-enacted the mayhem of the original riot. Police have ample legal powers to disperse disorderly assemblies, but doing so would be tactically difficult and would require enormous numbers of officers. It was better, from the police perspective, to allow a march – even one with the potential for disorder – than to ban it.

When police made it clear that no ban was being sought, they received information that the Defence Campaign now intended to participate in the main march, thus bringing them within a structure and discipline that made them manageable.

Using, rather than enforcing, the law

Police did impose conditions on both the two anti poll tax marches. However, they did so in pursuit of their own, rather than legally anticipated, purposes. Like the patrolling constables, senior officers *used*, rather than enforced, the law to extend control and avoid trouble (P. Waddington 1994).

The second anti poll tax march planned to process from Kennington Park, just south of the River Thames, to Brockwell Park in Brixton. The police negotiated a change of the assembly point, so as to move it further away from central London – the location of the earlier riot. However, the police and protest organizers now reached an impasse: the police aim was for the march to "go from nowhere to nowhere, via nowhere", which obviously conflicted with the desire of the marchers to process where they would be seen by bystanders. Accordingly, the protest organizers wanted the march to proceed along the Walworth Road – a shopping street in a side-street of which a market is held each Saturday. They proposed marching northwards from the assembly point in Kennington Park to the "Elephant and Castle" roundabout and then southwards along the Walworth Road to Camberwell Green (a major intersection) and thence to Brockwell Park.

Police had several objections to this suggestion. First, since the Labour Party headquarters is located in the Walworth Road and the most prominent group in the anti poll tax campaign was "Militant" – an organization that had been in acrimonious dispute with the Labour Party – the police feared that the party headquarters would become a focus for disorder like Downing Street had been on the first march. Secondly, if there was disorder in the Walworth Road, for whatever reason, the police foresaw that it would be as difficult to control as the mayhem that occurred in the West End on the evening of the earlier riot. They had a nightmare vision of

61

protestors running amok, looting shops, overturning and setting fire to cars, as had happened previously. Thirdly, they feared serious traffic congestion at the "Elephant and Castle". Finally, they were concerned that the route was almost circuitous and would, thereby, cut off residents within the circle from the wider world. The police were able to persuade the organizers to avoid the "Elephant and Castle" and the Labour Party headquarters, but could not persuade them to avoid the Walworth Road entirely. It was the only place where the marchers would acquire an audience.

Once it had been decided not to ban the march, the meeting called by the Assistant Commissioner had to decide upon whether to impose conditions. The major obstacle to doing so was legal. First, their actual concern was that, in the event of disorder, it would prove difficult to control in the midst of throngs of shoppers. However, the 1986 Act did not allow such grounds for imposing conditions; they would have to show that, by going along the Walworth Road, serious disorder became *more likely*. Secondly, as noted above, it would prove difficult to convince a court, if challenged, that proceeding along the Walworth Road would cause "serious disruption to the life of the community".

It was at this point that a subsidiary concern came to the fore as a possible justification: by marching northwards from Kennington Park, the procession would be heading in the direction of central London – the location of the riot. It was not unreasonable to maintain that some militant sections might refuse to turn southwards and would try to cross the Thames and enter central London. The police did not regard the prospect as at all fanciful; indeed they had already made plans to close all of the bridges across the river in the event of any such breakaway. The protest organizers had admitted to the existence of such militant factions within the Federation who were reported to resent being "banned from central London". Thus, the justification would be that, by marching northwards, serious disorder became all the more likely.

Nevertheless, the imposition of the conditions had to be managed with tact. Police understood that the organizers with whom they negotiated were more prepared to compromise than were the other factions in the Federation. They calculated that imposing conditions would not adversely affect their relationship with the organizers and might even "get them off the hook", because the organizers would be obliged by law to comply with police directions, rather than willingly agreeing to do so. The equanimity with which the organizers received the official notification that conditions were being imposed convinced police of their interpretation.

The police also sought to "soften the blow" by assisting the organizers in compensating ways. They understood that the Federation was short of funds and that the hire of two parks, plus facilities like additional mobile lavatories, would be an onerous financial burden. By allowing the march to assemble in a small residential road adjacent to the park, they had already made a concession designed to evoke co-operation. The opportunity to do more arose when the local authority that owned the park in which the rally was to be held began to raise objections, having been initially sympathetic. The police assisted the marchers by first of all pleading on their behalf for the park to be made available. The Deputy Assistant Commissioner for that area of London wrote personally to the leader of the council, pointing to the possibly dire consequences of disorder if the park was unavailable. Meanwhile, contingency plans were made to terminate the march on Clapham Common, a large park with public roads that traverse it. The police planned to close one of these roads and allow the rally to be held thereon, in the expectation that the protestors would spill on to the common. However, the fiction of using the closed road would obviate any necessity to seek local authority permission. Moreover, if the march was terminated at the boundary of the two local authorities that shared jurisdiction for the common, it would have been difficult to apportion responsibility.

This example illustrates that even the imposition of conditions need not be as brutally confrontational as many of those who subscribe to the "authoritarian state thesis" would have us believe. On this occasion it was a carefully managed exercise of balancing coercion and accommodation (P. Waddington 1994).

This accommodation did not prevent serious disorder erupting after the march when members of the Trafalgar Square Defence Campaign organized a secondary march to Brixton prison, where many poll tax defaulters and those suspected or convicted of offences in connection with the riot were being held (see pp. 52–4).

In the aftermath of the original riot and this more recent episode of serious disorder, the pressure to impose a ban on the final poll tax march was intense. Members of Parliament, the leader of Westminster City Council and other influential figures made it clear that they wanted the police to seek a ban. However, the police were disinclined to apply for a ban. There were all the problems rehearsed above, but there were others too. First, this final march was due to take place during the height of protest marches opposing the Gulf war. Individual marches cannot be banned under the

1986 Act: bans prohibit all marches of a particular type within a given area. Consequently, banning the anti poll tax march would have meant also prohibiting anti Gulf war marches. As one senior officer put it, this would be invidious when Britain was at war ostensibly in defence of democracy. Secondly, many of the most militant factions about which the police were most concerned had participated in the anti Gulf war marches without incident. Although the context was different, some senior officers anticipated a challenge to the ban based upon the good conduct of these groups. Thirdly, it was felt that, if the marchers were prevented from going near Trafalgar Square, they would make access to the Square a *cause célèbre*. Even as indignation against the poll tax declined, protestors might have continued to return to demand access to Trafalgar Square. Thus, it was decided not to apply for a ban.

Again, this was a situation that needed managing. It was not the protestors, however, who needed management on this occasion but all the offended groups that had been lobbying for a ban. The police met the most influential individuals privately to explain why they had decided not to ban the march. They also arranged a public meeting at Westminster City Hall, to which tenants', residents' and tradespeople's groups were invited. This "public relations offensive" was designed to explain police reasoning and defuse opposition. This did not prevent the leader of Westminster City Council appealing directly to the Home Secretary to impose a ban, but such a move was precluded because the procedure requires that a ban must be initiated by a request from the Commissioner and no one else.

One of the resources at the disposal of the police for defusing opposition was the fact that they had imposed conditions on the march. This, in fact, was almost entirely notional, for the route that was imposed was identical to the route that the organizers had proposed. It did, however, give the impression to concerned outsiders that the police were "doing something" and it marginally strengthened the hand of the police legally, for if any marchers diverged from the agreed route they would have been in breach of the conditions and could have been arrested and charged. However, since the Act requires that persons must knowingly breach conditions before they commit an offence, this was hardly of any consequence. The other resource, of course, that the police could employ to reassure influential critics was the size of the policing operation. This will be discussed later (see pp. 158–9); suffice to note here that a huge force of police was mobilized to provide "insurance" lest order was not maintained by the accommodative approach the police had taken.

Democracy and the law

Pragmatism was to the forefront in police decision-making regarding the anti poll tax demonstrations, but it was not the sole concern. Senior officers also thought that it would be undemocratic for a march on an issue of such sensitivity to be needlessly banned. Occasionally, the police see it as their duty to protect rights of protest by refusing to enforce laws that they believe are being applied unreasonably and undemocratically.

During the 1992 general election the police were approached by a group calling itself "the Anti-Election Alliance". This was based upon "Class War", a militant anarchist group closely associated with the Trafalgar Square Defence Campaign whose picket at Brixton prison turned violent. They planned to march along a circuitous route from Trafalgar Square, passing Downing Street and the Palace of Westminster. The police did not greet this announcement with any relish, but began to plan an operation on the assumption that the march would go ahead.

However, the Department of the Environment, which at that time was responsible for Trafalgar Square, refused permission for the Anti-Election Alliance to assemble and hold a rally. Senior police officers regarded this decision with abhorrence: it was unfair, legally dubious in their view, confrontational, but, worst of all, undemocratic. The police wrote to the Department objecting to this decision and asking for it to be reconsidered, but to no avail. Strictly speaking, any assembly or rally that does not receive the permission of the Department is in violation of the Trafalgar Square Regulations 1952 and those assembled could be dispersed, arrested or summonsed. It was decided by senior officers that no attempt should be made to prevent any assembly or rally, and that police action would be limited to reporting the names of the organizers to the Department of the Environment so that the latter could prosecute if they wished. When the anarchists arrived for their assembly, their leader approached the sector commander in charge of the Square and asked whether they were to be arrested. When the officer replied that police would only report them to the DoE, he perceived that "the wind was taken out of the sails" of the anarchists. Confrontation was avoided and arrangements for the march quickly finalized. The march itself proceeded smoothly and quickly. There were none of the various confrontations that police had feared and planned for. It was, in the police view, a "non-event".

But why did the police accept the in-the-job trouble that their decision not to ban the poll tax marches and confront the Anti-Election Alliance aroused? Apart from what appeared to be a genuine commitment to democratic rights, senior officers sought also to maintain their "room for manoeuvre". If they were to allow external pressures to dictate their course of action, they would jeopardize their independence from political control and be unable to pursue police, as opposed to other vested, interests. Although officers felt that their decision placed their careers at some risk, they equally felt compelled to back their own professional judgement against the judgement of others.

The Sessional Order

There is one legal restriction that senior officers are much more willing to enforce, despite the risks of confrontation and notwithstanding the legally petty status of the offence. This is the Sessional Order of Parliament. Each parliamentary session commences with the passing of an order in both Houses, each of which instructs the Commissioner of the Metropolitan Police to maintain unimpeded access of MPs and peers to the Palace of Westminster, and to keep highways free from obstruction and disorderly persons. The Sessional Order is implemented by the Commissioner making directions under ss.52 and 54 of the Metropolitan Police Act 1839. By custom and practice, this establishes an area approximately one mile in diameter to the north of the River Thames – the Sessional Area – within which protest is in effect forbidden. However, s.54 carries no power of arrest and police claim that it is difficult to obtain convictions in the magistrates' court. Yet the police feel compelled to defend the Sessional Area almost at any cost, because of the "grief" that they will receive if it is violated. It was the police view that MPs and peers were notoriously prone to complain to ministers and lay motions before the House if they believed the Sessional Order to have been breached (see pp. 121–2). Even the presence of protest placards in Parliament Square would, I was told, bring a complaint from Black Rod. It was in defence of the Sessional Area that police fought the "battle of Westminster Bridge" against a breakaway march of students in 1989 (see p. 17). We will see later (pp. 180–82) that police were prepared to make mass arrests to prevent gay rights activists from breaching the Sessional Order in 1992.

The Sessional Order creates a "ditch" in which the police feel compelled to "die". Yet, even here they tried to avoid confrontation with protestors if possible. When the issue was politically sensitive, they went to even greater pains to avoid confrontation. These were the circumstances that arose on the night that the United Nations' ultimatum to Iraq expired, heralding the outbreak of the Gulf war. A group calling itself the "11th Hour Committee" announced its intention to gather in Trafalgar Square and march to Parliament so as to coincide with the end of an emergency debate then being staged in the House of Commons. The organizers of the march did not officially notify the police of their intention. Still the police learned of it and made contact, warning them that the march would be in breach of the Sessional Order.

Thus, this march was doubly illegal: it was not notified under the 1986 Act and it breached the Sessional Order. Still the police did not seek to prosecute the organizers nor did they attempt to prevent the march by force. The strategy was to attempt to approach the organizers of the march as protestors assembled in Trafalgar Square on the evening of the protest. They would be asked not to *march* along the highway, but to *walk* along the footpath. This would be facilitated by the police, who would keep one footpath free of pedestrians and would escort protestors on to the central area of Parliament Square upon their arrival. In other words, compliance with the Sessional Order would be almost entirely notional, but the senior officer did take the precaution of obtaining the Home Secretary's approval for this course of action.

Even so, the organizer did not acknowledge responsibility for the protest and refused to negotiate an agreement with the senior officer who approached him as protestors assembled. The fall-back position for the police was to prevent the march continuing along Whitehall by placing a cordon of police across it. However, the footpath was to remain available and marchers were to be directed towards it. As the protestors streamed off Trafalgar Square and soon collided with the police cordon there was pushing and shoving, and some scuffles. Although a substantial body of protestors was successfully redirected on to the footpath, the cordon was soon overwhelmed by the sheer and unexpected size of the protest, and protestors began streaming down Whitehall towards Parliament Square. No further attempt was made to prevent this and, when they arrived at Parliament Square, a cordon of police was placed across the road to guide the marchers on to the central area and keep protestors away from the Palace of Westminster. A number of protestors then sat down in the highway partially blocking the Square, but police were able to keep traffic moving around the remainder of the Square. A number of people were arrested at this and another sit-down demonstration on the far side of the Square, but no one was prosecuted for failing to notify police of the march or for breaching the Sessional Order. However, there was some relief that, as the marchers arrived in Parliament Square, the light above the clock face (usually referred to as Big Ben) was extinguished, indicating that the sitting had ended and, therefore, that technically the Sessional Order no longer applied.

Two nights later there was a virtual replay of this protest to oppose the commencement of the bombing campaign. Again, protestors assembled in Trafalgar Square and attempted to march illegally to Parliament Square. Again, the police attempted to negotiate at the scene but were rebuffed. Again, the marchers collided with the police cordon, but this time it held and all of the protestors were shepherded on to the footpath. They made their way to Parliament Square, where the police stopped the traffic so that they could assemble in the centre of the Square. This the protestors did. They held their protest for some minutes before drifting away. On this occasion there were no sit-down demonstrations and no arrests.

Thus, even when protestors were clearly in breach of the law, the police were loath to enforce it. They reasoned that it was preferable to try and gain control over the march, illegal though it was, rather than to run the risk of a violent confrontation.

Conclusion

The police applied the same considerations to the policing of political demonstrations and marches as they did to other public order operations. Like officers engaged in routine patrol, they attempted to minimize trouble – either on-the-job or in-the-job. This did not mean that the policing of political demonstrations was identical to that of other operations, for protest demonstrations have the potential for creating particular kinds of trouble. It would, however, be a mistake to assume that in the hierarchy of organizational "disasters" (Thomas 1972) political protests figured most prominently. Undoubtedly, a successful attack on a royal ceremonial or a Hillsborough-like tragedy in Trafalgar Square were regarded as far more calamitous. Political demonstrations were problematic not because they threaten the most dire in-the-job trouble, but because the ability to forestall on-the-job trouble was thought to be restricted. Far from political demonstrations being opportunities for paramilitary excess, senior officers believed they must be approached with caution for fear of the police being accused of oppressive measures. It is in limiting the police's room for manoeuvre that the political overtones of demonstrations and marches were most acutely felt.

CHAPTER 4

Negotiating protest: policing by consent?

Introduction

The preceding chapter argued that police sought to exert extensive control over political protest, but were constrained to do so without the risk of confrontation. How, then, did the police try to extend control? The answer is that in public order operations they relied, as officers do in much of police work, on informal means. The principal method of securing compliance was through negotiation with the organizer of the protest.

Negotiation under the law

The government justified the notification requirement contained in the 1986 Act on the ground that it should spur the parties into negotiating mutually acceptable arrangements. Critics of the 1986 Act, on the other hand, feared that negotiations would be undermined because the police could rely upon their coercive powers to impose conditions and ban marches (Thornton 1985, D. Waddington et al. 1987). As Staunton puts it:

> If the Government's public order proposals become law, the relationship between the organisers of marches and the police will change from the present one of bargaining in order to reach an agreement, to one of outright conflict. The increased police discretion about which protests or demonstrations would go ahead is bound to lead to accusations of political policing. The demon-

strations which are so much a feature of a healthy democracy will be undermined. (1985: 7)

Robertson confidently asserts:

The notice requirements merely discourage sensible people from volunteering to "organize" a procession which would lay them open to a criminal charge if it took an unnotified turning or started an hour late because the band failed to arrive. (1989: 71)

The 1986 Act requires that notification should reach the police not less than six clear days before the intended date of the procession. The Act also requires that certain information be furnished, namely the date and time that the procession is due to commence, the place of assembly, the proposed route, and the name and address of the organizer. No estimate of the numbers likely to attend is required, even though this is crucial to police planning. Nor is there any obligation upon the organizer to participate in any further negotiations. Legally speaking, the organizer is entitled simply to furnish the minimum information and then leave the ball in the court of the police.

In fact, it is extremely rare that organizers restrict themselves to minimal compliance. Police evidence to the Home Affairs Committee (1980) estimated that 85 per cent of protest marches were preceded by negotiation. Of the 75 protest marches observed as part of this research, only three failed to notify police at all, which amounts to 96 per cent compliance. Just three gave less than the minimum notice and five more complied only minimally. On the other hand, 16 gave more than 90 days' notice, of whom five gave more than 180 days. The mean length of notice given by protest organizers was 55.5 days. Records of meetings between organizers and police were incomplete, but, of the 56 events for which records are available, there was at least one meeting for 22 of them, two meetings for 24, and 13 occasions when more than two meetings were held. All of this indicates eagerness to engage in negotiation, rather than the reluctance feared by some critics.

"Winning over"

On Friday, 16 October 1992, a meeting was hurriedly arranged at Scotland Yard with a representative of the National Union of Mineworkers. A few days previously, the government had announced plans to close 31 coal mines. The NUM had organized a mass lobby of Parliament for the following Wednesday (21 October) to coincide with the House of Commons debate on the issue. A lobby of Parliament can be held without notifying the police under the 1986 Act, but police were aware of it since officers who are posted to the Palace of Westminster are responsible for making arrangements for lobbies. Such was the anger of miners and many sympathizers that the NUM now felt that a lobby would not accommodate all those wishing to protest and they wished to discuss arrangements with police for some other form of protest in addition to the lobby. The meeting was held in a large conference room, was chaired by a superintendent from the Public Order Branch and comprised a further 14 officers representing the respective force areas and departments that might be involved. There was some concern expressed by some of the police present that such a turnout might be perceived by the organizer as "a bit heavy".

The NUM representative arrived, escorted by a police officer, and sat next to the superintendent. He immediately apologized for his casual appearance, explaining that he had been working throughout the night at NUM headquarters in Sheffield and had travelled down to London that morning. His apologies were jokingly brushed aside and he was offered coffee, which he declined. The superintendent introduced all those present, making light of the large number of police involved in the meeting.

The NUM representative then explained that events were moving fast and that he had been in effect incommunicado on a train all morning. He had, however, seen a copy of that morning's *Daily Mirror* newspaper, which had encouraged readers to join the NUM protest on the forthcoming Wednesday – an initiative of which the NUM knew nothing. He added that NUM headquarters had been deluged with offers of support from the most unlikely quarters. He explained how passengers on the train had applauded him when he came to alight at the station. He added that the taxi driver, realizing he was an NUM official, had refused his fare and told him to contribute it to the fighting fund. This caused much merriment amongst the police, some of whom began looking out of the window for the Second Coming of Christ!

Then the meeting got down to business. Police explained that they had been in touch with NUM headquarters which was now estimating that some 10 000 protestors would wish to show support for the lobby on the following Wednesday. Various options were discussed, and police officers rang personal contacts in different local authorities to discover the availability of various assembly places. Eventually, it was agreed that a march would be held from Kennington Park to a road just to the south of the River Thames, opposite the Palace of Westminster. The police would close the road to facilitate the dispersal of the march and delegations to the lobby would be allowed across Westminster Bridge to the Palace of Westminster. There was concern amongst the police that protestors would wish to go to Parliament Square in violation of the Sessional Order, and the NUM representative agreed that the union would provide stewards to prevent any mass movement of protestors into the Sessional Area and, therefore, any possible confrontation with police. There was shared concern at the potentially disruptive behaviour of "hotheads" and the NUM representative repeatedly reassured the police that the NUM wanted a peaceful protest, because they did not wish to lose the "moral high ground". For their part, the police replied that they accepted fully the good faith of the NUM. After a couple of hours the meeting was concluded and the NUM representative went to finalize arrangements with local authorities and other interested parties.

The situation remained fluid, however. By early evening, the police had received word from NUM headquarters that numbers on the march were now likely to exceed those that could be accommodated at the assembly point that had been arranged earlier in the day. Another meeting would be necessary the following day and an NUM delegation would arrive at Scotland Yard early the next morning. It was clear to the police that this was likely to be a major demonstration and the Commander who had been appointed as "Silver" decided that he should join the Saturday meeting.

Next morning, members of the Public Order Branch were having breakfast when a single woman representative from the NUM arrived. Expecting a delegation several strong, the staff at the reception desk failed to notify the Public Order Branch of her arrival and she was left waiting in the foyer for some minutes. When this was discovered she was hurriedly brought to the canteen and, amid much apologizing, offered breakfast, which she declined. Over coffee she was assured by senior officers that they wanted to do everything to facilitate the protest and she, in turn, reassured them that the NUM wanted no disorder or disruption.

A chief superintendent's office was then commandeered in which to hold the meeting, which was to last until mid-afternoon. Throughout the meeting, the representative needed to make several telephone calls to NUM headquarters in Sheffield. She offered to use a payphone, but the police insisted that she use one of their phones and the privacy of an office, for which the representative expressed effusive gratitude.

The police proposed that, in addition to and quite separate from the lobby of Parliament, there should be a march that would circumnavigate Hyde Park. They favoured this because, not knowing how many protestors would attend, they wanted a route that was relatively self-contained. It would minimize traffic congestion, and be near enough to central London to satisfy protestors, but outside the Sessional Area. For the police, the greatest worry was that protestors would seek to march *en masse* from Hyde Park to Parliament Square. They wanted to keep the two parts of the event – the lobby and the march – quite separate.

It was agreed with the representative that police would organize parking for coaches. For their part, the NUM would supply special labels, with unique serial numbers to prevent counterfeiting, for those coaches conveying delegations going to the lobby. This would ease segregation between lobbyists and other protestors. There were problems to be overcome ensuring that delegates to the lobby remained distinct from participants in the march, since they might each originate from the same coal-mining areas. However, the NUM representative agreed that the union would ensure segregation was maintained.

The NUM, having agreed to the Hyde Park demonstration, now needed permission from the Department of National Heritage (DNH), which administers the park. The DNH normally refused to accommodate marches on weekdays, and moreover the proposed route would require that the roads within the park be closed, something else that the park authorities were expected to resist. However, the police undertook to do everything in their power to persuade the park authorities to allow this demonstration as an exception. "Leave it to us," the police told the NUM representative. The park authorities also banned placards within the confines of the park. The representative was advised that placards should be issued as people left the park and collected again when they re-entered, but she was confidentially told that the police would not themselves enforce this regulation. Throughout these discussions the representative repeatedly remarked that it was "good" for her to see that the police were not simply an arm of the government and were willing to pursue the interests of the NUM – a union with which they had recently been in conflict during the miners' strike.

Sensitivities about the miners' strike arose when it was proposed that mounted officers should be on duty within the park. The police went to great lengths to reassure the representative that this would certainly not be an aggressive deployment. Mounted officers would be in their normal equestrian uniform and simply be acting in a crowd-marshalling capacity.

Still the representative was uneasy at the suggestion. It was agreed that mounted officers should be deployed, but that they would be withdrawn if any hostility was shown to their presence.

With the plan agreed, the representative telephoned NUM headquarters for final approval, but there was an objection to the rigid segregation of those on the march and those attending the lobby. Headquarters wanted delegates to the lobby to attend the march and then to adjourn to Central Hall (opposite the Palace of Westminster) from where the lobby would be organized. This aroused fears amongst the police that as the delegates adjourned they would be followed by a mass of protestors who would crowd into Parliament Square. However, after some further discussion it was proposed that lobbyists would witness the start of the march and then be escorted from the park to the lobby. This would involve complex arrangements being made to keep delegates separate from other protestors and coaches being parked so as to facilitate their departure, but the police were willing to do this. About one thing the police were adamant: once the delegates had left the park, no one else would be allowed to follow and this was accepted by the NUM representative, who promised that stewards would ensure that marchers complied with this requirement. Another phone call was made to NUM headquarters, only for the representative to return to say that on reflection the NUM now accepted the first plan. The representative expressed effusive apologies for wasting their time and gratitude for the understanding and flexibility the police had shown. The Commander replied that, if he was fired as a result of this operation, he would expect a job in public relations for the NUM!

In the event, the demonstration was held in accordance with the arrangements negotiated. Cordial relationships were maintained, so that when a radical group attended the march with a large banner on which was printed an obscene slogan, the "Silver" commander asked NUM stewards to have it removed. Several burly miners confronted the group, who were seen shortly afterwards, leaving the park with their offensive banner furled. Moreover, when another militant group staged a sit-down demonstration, stewards encouraged other demonstrators to continue. Another militant group did stage a breakaway march to Parliament Square, but were not supported by other demonstrators and were easily contained by police. Although there were a few anxious moments, the day's protest was concluded peacefully and without any arrests. There was an exchange of mutual thanks between the NUM and the Metropolitan Police.

The complexity and urgency of these negotiations were unusual, but this example illustrates many of the normal features of the negotiating process.

The police achieved their foremost aim (the segregation of the protest march in Hyde Park and the lobby in Parliament Square) and did so by "winning over" the organizer of the march. Let us, then, try to isolate the components of the negotiating process. It will be helpful to divide these into structural and interactional elements.

The structure of negotiation

Structural features of the negotiating process do not exist in order to induce organizers to agree to police proposals, but they tend to have this effect nevertheless – an effect of which experienced police officers are tacitly aware.

The "home ground advantage"

The first imperative of the police is to bring the organizer of the demonstration into negotiations, preferably on police premises. As soon as organizers consent to visit police premises the police acquire the "home ground advantage". Being a visitor to a police station has many compliance-inducing features. Organizers were isolated from others who might offer support and advice. Like any other visitor, they gave up their freedom of movement, because police premises need to be kept secure and, therefore, all visitors gave personal details to those at reception, wore a pass, and were also escorted wherever they went within the premises. Thus, from their arrival, organizers were required to comply with police demands.

One obvious reason why the police prefer to remain in their office and have organizers travelling to meet them is its convenience. It would clearly have been inconvenient and inefficient for a large delegation of police to have travelled to Sheffield, when the proposed NUM protest was to be held in London. But meeting on police premises can also be inconvenient; New Scotland Yard, for example, was woefully short of accommodation. The result was that meetings were almost invariably held in the private offices of senior police officers, as was the Saturday meeting with the NUM representative. This had its lighter side: for most of the period of research the occupant of the office suitable for larger meetings was an enthusiastic athlete. However, the use of his room obliged all the negotiators to sit amongst a variety of sportswear draped inelegantly over any suitable hanging space – an experience bound to break the ice! Not infrequently, senior officers found themselves being asked to vacate their offices for the duration of the meeting or returning to find their offices commandeered for negotiations that were in progress and being obliged to retreat uttering suitable apologies. The organizer might have witnessed either or both of these eventualities and appreciated thereby the inconvenience the meeting caused.

All of this places the organizer in the position of an intruder into the private world of the "backstage" of policing (Punch 1979). Organizers were obligated to submit to the social rules that govern the private space that they temporarily occupied: others moved freely, whereas they could not. "In jokes" circulated to which they were not privy; for example, the athletic senior officer's office was referred to by his colleagues as "the drying room". Visitors relied on the directions of their hosts and accepted their assurances that a particular place was suitable for holding a meeting, even if appearances suggested otherwise. The organizer was in the "hands" of the police, complying with their requirements and requests. Those "hands" might be quite accommodating, as the NUM representative found when she wanted to make telephone calls, but she was dependent upon the goodwill of her hosts.

Bureaucracy

The police organization is a bureaucracy that can also induce people to comply with police wishes. The police could not compel organizers to supply all the information they considered essential for planning the policing operation. They could invite the organizer to complete certain standardized documentation in the interests of efficiency. Letters can be lost but an official form containing a unique identification number, duplicated on a tear-off receipt handed to the organizer as proof of notification, gave the organizer a reasonable guarantee that their notification had been properly received. In return, the form asked for the name of the organization, the reason for the demonstration, the number of people likely to attend, whether petitions were to be delivered or meetings held before or after the march, and the names of any speakers who were due to address the rally. The organizer was not obliged by law to provide this additional information, but its presentation as an official form that did lawfully require the provision of *some* information and the failure to explain the scope of legal requirements seemed to act as a strong inducement.

This elicitation of additional information was not oppressive in any overt way; indeed it was treated, probably quite genuinely, as a routine chore. The absence of any sense of drama conveyed the impression that what was being asked was unexceptional and unexceptionable. If organizers had difficulties completing the form, police officers were anxious to assist, for example, by reading out the names of all the roads along which the march was due to proceed. They reassured organizers that incomplete information would be acceptable, while requesting that when full details were known the police be informed.

Another dramaturgical twist came in the "ceremony" of exchanging the "route form". It has been noted in Chapter 2 that the police rarely invoked their powers to impose conditions under the 1986 Act. However, they did seek, wherever possible, to meet the organizer in the few days preceding any march. Ostensibly this meeting was to allow the senior officer in charge of the march to establish contact with the organizer and "iron out" any last-minute problems. At this meeting, the organizer was, almost invariably, presented with three copies of the "route form", each of which had spaces for his or her signature and the signature of the police officer who had conducted the negotiations. Of the 75 operations for which documentation is available, the "route form" was signed on 48 occasions; the form was inappropriate for six others; conditions were imposed under the 1986 Act in two cases, thus obviating the need for a "route form"; and on two other occasions the march was cancelled before the form could be served. There were only three occasions where organizers refused to sign the form, since they had not notified police of the march and not entered negotiations.

The "route form" was, in fact, a standardized letter on official headed note paper that contained details of the agreed route and any "conditions" that had been "agreed". Its use was recommended by Lord Scarman's inquiry into the disturbances at Red Lion Square to ensure that arrangements were clear to all parties (Scarman 1975). In introducing this document, the police casually explained that the "standard condition" was that the march would not stop except on the instructions of police. This was the sole condition for six marches of the 75 files examined, and was omitted from only one form. A commonly applied additional condition was that vehicles were not allowed to take part in the march or, if allowed, that they would be restricted in number (usually to one) and follow at the rear. This was included on 35 occasions. More rarely, conditions were included that forbade participants covering their faces or engaging in other conduct that the police wished to discourage. Additional conditions of such a kind were included on 14 forms. It is important to note that the form was couched in the language of what the police will or will not "allow".

The point is that all of this is entirely extralegal: the police are not imposing conditions under the 1986 Act, they are simply describing what has been agreed. The organizer is under no compulsion to sign the route form, but in a context in which the police first sign each copy, as a mark of good faith, it is difficult for organizers to refuse. The solemnity of the ritualized exchange, in which the organizer and senior officer both received a copy, and the third copy was retained for the file, gave the impression that this document had much greater significance than it had in law. For the senior officer it was a weapon that could be used in further negotiations at the scene. If marchers were slow to leave the assembly point, then the organizer's attention could be drawn to the agreement they had reached and recorded on the route form. If there was any attempt to vary the route, then the route form could be wielded as a persuasive instrument. Far from its influence being diminished by its unofficial status, the fact that it was a record of agreement enhanced its power to persuade. Unlike the imposition of legally enforceable conditions, the imposition of "agreed conditions" can be passed off as "merely routine". Since it is a record of agreement, it is also non-confrontational.

Expertise

Police also had the advantage that they usually enjoyed a monopoly of expertise, which they used selectively to advise and assist organizers unfamiliar with practices and procedures, and in doing so guided organizers along a path acceptable to the police.

Organizing a demonstration not only entailed notifying the police, arrangements had also to be made with various authorities for a venue to assemble and to hold a rally. The police could and usually did inform organizers of the need to do this, furnished them with the necessary telephone numbers and advised them which official to ask for. They sometimes informed organizers of the regulations that governed such places as Hyde Park, and advised them how best to arrange for the distribution and/ or collection of placards, as they did for the NUM representative.

In deciding upon the exact route to follow, the police were also equipped and knowledgeable. The 1986 Act requires the organizer only to notify the police of the route to be taken; if the police object then they need to satisfy the quite stringent test of "serious disorder, serious disruption to the life of the community" and so forth. Police had a more pressing concern: to follow a route that presented as *few* problems as possible. Organizers rarely attended negotiations with their own map or any detailed route in mind. They knew that they wished to start at, say, Hyde Park and terminate at, say, Trafalgar Square. They then found that the police helpfully suggested a suitable route, proffering a map and pointing out the route, calling out the names of roads familiar to police officers but probably unknown to all but a handful of others. If the organizer did not like the route, then another was offered as an alternative. In this way, the organizer was induced to accept a "package deal" constructed by the police.

Sometimes, albeit rarely, organizers tried to go a different way. Relying on the authority that comes from familiarity and expertise, the police often simply announced that they never went along that route or stopped at that particular location. Sometimes they resorted to technical explanations, such as their disinclination to march the "wrong way" along one-way roads because of the difficulties this creates in directing traffic. These objections were typically quickly followed by offering an alternative, more acceptable to the police. Very rarely did organizers challenge these assertions or reject the alternative.

Of course, police were familiar with and knowledgeable about the topography of the area through which the march would go. What looked convenient on a map might have been less acceptable in practice. The police knew from experience how long it would take a march to proceed from one point to another. They knew about forthcoming roadworks and other likely obstacles. They were aware that, while it might seem sensible to enter, say, Hyde Park through one of its southerly gates, the gates are too narrow to facilitate ease of access. This local knowledge could readily be deployed to dissuade organizers from a course of action that did not meet with police approval.

Interactional practices and ploys

Negotiation is not a neutral process: the word implies that each party will seek to achieve its goals, possibly at the expense of the other. Police were seeking maximum control over the event and attempted, therefore, to persuade the organizer to see the wisdom of their viewpoint. In doing so they repeatedly employed what have been described in another context as "ploys" (see Sanders et al. 1989, but note Dixon 1992), some of which have already been noted. However, they did so with little or no deliberation: unlike officers interrogating a suspect, there was no prior discussion about how they might "play it". The ploys were embedded in the practices of negotiation and understood in terms of what constituted "competence" (Fielding 1984).

One practice that was notable for its absence was any reference to the law. The only occasions witnessed in which any reference was made to the

1986 Act at all were when senior officers who did not belong to the public order fraternity were involved. Referring to law was regarded by those who deal with demonstrations on a regular basis as gauche and a sign of amateurism. The NUM could not give six days' notification, but that was studiously not mentioned to either representative, for to do so might have injected an air of confrontation. If organizers proposed a course of action that was clearly illegal, police normally responded by referring to the likelihood that a passer-by might object, thus compelling the police to intervene. Thus, when the organizer of a march protesting at the treatment of "untouchables" in India proposed carrying placards containing large photographs of dismembered bodies, the police did not invoke the Indecent Displays (Control) Act 1981, as they could have done. Instead, they suggested that bystanders might be so horrified by the images that complaints might be made to police, thereby prompting them to act.

The one exception was the Sessional Order: not only was this referred to quite freely by police, but organizers planning protests when either House was sitting were routinely issued with one, and asked to sign another, copy of the Sessional Order. However, this was habitually presented as an obligation that Parliament imposed on the police, not as a law they had any discretion in enforcing. Thus, both NUM representatives were told that Parliament forbade marchers congregating in Parliament Square and even lobbyists would not be permitted to carry placards and banners.

Setting the agenda

The structural setting made the organizer a guest of the police in an unfamiliar environment in which movement was controlled. The disadvantage at which this put organizers was reinforced by the control the police exerted over the meeting itself. Habitually, the police chaired any meeting that was formally convened and determined the agenda. Even if it was a small meeting of the organizer and one or two officers, the police initiated the vast majority of discussion. If organizers interrupted and tried to raise issues of concern to them, they were likely to be told that "OK, but we'll come back to that later". Before the organizer was able to raise issues him- or herself, the chairman invariably asked other police officers whether they had any other relevant issues to raise. Thus police priorities were given pre-eminence. In the case of the NUM, it enabled police to establish as a first principle the inviolability of Parliament Square. This was followed by discussing detailed arrangements for the lobby, which reinforced its segregation from the march in Hyde Park.

The first item on the agenda of any meeting was, inevitably, introductions. At larger meetings the chairman introduced each of the police representatives. This was often the opportunity for making humorous or light-hearted remarks, for example, the often solitary constable present taking minutes was frequently introduced as the person who "did all the work". This was followed by inviting the organizer to introduce him- or herself. Unlike police introductions, the organizer was expected to say not only who he or she was, but also what position he or she held in the group or organization he or she represented, how that group was constituted, what its aims were and from where it drew its membership. The "openness" with which organizers explained all this was regarded by police officers as indicative of their good or bad faith and, just as important, their competence. Many protest groups were ad hoc and/or umbrella organizations comprising many constituent groups. Organizers who was fluent in their description of the organization and their rôle within it conveyed the impression of personal competence and of a protest group that was well organized, with whom the police could do business.

The remainder of the meeting usually followed a series of stock items: the time, date and place of the assembly; the route to be followed; the length of the rally; the numbers of people likely to attend; the groups or organizations that were likely to support the march; whether there was any likelihood of opponents disrupting or attacking the march or rally; stewarding arrangements; whether particular categories of people, such as children or the disabled, were likely to join the march; plans to hand in petitions; any intention to have vehicles on the march; arrangements made for coaches to drop off and pick up marchers at the beginning and end of the event. This information allowed the police to plan the type and scale of the operation to be mounted. It was also, of course, much more than the police were empowered to elicit by law alone.

Again, all of this was perfectly routine, even normal, but contributed to the organizer's lack of control over the situation. It was not his or her meeting, but the police's meeting. It was held on police premises, within their bureaucratic structure. They dictated the direction and pace of the meeting according to their priorities and preoccupations.

Authority to negotiate

The negotiations with the second NUM representative were quite unusual in one important respect, namely the rank and rôle of the officer with whom she negotiated. It was most unusual for an officer of such rank and responsibility to enter negotiations. In this case, speed was paramount and decisions needed to be taken authoritatively and urgently. Normally, the police negotiators did not have command of the operation and were subordinate in rank to the Commander. This allowed the negotiating officer the opportunity to avoid making a split-second decision without fully considering its ramifications, on the grounds that any contentious matter must be referred back to superiors. Indeed, the negotiations were always provisional, subject to ratification by superiors. This tactic was not exclusively used by the police; negotiators too often said that they had a limited mandate and that some decisions needed the approval of their respective executive committee. Some organizations delegated the task of negotiation to a particular member or officer, who was not truly "the organizer". Police resisted attempts by organizations to distance negotiation from ultimate decision-making. They sometimes asked the organizer if he or she had the authority to negotiate and, if not, insisted that those with that authority attend in person. Here the law came to the aid of the police, but doubtless not in the way that legislators envisaged. For the person who notified the police became in law the "principal organizer" responsible for the march. The police sometimes drew this to the attention of the representative and asked if he or she was willing to shoulder that responsibility. In the case of the NUM the police were unusually willing to negotiate with a representative who had to ratify arrangements with headquarters.

Responsibility

More routine was the way in which police tacitly sought to impose responsibility upon the NUM, for example, by encouraging them to provide labels for coaches, arranging for stewards to prevent mass movement to Parliament Square, ensuring sufficient "entertainment" in the park to occupy the attention of protestors, and so forth.

It has already been noted that the police routinely elicited various information about what the organizer envisaged so that they could plan the policing operation. This process also had the consequence of implicitly making the organizer accountable to the police for the arrangements they had made. To the extent that the organizer had made detailed provision, the police showed approval, as they did to the NUM representative who had draft copies of the labels to be used to identify coaches. Where an organizer had failed to make arrangements or was ignorant about possibilities (such as the number of coaches booked by supporters travelling from outside London and their parking arrangements), then their status was diminished in the eyes of the police. The organizer would then find him- or herself virtually instructed about what was required. "What you need to do now is this . . . and then you must do this . . ." This reinforced the gap between the knowledge and expertise of the police and the ignorance of the organizer, adding to the dependence of the latter on the former.

Of particular concern to police were arrangements for stewards to be provided and briefed. They repeatedly emphasized that it was the organizer's protest, not that of the police. It was up to the organizer to ensure that those attending the protest acted properly and the police would take action, at least in the first instance, only through stewards acting as intermediaries. The police would act directly only if the stewards could not cope or something occurred that was so outrageous that the police could not ignore it. The message was clearly conveyed that it was far better for the organizers and the group he or she represented to "police themselves" than to have the police intervene. Virtually all organizers were furnished with a leaflet offering officially sanctioned advice. To ensure close co-ordination between stewards and police, a junior officer was sometimes appointed as a "steward liaison officer" for larger marches and arrangements were made, where possible, for them to attend any stewards' briefing.

There is little doubt that most police genuinely believed that it was mutually advantageous if marchers "policed themselves". Indeed, they valued those organizations most that were best able to do so. Thus, trade union marches were regarded with something approaching affection, because they were well organized and stewarded. Officers valued the co-operation and envied the relatively unfettered power of stewards who, like those at the NUM march, would "turf out" unwelcome "extremists". Equally, there was no doubt that police regarded stewarding on most marches as extremely poor or non-existent. It was a source of repeated complaint.

Why, then, did police pay so much apparently futile attention to stewards? Since they envisaged that they would normally find themselves stewarding the event and would always need to have sufficient officers available for this purpose, why did the police not simply accept reality? Why did they try and persuade organizers to have protestors "police themselves"? Whether intended or otherwise, asking about the stewarding arrangements added to the pressure upon the organizer. It reinforced the sense of responsibility: it was their march; it was for them to ensure good behaviour; they must supply and brief stewards, who must be clearly identified. In other words, by organizing a march, the organizer was assuming a considerable measure of responsibility, and appropriate arrangements should have been made. If there were problems, responsibility would rest with the organizers, not the police.

Apart from imposing a sense of responsibility on the organizer, this tactic also served to marginalize "extremist" groups that might be attracted to the march. Once responsibility for the outcome of the march was accepted by the organizer, he or she acquired a shared interest with the police and a shared perspective towards those who might be considered "troublemakers". This assisted police in isolating such groups and legitimated any coercive action the police felt they needed to take. For example, they sometimes prevented certain groups taking a position at or near the head of a march, it was hoped at the request, or at least with the agreement, of the organizer. This action was ostensibly taken on the grounds of protecting the organizer's proprietorial rights in the event, but also served the police's interest in preventing groups that were difficult to control from leading a march, and possibly leading it astray. More commonly, the union of interest between police and organizers simply facilitated the flow of information and intelligence.

Ganging up

The weight of responsibility was added to by other agencies who combined with police to impose requirements. Marches almost invariably needed either to assemble or to conclude on privately owned property. In consequence, the organizer was obliged to obtain the permission of the owner of the property on which they assembled or dispersed. Usually, the owners were a public body: Hyde Park and Trafalgar Square were the responsibility of the Department of National Heritage (formerly the Department of the Environment), and various London boroughs were responsible for other favoured assembly and rally locations, such as Marble Arch (Westminster City Council), Geraldine Mary Harmondsworth Park, Kennington Park and Brockwell Park (Lambeth), Clapham Common (shared between Lambeth and Wandsworth), and Battersea Park (Wandsworth). These bodies enjoyed the privileges of ownership, which in the case of Hyde Park and Trafalgar Square were underpinned by statutory regulations. They could refuse permission for protestors to gather: for example, assemblies or rallies were forbidden in all the royal parks other than Hyde Park. If they allowed protestors to meet on their property this was subject to contractual arrangements. For example, protestors were required to provide a deposit, or to insure the owners against loss, or were charged for the collection of litter in some parks.

For the police this offered the opportunity of "playing both sides against the middle". On the one hand, owners of such locations relied upon the police to safeguard their interests. Indeed, the Metropolitan Police were (until February 1993) contracted routinely to police one of the most heavily used assembly and rally locations, Hyde Park. In any event, the police had almost invariably developed a good working relationship with those responsible for administering these various locations. Liaison often occurred between the police and the owners before permission was granted to assemble or hold a rally. The owners often imposed conditions more onerous and subject to more direct penalty for non-compliance (such as withholding a deposit) than could the police. On the other hand, the police could conspire with the organizers to circumvent the unreasonable demands of the owners and their agents. When the police indicated to the NUM representative that they would not enforce the park regulations forbidding placards and banners, they were employing a commonly used tactic. In so doing, the police became an "ally" of the protestors deserving reciprocation. Not only was it "good" for the NUM representative to see the conflict of interest between police and park authorities, and how the police tried to protect the miners' interest, it was also good for the police that she recognized what they were doing on the union's behalf.

On one occasion, the police became involved in the internecine politics of a protest organization, ganging up with an organizer with whom they had developed a good working relationship so as to prevent her dismissal. The police were concerned that members of the executive committee of the organization had evidently begun to distrust the close relationship that had developed during the course of a protracted campaign. A replacement organizer arrived to conduct negotiations for one march, accompanied by her displaced predecessor. The police were noticeably less accommodating to the interloper than they had been hitherto to the predecessor. Instead of assisting, they allowed the replacement organizer to encounter all manner of problems for herself, thus obliging her to rely upon her predecessor for assistance. The march was predictably a shambles compared with those that had preceded it. Needless to say, the original organizer was reinstated for the remaining marches in the campaign and the previously good working relationship resumed.

Either way, the police used their pivotal power as the third member of a tripartite relationship to form coalitions with whoever served their interests.

Favours

The police did many favours for the NUM both great and small: they waived all reference to the 1986 Act; they arranged coach parking for both marchers and lobbyists; they interceded on behalf of the NUM with the park authorities to allow a march that otherwise would have been forbidden; they were willing to make complex and special arrangements to facilitate the attendance of lobbyists at the march; and they allowed the representative to use their telephone. Likewise, when the TUC sought to march the following Sunday there was nowhere available in which to hold the rally, mainly because a group of expatriate Indians were holding a rally in Hyde Park before marching to the Indian High Commission. Again, the police prevailed on the Department of National Heritage to allow an exception to the rule that only one rally was allowed in Hyde Park on any day. They then persuaded the other protestors, whose protest had been arranged for the same Sunday, to hold their rally a little earlier than planned and then, because of unforeseen problems on the day of the march, to move their small rally from the park to Marble Arch. Nor was this exceptional; police frequently did favours for all manner of protest groups.

This assistance was not offered out of largesse, but from a practical concern to win the co-operation of organizers. The police sought reciprocity from organizers: by doing favours, they expected organizers to offer compliance in return. This was why they preferred organizers with whom they could establish a relationship of mutual benefit. Thus, during the Gulf war the police assisted the Campaign to Stop War in the Gulf to arrange facilities and, in return, on one occasion obtained the agreement of the Campaign to alter their proposed route so as to avoid encircling the Ministry of Defence at a time when officials were working in the building.

Spurious friendliness

Doing favours, offering advice and guidance, and forming alliances are merely the most explicit expression of the general atmosphere of amicability that pervaded most meetings between police and organizers. As both NUM representatives found, organizers were welcomed with broad smiles and introductions were accompanied by shaking hands. Joking was a familiar part of the exchange. Police officers took the opportunity to be ostentatiously helpful. Officers expressed pride in their ability to "get on with" a broad cross-section of protest organizers, eagerly dropped the names of those with whom they were familiar (most notably former presidents of the National Union of Students now prominent in public life) and retailed

86

stories of having been invited to parties hosted by organizations across the political spectrum. On the sole occasion observed when organizers rejected such overtures and impugned police motives (the Anti-Election Alliance), officers genuinely took umbrage. The refusal by a representative of this anarchist group to shake hands, and his overheard suggestion that the police's contempt for him and his colleague was palpable, were the subject of resentful comment and gossip for weeks afterwards.

On the other hand, although the police might have genuine affection for some organizers, the appearance of friendliness was often a studied performance. Almost unfailingly, organizers' veracity and competence were subjected to withering scrutiny the moment they left the negotiating meeting. On some occasions, police officers, who a few minutes earlier were friendly to the point of being unctuous, denigrated the organizer's personal qualities. For example, one organizer had hardly left the room before one officer loudly proclaimed that he was a "lying, cheating, scheming little git". Indeed, all organizers tended to be regarded with suspicion.

The friendliness shown by the police was a device that was consciously manipulated to achieve their goals. The task of negotiation, for the police, was to persuade the organizer to hold a protest or other event that was minimally disruptive. Confrontation was merely an obstacle to persuasion, whereas friendly advice and guidance were an aid.

Consensual values

How, then, did police object to organizers' plans without overt confrontation? We have seen that the law was of little assistance and was thought to be confrontational. If police objected to some proposed course of action, they relied upon consensual values, the most commonly invoked one being "safety". The police presented themselves as concerned primarily with the safety of the marchers and other road-users. This was a genuine preoccupation of the police, but also allowed them to object to proposals that threatened other interests.

The clearest illustration of this was to be found in the strong opposition that organizers encountered to any proposal to have a vehicle at the front of a march. From an organizer's point of view there might have been compelling reasons to head the march with a vehicle. For example, a flat-back lorry could carry a brass band, or loudspeakers that could blast out the message of protest, or it could carry placards and banners aloft explaining their grievance, or icons, such as model Scud missiles being used to bombard minorities in Iraq. They found, however, that the police were implacably opposed to any vehicle at the head of a march. They were repeatedly told that petrol or diesel vehicles were ill suited to being driven for protracted periods at walking pace: diesel engines, in particular, tend to disgorge oily smoke that engulfs the front ranks of marchers. Such vehicles tend to break down, necessitating the march passing it and venturing out into the path of oncoming traffic – a dangerous and disruptive manoeuvre. Vehicles tend to attract marchers, who walk alongside them, and try to jump on to them with the attendant danger that people will fall under the wheels and be injured or killed. The police allowed a vehicle at the rear of marches, if the organizer insisted, but that was a concession usually justified if it was necessary to carry equipment from the assembly to the rally, or to ferry the disabled, or collect those too young or too old to walk the full distance.

There was, however, a contradiction in the police argument, for marches were almost always headed by a vehicle – a police control van. Control vans were equipped with writing desks, police radios tuned to various frequencies and mobile telephones. Their crews were responsible for radio communications and any administrative duties, such as logging events. They were habitually used to lead marches, being equipped with a large checkered dome that contained a flashing light designed to warn other road-users of the presence of a march. Not only were these vehicles petrol driven, they were also rather ancient ("R" registered) and prone, in their dotage, to break down. On one occasion, marchers assisted police in pushing a disabled control van to one side, in order that they could pass it. When a breakdown occurred, police immediately replaced the broken-down vehicle with an alternative petrol-driven vehicle. What was the difference between a police petrol- or diesel-driven vehicle and a similar vehicle provided by the organizers? The answer is that the former was under police control and the latter would have been under the control of the protestors.

We have seen that the police sought to exert maximum, but subtle, control over the conduct of marches. A vehicle at the head of the march was a useful adjunct to maintaining control, because it led the way. A police vehicle led the marchers along the prescribed route at a pace dictated by the police commander. The police vehicle could be instructed to speed up, slow down or even stop, if conditions required it. For example, if the march began to straggle or gaps appeared, then the commander asked the control van to slow down, so that those at the rear could catch up. There would not have been as much control over a vehicle arranged by the protestors themselves, which might have diverged from the route, wittingly or not, leading the rest of the march astray. In addition, when vehicles carry passengers the latter are not as preoccupied with the march as those who walk; they are free to chant and to drink, and, in police eyes, to act irresponsibly in a highly visible way. Should the police wish to intervene, passengers on a lorry could occupy the "high ground", making police action physically difficult and highly visible. Finally, if disorder erupted, a vehicle like a lorry could become a mobile barricade and a ready supply of ammunition for petrol-bombs, as occurred on 24 January 1987 outside the *Times* newspaper plant at Wapping. From the police point of view, these were compelling grounds for excluding vehicles from marches entirely, particularly at the front, but they were reasons that remained undisclosed.

These undisclosed reasons for seeking to prevent vehicles heading marches did not, of course, invalidate the arguments based upon the safety and convenience of marchers. Indeed, the police were about to experiment with an electrically powered control vehicle, thus eliminating the apparent contradiction in their stance towards petrol- and diesel-driven vehicles. The point is that overt arguments can serve covert purposes.

The other argument that was commonly used appealed to both consensual values and self-interest: it was that the marchers should minimize disruption to others. Police explained that, while they appreciated the quite understandable desire of the protestors to gain maximum publicity for their cause, organizers were also reminded that, if their march created too much disruption, especially traffic dislocation, their cause would be harmed. The police also assumed the mantle of impartial guardians of the public interest, explaining that they were duty-bound to balance the rights of the protestors to demonstrate with the rights of other citizens to go about their business without undue hindrance. Rarely did such appeals fail to persuade organizers to agree to arrangements that satisfied police requirements.

Precedents

Through these means the police attained their goal of achieving far more control over the event than the law allowed, and did so without risk of review by the courts because it was obtained by consent. In most cases observed, this was facilitated by the organizers themselves, who seemed quite willing to accept police requirements. It was quite rare for an organizer to resist. Indeed, in most cases the protestors were so few and so compliant that little difficulty would have arisen even if they did not accept police conditions. Yet, even in these cases the police insisted that, for example, there should be no vehicles at the front or in the midst of a march.

Why did they bother to do so? The reason was to avoid "giving anything away" and creating a precedent thereby. Police experience was that the organizer of any one demonstration often participated in others. If the police allowed, say, a vehicle at the front of one march, the organizer of a later event would have the opportunity of asking why similar arrangements were not extended to his or her protest. By applying what amounted to a blanket policy, the police avoided the issue arising at all. Moreover, since they frequently knew so little about the organizer, the group he or she represented and who was likely to be attracted to the march, they felt that caution was always necessary.

Democracy

The police typically tried to maintain control over this web of relationships by isolating the various parties. Organizers negotiated with the police alone, which allowed the police selectively to disclose information, such as the nature of restrictions imposed by the Sessional Order. This, of course, was intended to enhance police power and might be regarded as a restriction on civil liberties achieved by duplicity and deceit. The alternative might be a more open democratic approach whereby all the parties meet under independent chairmanship to reconcile competing interests. For example, in many other countries it is the local authority that is responsible for negotiating suitable arrangements with demonstrators. This was commended to the House of Commons Select Committee by various witnesses as a transparently more democratic procedure (Home Affairs Committee 1980).

Something akin to such a forum has actually been created in connection with the Notting Hill Carnival (see pp. 18–20). After the disorder that ended the 1987 carnival, the then Deputy Assistant Commissioner responsible for the area of the force, Paul Condon (later to become Commissioner), proposed the establishment of an ad hoc support group. This comprised, at the time of this research, representatives of various interested parties: the police, the carnival organizers (Notting Hill Carnival Enterprises Limited [NCEL]), the Home Office, local authorities responsible for the area in which the carnival was held, funding organizations, and local residents' groups. It met under an independent chairperson: an Afro-Caribbean lady who had long been active in community relations. The secretary to the group was provided by the police, and this rôle was performed by an inspector who was devoted full time to planning the policing of the

90

carnival. Its meetings were held in public (although it seemed that few members of the public attended) in Kensington and Chelsea town hall. Planning for the 1991 carnival commenced almost immediately after the 1990 carnival. The debriefing meeting from the preceding carnival held in October 1990 highlighted the positive and negative features of the previous August's carnival and thereby set the agenda for the forthcoming series of negotiations. The support group met again in January, and from March onwards met monthly up to the staging of the carnival in late August. At each meeting there were reports from each of the principal parties, most crucially the chairperson of the NCEL, the Deputy Assistant Commissioner, the local authorities and funders.

The settlement arrived at after the 1987 and 1989 disorders was considered by NCEL to be too restrictive. NCEL sought to slacken restrictions, whereas the police were equally intent on containing the carnival within its current, quite restricted, bounds. Indeed they sought to strengthen control through more effective stewarding and better overall organization. One focus for dispute was the issue of the time at which the carnival should close. As part of the 1989 settlement, this had been agreed as 7pm, but NCEL wanted it to be much later, and suggested a 10pm close-down. For police, the 7pm closure was a victory that they treasured and they vigorously resisted any concession. It was their view that crime and violence increased enormously after dark on the Monday, and, since it took two or three hours for carnival-goers to drift away, an early closure was essential. There were also cost considerations for the policing of the event. As it was, maintaining a large force of police for three further hours of carnival would have proved extremely expensive.

The police succeeded in achieving their aims as comprehensively as they routinely did in less open negotiations. How was this decision and others so in line with police interests arrived at and what does it suggest about the operation of this kind of open forum?

Spurious friendliness

Police tactics in the support group were remarkably consistent with their approach to private negotiation. First, they avoided outright confrontation by emphasizing how all those involved in the support group were partners working towards the same end. Like their colleagues engaged in more private negotiations, they cultivated the appearance of friendliness and expressed genuine affection for many of the others involved. Their tactics were eagerly to acknowledge the success of the previous year's carnival, which had been free from disorder, but cautiously to note that this testified to the effectiveness of the early closure, compared with crime-ridden previous years, and that, even so, crime began to show an increase once darkness fell. Secondly, again like their colleagues elsewhere, they appealed to the self-interest of NCEL. Carnival, the police said, was "calming down" and it should be left to stabilize its new, more positive image. Perhaps in the indefinite future the situation could be reviewed, but now was not the time to rock the boat.

Favours

External conditions enabled the police to pursue the strategy of presenting themselves as collaborators in a joint enterprise, rather than as an obstruction to others' goals. NCEL had taken over responsibility for organizing the carnival after the 1987 disorders, with a mandate to transform it from a somewhat chaotic street festival into a commercially successful cultural celebration. This transformation required sponsorship, all the more so because funding from public bodies was being reduced and would cease entirely in a few years' time. If the carnival was to survive it would need to change its image and this was frankly acknowledged by NCEL, which foresaw future carnivals being patronized by families rather than the "young and tough". Police argued that a later closing time threatened that prospect for the future, the increasingly positive image of the carnival and the likelihood of sponsorship. Sponsorship deals needed the endorsement of the police, local authorities and central government, and that endorsement was implicitly conditional on the existing closure time. In other words, significant parties (including the police) were willing to do favours for NCEL, provided NCEL "played the game".

Ganging up

The police did not need to oppose a later closure too overtly, since other representatives did so more effectively. Outright, indeed vociferous, opposition was voiced by representatives of local residents. One of the senior officers privately remarked to colleagues that in order to achieve their aims the police needed to do nothing other than sit back and allow the residents and others to do the police's opposing for them. It was difficult for NCEL to dispute the legitimate vested interest of the residents, or to minimize the disruption that many endured during the carnival when they were unable to drive cars into their own neighbourhood or to walk to their houses without identification that allowed them through police sterile areas, and when they

92

suffered carnival-goers using gardens as lavatories and other depredations. A non-police coalition of residents, local and central government representatives, and funding bodies was also instrumental in pressing for more money to be spent by NCEL on more effective stewarding, another police interest.

Reliance on others for support was not, however, an untrammelled blessing for the police. Since others had their own perceptions of the carnival and vested interests, they could not be relied upon to support all police aims. The skilful appeal to the interests of other representatives by NCEL could secure the interests of the latter at the expense of those of the police. For example, police had hoped to receive the support of residents' representatives to defeat a proposal by NCEL to install "bar sites" in the carnival area. These were mobile licensed retail outlets for the sale of alcohol whose operators were to pay a fee to NCEL for permission to operate. Police had two principal fears: first, if these bar sites proved successful they would present targets for robbery. Secondly, the presence of bar sites would increase pressure for police to prevent the casual sale of alcohol by small traders and this would be a recipe for confrontation on the streets that might provoke disorder. NCEL were able to persuade other members of the support group that bar sites were a legitimate means for NCEL to generate the necessary income needed to place the carnival on a sound commercial footing. This appealed to the financial interests of funders and appealed also to residents, who were offered the prospect of the more regulated sale of alcohol.

A different kind of problem arose over the enforcement of health and safety. At first police warmly welcomed a highly critical report on standards of health and safety at the carnival by members of a local authority Environmental Health Department. The report advocated the imposition of severe restrictions on the levels of sound emitted by music amplification equipment and improved standards of hygiene of cooked food. This promised to regulate two features of the carnival that the police had been seeking to control for years without much success – sound systems and traders. And it did so in pursuit of consensual values – health and safety. Used with discretion it would add to the police armoury a means of bringing further pressure to bear on operators of sound systems. However, police attitudes became more equivocal as it became clear that the Environmental Health Department insisted on operating independently and in ways that the police feared might create confrontation. At a private meeting between the police and the senior Environmental Health Officer, an attempt was made to secure an undertaking that any enforcement action would be taken only with the agreement of the police. Her refusal to subordinate her enforcement priorities to those of the police transformed health and safety, in the eyes of many sector commanders, from a weapon in the police armoury into a loose cannon.

Marginalizing troublemakers

In police eyes, the Notting Hill Carnival equivalent of "extremists" was a group of prominent local people associated with the "Mangrove" restaurant and community centre. Relations between the police and the Mangrove had been turbulent for many years, since this had been a centre of local (and to some extent national) resistance to what was regarded by members of the Afro-Caribbean community as police harassment (for a history of the carnival see Cohen 1980, 1982, Gutzmore 1982, and Pryce 1985). The situation came to a head in 1987 when police mounted a drugs raid on the Mangrove and arrested its proprietor, Frank Critchlow. Critchlow was subsequently acquitted, after it was alleged that drugs had been planted by police during the raid. During the period of this research, a civil action by Mr Critchlow against the Metropolitan Police was outstanding (and was settled out of court shortly after the conclusion of the 1991 carnival).

Prominent members of Mangrove had also played a leading part in the organization of the carnival until they were superseded by NCEL. Police favoured the more accommodating style of NCEL, and sought to do nothing that would undermine the NCEL's position within the local community. This gave NCEL greater influence over the policing of the carnival than would otherwise have been the case. NCEL could withdraw accommodation – a significant threat to police interests. The police felt obliged, therefore, to reciprocate, provided their interests were not threatened too directly. The description of the sterile areas as "safety zones" was one such concession. Another was to change the title of the document formally drawn up that set out the respective rights and duties of NCEL and the police. It had hitherto been described as a "Notice of Agreement", but this suggested to the NCEL that they were subordinate to the police. So the title was changed to that of a "Code of Conduct", which, in the view of NCEL, indicated an agreement between equals. Symbolic gestures of this kind and a general aura of support were within the gift of the police and they were willing to give them.

More significantly, the police were prepared to "gang up" with NCEL against others involved in the carnival whom they sometimes accused of being insufficiently accommodating of NCEL's legitimate interests. They were critical of the local authority for refusing to make available a small park, Horniman's Pleasance, at the times NCEL wanted to stage the curtain-raiser for the carnival, a steel band competition called "Panorama". This was staged on the Saturday prior to the commencement of the carnival the following day. NCEL wished to hold it during the evening, but the local authority insisted that the normal closing time for the park must be adhered to. In the event, organizational chaos meant that the competition did not begin until after it should have concluded. Police suspicions were aroused and they privately accused the organizers of engineering the delay, but they were no more prepared to enforce the closing time of the park than their colleagues in central London were prepared to enforce the regulations of Hyde Park against protestors. Indeed, they went further, assisting in making hurried changes to plans on behalf of NCEL, using police vehicles to tow a trailer on which a steel band was conveyed, and eventually announcing the results of the competition over the public address system of a TSG personnel carrier. As the commander responsible for policing "Panorama" remarked at the time, while he would have preferred a better-organized event, the chaos gave him the opportunity to cement good relations with NCEL. It also prevented the former organizers from being able to criticize NCEL for any conspicuous failure.

Consensual values

As in other, more private, negotiations the police employed the "safety" issue to their own advantage. They repeatedly emphasized the priority they gave to ensuring public safety and played down their rôle in the maintenance of public order. Although no doubt to a large extent genuine, restrictions could be imposed in the name of safety that would have been contested if presented as an anti-crime or public order measure. One major issue was the creation of "sterile areas" throughout the carnival area. Various streets in the carnival area were closed to access by anyone other than the emergency services and residents. The most important of these, from the police point of view, was a street that connected the main location for police reserves with the centre of the carnival area and its most sensitive symbolic location, the All Saints Road. This enabled riot police unimpeded access to the heart of the carnival area. It, and other smaller sterile areas, also offered safe havens into which suspected offenders could be rushed immediately after arrest, thus minimizing the opportunities for bystanders to try and rescue suspects and create thereby a confrontation. Police wanted more and bigger sterile areas, but they believed that the NCEL wanted fewer and smaller ones, for not only did they occupy valued space, they also represented a symbolic reminder of the recent troubled history of the carnival.

The police strategy for resisting any reduction in sterile areas rested on "safety". The nominal purpose of these areas was not to tackle crime and public order, but to ensure public safety. The density of crowds at carnival made access for emergency services difficult anywhere within the area. The police maintained, that in the event of a major disaster, it would be crucial to obtain speedy access and this the sterile areas would facilitate. In addition, the presence of empty streets would allow escape for carnival-goers caught in a crushing incident. In recognition of this, the police renamed these areas "safety zones". As it happened, when the carnival was closing on the Monday evening in 1991 a canister of CS gas was released by someone in the crowd in the All Saints Road. This caused a stampede of people seeking to escape the choking gas and the sector commander hurriedly ordered the opening of barriers into the central "safety zone". The stampeding mass of people were able to escape in safety and were then escorted through the empty streets to an exit away from the CS gas. Later the sector commander observed, somewhat to his apparent surprise, that the "safety zone" had performed its nominal purpose effectively and that this incident could be used to strengthen the hand of the police in future negotiations over the size and location of "safety zones".

Negotiating in public

How then did this exercise in public negotiation differ from those normally conducted in private? The outcome was remarkably similar: the police secured their primary interests without confrontation. Police success owed little or nothing to their legal powers, which were hardly ever mentioned. It was a political success, in much the same way that they succeeded politically in private negotiations. What was different was the part played by third parties. They largely did the police's bidding in "ganging up" to defeat proposals made by the NCEL. In part this was because police interests and those of the groups represented on the support group coincided. This is hardly surprising: groups that cause disruption to the normal life of communities, be it by protest or by mildly rebellious street festivals, tend to be drawn from the more marginal sections of the population. Their powerlessness is not diminished by representation on open democratic decision-making bodies, like the support group. On the contrary, their dependence on the powerful becomes more evident than before. Ranged against them are representatives who may be prepared to tolerate their activities, even facilitate them, but only on terms that are acceptable to those with power. In the case of the carnival, the threat of disorder and crime was so pervasive that the police did not even need to raise it. They could rely on threats to "public safety" to mobilize opposition.

These observations echo those of Morgan (Morgan & Maggs 1984, 1985a, 1985b, Morgan 1987, 1989), whose research on consultative committees set up following Lord Scarman's report on the Brixton riot (Scarman 1981) arrives at much the same conclusion. This has wider implications for the notion of democratic control of the police, for such a concept fails adequately to recognize the realities of power relations. The powerless are not empowered by formal constitutional arrangements. If they were, then the struggle for equality would have been shorter and more successful than it has been. Relatively powerful interests on the carnival support group prevailed because they were financially powerful, well organized, and able to form coalitions. The NCEL, on the other hand, were isolated, financially dependent and represented marginal interests. Democracy, in this instance, was not liberating, but a controlling device.

A departure from the norm

The success the police enjoy in achieving their ends by these means is so common that it is difficult to affirm that the elements identified above have the impact that has been attributed to them. There was, however, one negotiation that differed significantly from the pattern. It was not associated with protest or dissent, nevertheless it resulted in a major public order operation involving over 1400 officers. It also generated a tremendous amount of antipathy on the part of senior police officers towards the event, more or less open confrontation with the organizers and an acrimonious "debriefing" when the parties eventually gathered together to review the operation. This event was none other than the "Pavarotti in the Park" concert in Hyde Park, which celebrated the famous tenor's 25th anniversary as a professional singer.

Conflict arose from contradictory views of the police rôle.[1] The impresario's relationship with the police was mediated through the park authorities. He saw his function as simply staging a free classical music concert. In his view, the police had responsibility for the surrounding area and would need to be consulted about traffic management around the park, but had no responsibility for crowd management within the park. They certainly were not asked to control the event itself, for the impresario regarded control of the event as his responsibility.

The police view was fundamentally at odds with that of the impresario: for them this concert represented a major public order operation. Their chief concern was to avoid a public safety disaster on the scale of the Hillsborough tragedy (Taylor 1989). The memories of many senior officers stretched back to the "Royal Fireworks" – a firework display staged in Hyde Park on the evening before the wedding of the Prince and Princess of Wales. The consensus was that an estimated 250 000 people had apparently attended the event and at its conclusion there was nearly a disaster as the crowd tried to leave the park through the few narrow exits, resulting in severe crushing. The police feared a repetition of this situation at the Pavarotti concert, with possibly more serious consequences. Secondly, they also feared that they would be expected to assume responsibility for crowd management within the park. One reason for this fear lay in the curious status of Hyde Park, which at that time was policed by officers from the Metropolitan Police under a special agreement with the Department of the Environment. Their apprehension was reinforced by the impression they gained from contacts with the park authorities. To ensure public safety in Hyde Park would, in the estimation of the police, have required an enormous force of officers. This led to their third concern: that if, by the use of police resources, the concert was a success, then it was likely to be followed by other similar events. The royal parks were about to be given "agency" status within the Department of the Environment and the police believed that the parks would be under pressure to generate income by such means as staging concerts. The more successful the park authorities were in doing so, the more demands would be placed on police resources. In sum, this led to a police view that the concert should not have been staged at all, and that they wanted no part in it.

At first sight it may appear that the police and the impresario held complementary perspectives: neither saw much of a rôle for the police. The problem was that the police could not remain remote from the event. First, they felt that, without a force of stewards adequate in number, training and organization, a disaster might well occur. They doubted the capacity of the organizers to mobilize such a force of stewards and considered themselves duty-bound to provide sufficient officers to intervene if disaster threatened. Thus, they mounted a major public order operation. Secondly, they could not avoid responsibility for the area surrounding the park. They imagined that a concert expected to attract a huge audience to a venue in central London on a weekday evening would cause traffic dislocation and this needed to be catered for. Thirdly, they had responsibility for protecting the various VVIPs that were expected to attend, such as government ministers and members of the royal family. For these reasons, negotiators aimed to exert as much control over the staging of the event as they could, without becoming directly responsible for the arrangements within the park. The principal resources available to negotiators were the same informal means that were habitually employed in negotiating protest demonstrations, but they were far less effective in this case.

What distinguished these negotiations from others was that the usual balance of power was significantly disturbed. Unlike protest demonstrations, where organizers typically approach the police unprepared and can be steered to achieve police goals by the provision of advice and guidance, the police found themselves confronting a well-organized impresario who knew exactly what was wanted and how it was to be achieved. They felt that their attempts to gain control through the provision of advice and guidance were spurned. The impresario, on the other hand, insists that police advice was actively sought but not forthcoming at an early stage, and that when it was eventually offered it was meddlesome interference in an activity in which his organization was more expert than the police. Either way, self-assertive businesspeople not only resisted police influence, but also were not at all hesitant in making demands and couching them as such. Thus, instead of an organizer who readily yielded to subtle police pressure, the police found themselves dealing with an organization that resisted and challenged the influence they sought to bring to bear. Instead of amicability, relations between the police and the impresario quickly degenerated, with the police reserving far more hostility towards this event and the organizers than was witnessed on any other operation.

The police were also placed in the position of "playing away", rather than having the "home ground advantage" they were accustomed to. Hyde Park is private space over which the police were unable to exert any significant control or influence. It was a repeated source of complaint that, had the event been staged in a purpose-built stadium, they would have had much more control. As it was, they felt that in crucial respects they were presented with a *fait accompli*: the concert would be held on a weekday evening in Hyde Park.[2] They felt that they were required to manage the consequences of those decisions, without the opportunity effectively to influence the decisions themselves.

The police lost the "home ground advantage'" in other respects too. Although meetings were held on police premises, the impresario and his representatives were not overawed by intruding into the "backstage" areas of policing. They regarded security procedures at Scotland Yard and other police premises as irksome, rather than intimidating, and were quick to complain about being kept waiting. Most importantly, the police rarely chaired meetings and were invariably outranked by other interested parties. The fact that the concert was to be attended by royalty and other VVIPs, and that some of the proceeds were to be donated to the Prince of Wales' Tree Appeal, meant that the police confronted powerful interests. It was the police who were relatively isolated, rather than the organizers of the event. Instead of "ganging up" with others to defeat proposals, they found that others were "ganging up" against them.

Not only did the police find that they were able to exert little control over arrangements within the park, they had no more success in controlling provision outside. This is illustrated by the issue that came to dominate negotiations – the closure of Park Lane. The police had sought to resist any proposal to close Park Lane at the end of the concert to facilitate egress from the park, while making contingency plans to do so in order to safeguard pedestrians, if this became necessary. They sought to draw a distinction between the private interests of the impresario and the park authorities, and the public interest represented by the threat of traffic congestion. However, during negotiations a relatively junior officer was pressured in effect to concede that Park Lane would be closed, and senior officers subsequently, and reluctantly, felt compelled to accept this concession because of the obvious threat to public safety as people left the park.

With few of their non-confrontational sources of power and influence available to them, the police adopted an increasingly confrontational stance. Of course, the Public Order Act did not apply in this instance and, because the concert was to be held in a royal park, which benefits from Crown immunity, an entertainments licence was not needed. Nevertheless, the police strongly objected to the arrangements for crowd management within the park and pointed to how these deviated from proposed government guidelines on how such events should be managed. By these means they hoped to embarrass the park authorities into addressing their concerns regarding the physical layout and number of stewards on duty. When this did not have the impact that the police had wished, they eventually enlisted the Home Office, resulting in an exchange of letters at ministerial level with the Department of the Environment. This led to concessions by the park authorities, allowing the Safety Officer for Westminster City Council to act as an adviser and thus, through this route, to require that some of the anxieties of the police be addressed.

Despite these concessions, the police remained dissatisfied with the event and published a lengthy document itemizing their complaints. At a subsequent "debriefing" held at the Department of the Environment, there was an acrimonious confrontation with the organizer and the relationship between the police and the park authorities came under severe strain.

What distinguished this event from others observed was that the police did not "organize it for them". They confronted a powerful organizer and lacked many of the resources they would normally use to achieve their purposes. Instead of relying on guile to achieve their ends, they resorted to official means and open confrontation.

Conclusions

What is so remarkable about most negotiations is that, in stark contrast to those concerning "Pavarotti in the Park", they are so ordinary and amicable. Certainly, these observations refute the fears and expectations voiced by most advocates of the authoritarian state thesis. Negotiation had not been abandoned in favour of reliance upon coercive powers, because those coercive powers – formidable as they might appear – were regarded as an obstacle to the police achieving as much control over the event as they sought. By "winning over" the organizer, the police achieved much more extensive control over the conduct of the march than the law alone would allow.

However, although the process of negotiation might appear as a victory for "policing by consent", the extent to which the organizer genuinely consented may be doubted. As in other areas of police–public encounters, the balance of power and advantage usually lay firmly in favour of the police. Negotiation was less a process of "give and take" and more that of the organizer giving and the police taking. The police were enormously successful at ensuring that protest took place on their terms. Is this because police negotiated in "the shadow of the law"? That is, did organizers consent because they knew or feared that they would have been coerced if they did not? Resolution of this issue would require data regarding the perspective of organizers that is unavailable here. There was, however, no overt indication that this was so.

There is, however, another simpler, more obvious and compelling explanation. As the example of the NUM march illustrates, the police had a far more potent source of power than the law – they provided a service. The NUM march took place on terms dictated by police, but it did take place. Had the police not gone to some considerable lengths, there would probably have been no NUM march. For marches generally, it is the police who will close assembly areas to traffic, escort the march through congested streets and protect it from ill-disposed opponents. The police could have in effect banned a march in central London by the simple expedient of refusing to accompany it. On one occasion this is in effect what they did: only a handful of marchers turned up at the assembly and, after waiting some considerable time to allow latecomers to arrive, the officer in charge announced, to the protests of the would-be marchers, that he refused to "bring London to a halt" for such a small number and dismissed all his officers. He did not attempt to prevent them marching (for he had precious few officers left who could be used for the purpose). He simply refused to *facilitate* the march. The marchers were obliged to accept the alternative of holding an assembly at a nearby location, because there was no way they could have hoped to cross the heavy traffic in the main thoroughfare along which they had intended to process.

Thus, the police have much to offer a protest organizer, but they seek something in return; it is after all a *negotiation* and that implies that the police have aims they wish to achieve. Those aims go well beyond strict compliance with the law: they seek a *minimally* disruptive demonstration, not just something that avoids "serious disruption to the life of the community"; they want *control*, not just compliance. Of course, had the police refused to assist the NUM in organizing their protest, they would have run the risk that a large number of disorderly protestors might have descended on Parliament Square, causing trouble for the police. The process of negotiation, then, involved an exchange in which the protest organizer achieved his or her basic aim, the holding of a protest demonstration, in return for doing so in ways that conformed to the police's basic aim, the avoidance of trouble.

What made the negotiating process so ordinary was that the police used methods commonly employed in social and business exchanges, rather than the formalities of the law. Police officers recoil from the suggestion that they are sometimes deceitful, but deception is a routine feature of social exchange. Their friendliness towards organizers was often "spurious", but no more so than that displayed by a salesman to a customer. Police used their expertise and knowledge to secure their aims, but in the manner of a coach steering an athlete to greater achievements (Strauss 1966). Other enforcement officials also adopt such an accommodative approach so as to achieve wider goals. Amongst Environmental Health Officers (EHOs) (Hutter 1988) this was exhibited through the use of tactics designed to persuade and cajole that are remarkably similar to those used by officers negotiating arrangements for marches. For example, businesspeople were persuaded to improve standards by appealing to their sense of responsibility, just as police appeal to consensual values; like the "route form", informal letters were used as instruments of mild pressure; and, just as police did favours for march organizers, so EHOs turned a "blind eye" to minor transgressions in return for adherence to important standards.

Marchers have a right to process where and when they wish, unless the police take (what they regard as) the legally precarious path of imposing conditions or seeking a ban. However, without police assistance that right is inconsequential, for although an organizer could, in principle, opt to comply only minimally with the requirements of the 1986 Act, by simply giving notice of a route, the police, by the same token, would be under no obligation to stop and/or divert traffic. As the Greater London Council (1986) correctly remarked, "The police will always be negotiating from a position of strength" (p. 34), not, as they imagined, the strength of the law, but the strength of their social position. As one police officer so graphically expressed it: "If it came to a contest between marchers and a London bus, my money is on the London bus!"

Notes

1. Because of the acrimonious dispute that developed between the police and the organizer it is impossible to give an uncontested version of events. I will concentrate here upon how the police saw the situation develop, relying upon fieldnotes supplemented by the official police debriefing report, noting where disputes arose.
2. The impresario insists that various alternative dates were initially open, but that the police failed to attend meetings to which they were invited when decisions were made.

CHAPTER 5

Relationships

Introduction

Research on policing has emphasized the ubiquity with which police rely on stereotypes (Skolnick 1966, Holdaway 1983, Policy Studies Institute 1983, Brewer 1990). It has also repeatedly been found that the police jealously guard their "backstage" areas (Punch 1979) and seek to exclude those who, like lawyers, might seek to challenge their control of their working environment (Holdaway 1983). This touches on the general issue of police–public relations and the democratic control of policing. Those issues are no less real in the context of policing political protest. In this chapter we will explore police stereotypes of protestors, and their relations with third parties with a vested interest in protest.

Intelligence and "commonsense"

Agents provocateurs, informers and police spies play a prominent part in the liberal demonology of public order policing, often with good reason (Marx 1974, Brodeur 1983). Intelligence services the world over have paid attention to domestic social movements, especially the more radical and militant amongst them (Bunyan 1976). In Britain, the police Special Branch are mandated to counter "subversion". Whilst this principally entails operations against terrorist organizations like the Provisional IRA, it has also led Special Branch officers to interview peace movement activists who have written letters to the press (Loveday 1984). Throughout the miners' strike there were repeated allegations of telephone tapping, infiltration and surveillance. Concern about police intelligence-gathering was vindicated by the then Chief Constable of Devon and Cornwall, John Alderson, who instructed his officers to destroy many secret intelligence files that apparently consisted of unsubstantiated rumours and gossip. An inquiry by the Home Affairs Committee (1985) suggested that greater restrictions should be imposed on intelligence-gathering, especially of domestic social movements. On the other hand, some social movements are clearly sympathetic to terrorist organizations, and some undoubtedly engage in serious criminal actions. The "spiking" of trees by "Earth First!" activists has caused injury and death to loggers (Lange 1990, Short 1991) and during the miners' strike a taxi driver was killed when striking miners dropped a lump of concrete on his car in an attempt to prevent a strike-breaker going to work. These are crimes that the police are duty-bound to prevent. It is doubtful whether many liberal critics of police intelligence activities worry about the possibility that extreme right-wing organizations orchestrating violent protests against refugees in Germany are infiltrated by the police. Indeed, they may be concerned that they are not.

The rôle of Special Branch in the public order operations that I observed was notable mainly for its absence. This is, perhaps, surprising, since a major function of the Public Order Branch was intelligence – soccer intelligence. Officers in this part of the Branch collated information from around the country and issued assessments of the potential for disorder for soccer games occurring nationwide each Saturday. Some public order operations had a soccer-related component that brought soccer intelligence to the fore. For example, there was sometimes concern that football supporters might be tempted to oppose certain protest groups, such as the peace movement or gay rights activists. When this arose it was notable how much information was readily made available by the soccer intelligence unit to senior officers planning the operation. Senior officers were told which London soccer clubs were playing at home or away on the day in question and which supporters were likely to be *en route* through the capital to matches elsewhere. The pubs at which fans tended to congregate were identified and the inclination of hooligans to oppose or attack protestors was also assessed. On the basis of this information, senior officers were able to suggest alterations to the route of a march and make contingency plans to protect marchers.

Another area in which intelligence informs public order operations is royal ceremonials. For these events a "security co-ordinator" was appointed and he normally briefed officers on the likelihood and nature of any terrorist threat. The kinds of weapons available to terrorist groups and their potential were assessed, so that adequate counter-measures could be taken. Moreover, officers were alerted to the identity of individuals with a known hostility towards or fixation with the royal family, referred to as "royal watchers".

The capacity of the police to mount intelligence-gathering operations and to inform public order policing was, therefore, apparent. It was equally apparent that that capacity was infrequently used with regard to the policing of routine public protest. The briefing of officers on such operations routinely included an opportunity for the Special Branch assessment of the likelihood of disorder to be given, but Special Branch officers only rarely took the opportunity to provide such a briefing. Frequently, the senior officer giving the briefing asked if a representative of Special Branch was available, only to be met with silence. More frequently, but still uncommonly, there was a written assessment that was only read out or paraphrased on a few occasions. Though they were probably incomplete, the files on 77 of the operations observed contained written assessments for 21 of them. Four of these assessments were that the march would be "peaceful"; in 12 cases the assessment was that the event would be "peaceful, but isolated incidents of disorder were anticipated or possible"; three further cases were thought to verge on "civil disobedience anticipated or possible"; and the remaining two cases were rated as having potential for violence, either from participants or from opponents of the march.

Irritation was commonly expressed by senior officers at what they perceived to be the lack of service they received from Special Branch. The Branch was often the butt of sarcasm and sardonic humour. Officers complained that they obtained a deeper understanding of protest groups by reading the press than they did from the Special Branch, whom they accused of obtaining information from the same newspapers. There may have been some substance in this allegation: in an attempt to ingratiate myself with a Special Branch officer I handed him a copy of a special issue of *The Independent* newspaper published exclusively for, and distributed free to, students. The main story was about student opposition to government plans for higher education and the protests that it was likely to arouse. He took the newspaper eagerly and thanked me several times when subsequently we met. The newspaper, he assured me, had proved very informative!

On the rare occasions when Special Branch officers did make a contribution to public order operations, their contribution appeared benign. Special

Branch officers were able to inform their public order colleagues of the financial difficulties being experienced by the anti poll tax campaign and of the internecine conflicts between different factions within it. This enabled the police to make valuable concessions to the organizers of the second anti poll tax march (see p. 63). Special Branch officers also tried to counter any tendency by their colleagues to over-react. For example, officers were briefed on one occasion that the Socialist Workers' Party was a prolific printer of placards bearing "catchy" slogans. Officers were warned not to confuse the number of demonstrators carrying such banners with the size of SWP support. Marches by émigré groups were sometimes openly attended by Special Branch officers, who chatted amicably with organizers. On several occasions, the officers were able to brief the senior officer at the scene regarding the factions present at the assembly, usually to confirm that more extremist groups were not in attendance. The possession of intelligence should not, therefore, be simply equated with heavy-handed suppression of minorities. An intelligent response is usually more selective and discriminating than an unintelligent one, and from the little that was seen in connection with public order policing it was so here too. If there was a problem, it lay in the absence of intelligence, not its abundance.

Intelligence is not a function that any organization can afford to do without. If public order operations are to be planned, then they must be based on certain expectations. For example, some estimate of the number of people likely to attend is crucial to determining the size of the police contingent. Since the principal motivation amongst police officers – I have argued – was the avoidance of trouble, there should be a strong incentive to assess the likelihood and nature of any trouble they were likely to encounter. How, then, was intelligence gathered? The answer is that it was gathered informally and subject to the occupational "commonsense" of police officers. In other words, it was stereotypical "recipe" knowledge.

"Good protestors"

What did the police value in protest organizers? Two qualities had overwhelming significance: good faith and competence. The more abundant these qualities were in a protest organization, the more police believed they could control events and the more "comfortable" they felt. An organizer acting in good faith shares a common interest with the police in holding a peaceful and minimally disruptive protest. Thus, established and institutionalized social movements were thought to have a vested interest in peaceful protest. Protestors who occupied a position outside institutionalized

107

politics were assumed to have little incentive to show good faith, for they had little to lose.

This is illustrated by the varying attitudes taken by the police to different organizations protesting about the Gulf war. The major protest organization was the Campaign to Stop War in the Gulf, which was an umbrella group whose main constituent was the Campaign for Nuclear Disarmament. This organization satisfied all the criteria to qualify as "genuine protestors". Relationships were amicable throughout the period of opposition to the war, and when a dispute arose between the Campaign and the Department of the Environment, the police intervened on the Campaign's behalf. There was reciprocation: on the one hand, the Campaign changed the route of a march to avoid encircling the Ministry of Defence (see p. 86); on the other, the police provided additional protection to marchers at the Campaign's request following an incident when a bystander threw a flour-bomb at a march. At the end of one march, a member of the Campaign approached the police control van and asked if there had been any arrests. The experienced sergeant in charge of the van replied that there had been none and had a brief and amicable exchange with the man. As the man walked away, other officers asked who he was. The sergeant replied that he was the legal adviser to CND; "He's been around for years," he added, "he's OK."

Other anti Gulf war protest groups were viewed with far more antipathy. One group that created particular trouble for the police was the 11th Hour Committee, which organized the illegal marches on the nights of the expiry of the UN ultimatum and the commencement of the bombing campaign and the land war (see pp. 66–8). The fact that the 11th Hour Committee's publicity gave the same address as that of the Campaign led to suspicions that it was simply the Campaign in militant guise. Those suspicions were allayed by two incidents that confirmed that the Campaign and the police shared compatible aims. The first was when stewards for the Campaign asked police to remove from a march a group displaying a banner calling for a sit-down demonstration in Parliament Square (see p. 162). The second was when a group entitled the "Internationalists" announced their intention of marching from the termination of a Campaign march in Hyde Park to the American embassy. Police feared that this would attract huge support and might lead to a confrontation at the embassy. So did the Campaign, who, when told of the "Internationalists'" plan by the police, hurriedly re-arranged the route of the march and with police assistance held the rally in Trafalgar Square, far from the embassy. A handful of "Internationalists" left the rally under police supervision, but attracted no large following.

One of the characteristics of the Campaign that left senior officers feeling "comfortable" was the type of person attracted to their demonstrations. The fact that most protestors were "old-fashioned CND types" was taken as evidence that there was little likelihood of disorder. Even when the 11th Hour Committee staged sit-down demonstrations in Parliament Square, senior officers regarded demonstrators with good humour, often remarking on the sense of *déjà vu* it gave of 1960s' CND campaigns. It was generally thought that large demonstrations attracting a predominance of "genuine protestors" were a reasonable guarantee against disorder, for they "swamped" the militants. Another "good sign" was the presence of large numbers of women and children. Children posed problems of safety and control, but police believed that groups intent on disorder did not normally invite women and children.

Tolerance was not necessarily exhausted by disruption. A National Union of Students' protest against government policy on higher education in February 1992 involved repeated brief sit-downs by demonstrators *en route* causing some disruption. One faction also diverted from the agreed route and began marching towards the Sessional Area. Police had made detailed contingency plans to "defend Westminster" – here they were prepared to "die in a ditch". TSG officers were deployed and formed a cordon across the street to stop the breakaway faction, which then decided to rejoin the main march. Along the length of the march, TSG officers were deployed to cordon intersections to prevent any further diversion. One might imagine that all this would have generated antipathy, but casual comments made at the time and during the debriefing that followed gave the opposite impression. Senior officers unanimously viewed the students' antics with wry amusement and dismissed them as "just kids".

The antithesis of good faith lay in organizers having their own hidden agenda, which the police were, by definition, unable to control. The clearest examples of this were militant extremist groups that, it was feared, used protest as a cover for violent confrontation. Another type of organization whose good faith the police doubted were commercial groups, the most notable being the organizers of "Pavarotti in the Park" (see pp. 97–101). In these instances, the hidden agenda was assumed to lie in the commercial interests of the entrepreneur. Police feared that entrepreneurs would sacrifice disruption and public safety (though not disorder) in the pursuit of profit. It was mentioned previously (see p. 100) that on the occasion of the Pavarotti concert the impresario demanded the closure of Park Lane. However, that was far from the only cause of conflict – although it was the major bone of contention. Another confrontation arose over the allegation that the impresario intended to charge coaches a fee for parking in Hyde Park. The police felt that, while this would generate income for the impresario, it was thought likely to create problems for the police, since it would dissuade some coach operators from parking in Hyde Park and encourage them to seek on-street parking in the West End, with consequent traffic congestion. They protested vigorously to the park authorities to ensure that no charge was levied.

The commercial agenda remained hidden, in the view of police, when an organizer purported to be engaged in a philanthropic venture. Hence, another event that generated surprising antipathy amongst senior police officers was the annual London Marathon, which cut off large parts of London for several hours.

The more assured the police were that the organizer had good faith, the more they relied on the protest being held in accordance with plans. There was little necessity for accommodating unforeseen contingencies. On the other hand, if the police doubted the good faith of the organizer, they needed to ensure a capacity to assert control through their own resources and invested heavily in "insurance". Thus, even though the police eschewed any responsibility for crowd safety within the confines of Hyde Park during the Pavarotti concert, they still mobilized a force of approximately 1400 officers to intervene if a disaster threatened. This was because they doubted the ability of stewards to avoid a disaster if it threatened.

Competence meant the ability of the organizer to "deliver" whatever had been negotiated. Police valued most those organizers who knew what they were doing and did it. These groups were regarded as "professional protestors" and included the trade unions, the Campaign for Nuclear Disarmament, the National Union of Students, Anti-Apartheid and similar established social movements. Their officials were familiar to police officers and they possessed a bureaucratic structure that meshed easily with that of the police. A person in a position of formal authority accepted the rôle of organizer with whom the police could negotiate. The organization had the resources to achieve agreed goals. For example, the police could rely on the provision of a stage and amplification equipment for speakers at a rally, thus avoiding the possibility that the rally would degenerate into a series of factions, each acting independently. The most important resource, so far as the police were concerned, was the provision of properly trained and briefed stewards, like those at the NUM assembly who ejected the militant faction with the obscene slogan (see p. 74). On the TUC march the following Sunday, sellers of left-wing newspapers, who frequently obstructed the footpath to the frustration of the police, found themselves unceremoniously brushed aside by stewards, who were asked by the police to keep the footpaths clear.

Least favoured were temporary loose alliances of many discrete protest groups. Here the opposite circumstances appertained: police could not be sure whether the organizer had genuine authority to negotiate. There was always the prospect that the executive committee would overrule any agreement arrived at, or that a faction would unilaterally opt out of the agreement. There may also have been doubts about the authority of the organizers to ensure the protest went according to plan. Stewarding could prove to have been ill organized because stewards were provided by various factions.

There was one qualification to this emphasis on competence, for, provided an organization acted in good faith, a lack of competence could be turned to police advantage. It enabled the police to "organize it for them", and thus have the protest conducted on their terms. The disadvantage, of course, was that this was expensive on police resources.

Gathering information

How did the police establish the good faith and competence of protest organizers? First, to the extent that the police could understand and appreciate the nature of the grievance, the more comfortable they felt about it. This need not entail agreement with the aims of the protest group. For example, most of the police officers involved with policing the anti Gulf war marches firmly supported the war, but could none the less appreciate protestors' antipathy to it. Sometimes they privately sympathized with protestors, as many of them did with the miners facing pit closures. On the other hand, many officers found it difficult to understand the demand for gay rights, still less to sympathize with it. Sometimes they were simply ignorant of the grievances that were being expressed, especially against foreign governments, or unable to appreciate the perspective of cultural or religious groups with whom they were unfamiliar.

Secondly, knowledge of organizations was derived directly from past experience. Protest groups that had demonstrated their competence and good faith in the past were trusted. This was another reason why "professional" protest organizations, like the trade unions, were preferred; they had a "track record" that inspired confidence. Often police officers built up a personal relationship with senior figures in these organizations.

111

Thirdly, organizers were judged by how they acted during the negotiating process. Did the organizer reciprocate friendly overtures made by the police? Did the organizer display confidence and familiarity with procedures and arrangements? Was the organizer helpful? This last consideration was probably the most significant, for it amounted to a material reciprocation of police efforts at assisting the protestors. Helpfulness was expressed in a variety of ways. For example, one organizer reported that, while he had been waiting in the foyer of the police station, he had overheard a police officer call out to a colleague the number of the security code controlling the entrance door, thus breaching security. The fact that he had reported this, allowing the number to be changed, led to a significant increase in trust. Most often helpfulness was shown in providing information and making arrangements in relation to the protest itself. For example, a student leader explained that it was currently fashionable in student protests for marchers periodically to pause, allow a gap to emerge in the march and then run to fill it. This rushing unnerved police and she offered suggestions as to how the stewards and police could work together to minimize the problem. Most frequently, organizers were used as a source of information about other protest groups. Their willingness to do so was treated as an indicator of their good faith.

"Genuine demonstrators" and "the opposition"
On this informal basis police frequently drew a stereotyped distinction between "genuine demonstrators" and "the opposition", which corresponded surprisingly closely to the distinction drawn in routine police work between "ordinary decent people" and the stratum of society variously labelled "slag", "towrags" and "scrotes", and whose American and Canadian counterparts are known as "scumbags" and "pukers" respectively (Cain 1973, Holdaway 1983, Policy Studies Institute 1983, Ericson 1982). This stands in stark contrast to Brodeur's assertion that "The tendency to confuse lawful dissent with illegal behaviour is, in my opinion, an insuperable feature of policing political activities" (Brodeur 1983: 511–12). On the contrary, there was, in the eyes of police officers routinely engaged in public order policing, a clear distinction to be drawn between the perfectly lawful dissent of "genuine protestors" and the illegal behaviour of the "opposition".

"Genuine protestors" consisted of ordinary people who rarely protest, but felt strongly about a specific issue and wished to express their grievance. "The opposition" were the "rent-a-mob" of the extreme left, who protested about virtually everything, which, in police eyes, disqualified them from genuinely feeling strongly about anything. Their motivation was perceived to be to "fight police officers", albeit that they were opportunistic in doing so. The prime exemplar of "the opposition" was the Socialist Workers' Party (SWP), which was perceived to be highly disciplined; so much so that the police claimed that they could precisely estimate the size of the SWP contingent from whether a London (700) or national (2000) "call out" was "issued". The overlap between the SWP and, until recently, the premier anti-fascist organization, the Anti-Nazi League (ANL) (Brittan 1987), encouraged police in the view that the hostility between groups like the National Front and British National Party, on the one hand, and the ANL, on the other, was simply a clash between "right" and "left".

To judge from casual remarks, right-wing groups were held in no more affection than were the radical left. Supporters of the National Front and British National Party were dismissed as "away day football hooligans". Indeed, close attention was paid to which soccer clubs were playing and where, because it was feared that soccer supporters might attack certain protests, such as the peace movement and gay rights campaigners. They were thought to have little understanding of the ideology that they notionally supported, but to be attracted by the prospect of fighting with their opponents. The only advantage they enjoyed over their opponents, in police eyes, was that they rarely attacked the police themselves.

This characterization of protestors reflected what social psychologists call the "ultimate attribution error" (Pettigrew 1979). This is to explain the behaviour of others by referring to some innate trait or disposition. Hence, the reason militant radical groups fought police was because they *enjoyed* fighting police. When the person or people behave out of character, then various devices can be deployed to discount this departure. The apparent reasonableness of an extreme right-wing organizer was discounted by referring to the extreme racist views he expressed on protest platforms. Likewise, the observed failure of the SWP to confront police on any given occasion was attributed to opportunistic factors, such as the evident preparedness of the police for any such confrontation.

Of course, it is far from fanciful to assume that far left and anarchist groups have a deep antipathy to the police. Equally, it seems that a more adequate explanation for violent confrontation lay in the immediate circumstances that provoked it. This was illustrated in the contrast between the behaviour of counterdemonstrators at two British National Party election meetings held in almost identical conditions. Both were held in Bethnal

Green: the first during the general election campaign and the second, a few months later, during a local government by-election campaign. Counter-demonstrators gathered outside the hall in which the meeting was being held and, as supporters of the BNP were being led in, they voiced their opposition and threw missiles. What differed significantly was the level of violence and hostility directed at police. At the first election meeting, having shouted abuse and thrown missiles at the BNP supporters, hostility continued to be shown to the police throughout the remainder of the evening. Counter-demonstrators taunted police with the accusation that they "protected fascists" and demanded entry to what should have been a public meeting (see p. 126). On the second occasion, the police not only escorted supporters of the BNP into the hall, but also mounted an operation to arrest those amongst them suspected of attacking left-wing newspaper sellers a few days previously. As the BNP supporters filed into the hall, individual counter-demonstrators identified suspects, who were then arrested in full view of the counter-demonstration. In addition, when some BNP supporters made Nazi-style salutes in the direction of the counter-demonstrators, they too were arrested. Immediately, the chant "Police protect the fascists" ceased, and once the BNP supporters were safely inside the hall, hostility subsided and the counter-demonstration was concluded. There may be little that the police can legitimately do to avoid being seen to "protect the fascists", but the hostility shown by anti-fascists to the police seemed largely attributable to the unenviable position that the police occupied on such occasions, rather than to any innate propensity of anti-fascists to attack the police.

Distinguishing major and minor operations

Stereotyping plays an important part in the crucial designation of operations as major or minor. It is here that past experience and "commonsense" have their most apparent impact (see pp. 107–11). Two considerations seemed to be uppermost in determining the scale of the policing operation: the size of the event and its "potential" – that is, potential for *trouble*.

Demonstrations thought likely to attract large numbers of supporters normally received significant policing, because of the disruption caused by the presence of a large crowd, however well disposed it might have been assumed to be. However, if the demonstrators were composed mainly of "genuine protestors", they did not attract great concern. Thus, throughout the Gulf war large marches by Kuwaiti nationalists in support of the UN received minimal police planning. The "March for Christ", which mobilized 50 000 supporters, was regarded as a major event, but one that was problematic only in so far as it created traffic congestion. Protests by oppositional groups who were thought unlikely to attract extremist factions were also regarded with equanimity. Thus, a demonstration by an expected 2500 supporters protesting at violence against women was commanded by a chief inspector and controlled from a control van at the head of the march. Likewise the annual National Anti-Vivisection Society protest, expected to be supported by 9000 marchers, was thought to pose little threat. Well-stewarded events, like the massive TUC march held to protest against the closure of 31 coal mines, were major, but unproblematic, operations.

Small protests, such as the Tibet Support Group and the Wildlife Campaign, which have protested annually for several years without problems, were dismissed as "nothing jobs". So too was a march of hospital workers, who marched from their hospital to the TUC headquarters where they aimed to demand more vigorous opposition to health service cuts. These were regarded as so unproblematic that I had difficulty in convincing staff of the Public Order Branch that I needed to be informed of their occurrence.

Protests that were known or thought likely to attract "the opposition" as supporters were regarded as much more problematic and received more police resources than the numbers attending would otherwise have merited. Thus a relatively small march, expected to be 1500 strong, to protest at the presence of the British National Party's "bookshop" in Bexley, south London, received the attention of a Commander as "Gold" and 741 officers, including 12 mounted officers. This was because it was feared that this march would attract "the opposition", in the guise of the Anti-Nazi League, who might prove difficult to control. Likewise, many of the Gulf war marches were regarded as problematic, not because the organizers were hostile to the police but because it was expected that radical militant groups would be attracted to the protest.

One category of marches proved particularly problematic for police to plan for. These were those held by nationalist groups protesting at conditions in their homeland. Twenty-two of the marches were of this type, held by groups including Sikhs, Indian "untouchables", Tamils, Iraqis (pro and anti the regime of Saddam Hussein), Kurds, Sudanese and various Islamic groups. They tended to recruit relatively few supporters and have the advantage, so far as the police were concerned, that either their existence was known only to the nationalist or religious community from which they were drawn, or they were actively hostile to domestic left-wing groups. On the other hand, they tended to be a relatively unknown quantity so far as the police were concerned. Frequently, these protests were organized by ad hoc umbrella groups, the support for which was difficult to estimate. Moreover, they often lacked the organizational structure that police found easy to work with. Leadership was established not bureaucratically, but according to traditional considerations that were a mystery to the police and may have been unclear to the participants. One of the horror stories often told or referred to by officers with experience of public order was of a protest against Salman Rushdie's book *The Satanic Verses* in 1990. According to police accounts, the leaders of different mosques present at the protest disagreed about various aspects of the demonstration previously agreed with the police. There were allegedly protracted and fractious discussions in Hyde Park, until a group of younger protestors surged out of the park *en route* to Parliament Square. This was quite contrary to the agreement reached, and police needed to be hurriedly mobilized to prevent it. The result was a violent confrontation in Parliament Square. Certainly, I witnessed the refusal of various factions to comply with the agreements that had been made. A source of repeated irritation to police officers was the insistence of leaders of different factions each to address the rally before setting off on a march, thus causing delay and, therefore, both inconvenience and possibly significant cost to the police in overtime payments.

The lack of knowledge and understanding of their grievances also meant that the behaviour of such groups was unpredictable from the perspective of the police – an unpredictability that was stereotypically reformulated as innate "volatility". Where the grievance was understood, perhaps because it received the attention of the news media (as did the plight of the Kurds in the wake of the Gulf war), then police found empathetic (and often sympathetic) understanding easier, which aided both negotiation and planning. Equally, when a nationalist group mounted a series of protests, then the police were progressively able to predict their actions and the scale of the appropriate policing response. One such example was the reaction of Kurdish nationalists to the "spring offensive" by the Turkish military in Kurdish areas of Turkey. On 14 March 1992 the Kurdistan Front held a march that was policed by a chief inspector and 79 officers. A week later a similar march was commanded by a superintendent and another the following week was commanded by a chief superintendent and 146 officers. What transformed the police response to these marches was that, after the first of them, a group of Kurdish nationalists had violently attacked the Turkish embassy and other official Turkish premises. This resulted in the Kurds being reassessed as "a problem" deserving serious attention.

It was not only the nature of the protestors themselves that determined the potential for *trouble*; the police needed to be alert to the political context in which the demonstration occurred. There were two principal contextual features to which police attended. First was the likelihood that the demonstrators would be opposed or attacked by counter-demonstrators. This is a recipe for on-the-job trouble and the organizations most closely associated with such confrontations were far-right, neo-fascist groups. Their marches, election meetings and annual general meeting were expected to attract counter-demonstrators intent on preventing them from holding their event, by force if necessary. Thus the police routinely mounted large operations to prevent violence erupting between these opposed groups.

An example of the scale of such operations was the annual general meeting of the BNP. This was not a march or public assembly and, therefore, the BNP were not obliged to notify police. Nevertheless, the police had learned from experience that the BNP held their AGM on a particular Saturday each year, and a similar lesson had been learned by the opponents of the BNP. In an attempt to prevent opponents breaking up their AGM, the BNP kept the venue for the AGM a closely guarded secret, refusing even to tell the police where it was to be held. Instead, they annually gathered at the same location in central London and then played a game of "cat and mouse" with their opponents, arriving at their eventual destination by a circuitous and devious route. To police the operation in October 1992, when 100 BNP supporters were expected to be confronted by 300 opponents, a Commander was designated "Gold", a chief superintendent with considerable public order experience was "Silver", 476 officers were deployed, of whom all but a handful were TSG or mounted officers, and the operation was controlled from the Special Operations Room. Police monitored the movements of both groups, using helicopter surveillance and communicating by encrypted radios immune to scanners. Whenever there threatened to be confrontation, police forcefully intervened to keep the rivals apart.

Secondly, the context may be affected by much wider considerations that would create in-the-job trouble. One clear example was the holding of the "Group of Seven" annual meeting in London in July 1991. This high-profile event, with its strong security implications, was also the occasion for a march demanding that the accumulated debt of Third World countries should be cancelled by developed nations, specifically the "Group of Seven". An operation commanded by a Commander as "Gold", chief superintendent as "Silver" and 398 officers controlled from the Special Operations Room was mounted to police what were eventually estimated as 870 protestors.

117

In sum, where the police feared trouble – either on-the-job or in-the-job – they mounted a major operation. In the absence of good intelligence about who would be attracted to demonstrations and their intentions, police relied on their stereotypical recipe knowledge.

Third parties

Maintaining police control of an operation is facilitated by the exclusion of third parties. Police officers are aware that in routine patrol work they can rely on their "low visibility" (Goldstein 1960) to resolve incidents informally (Chatterton 1983). Police routinely try to keep "challengers", such as lawyers, doctors and social workers (even senior officers), at arm's length and to "stage manage" any unavoidable encounter (Holdaway 1983). The policing of political demonstrations shared many of these features, save for the obvious and important fact that it tended to be highly visible. Police preferred negotiations to be conducted with a lone negotiator or a small contingent. As has been noted already (see p. 90), they tried to avoid negotiations that were subject to ratification by an executive committee because attempts at persuasion could not extend to those who were remote and invisible. Only barely more tolerable, from the police point of view, was the presence of "advisers" in the negotiations. Again, negotiations were hampered if there were people present who were knowledgeable enough to dispute the police version of events.

However much police attempted to restrict the involvement of others, public order policing almost invariably entailed other agencies. Chapter 4 described how this could be turned to police advantage during negotiations (see p. 111), because they exploit their pivotal position to form coalitions with organizers or officials. The relationship with agencies such as the royal parks division of the Department of National Heritage was genuinely ambivalent. On the one hand, they were regarded as a useful ally; for example, officials routinely notified the police if they were approached by organizers for permission to hold an assembly or rally in Hyde Park or Trafalgar Square. On the other hand, restrictions that officials were duty-bound to enforce in the royal parks were regarded as irksome by the police. Although police routinely informed protest organizers of the regulations restricting banners and placards in the park, they resisted pressure from officials to enforce them more rigorously. To do as officials requested would have been needlessly confrontational in the eyes of the police –

risking a riot in order to stop placards entering the park struck them as an absurd equation. Likewise, they refused to enforce regulations preventing prayers being said by Islamic groups, or food being served at Sikh assemblies. On the other hand, the restrictions on the number of vehicles allowed in the park were more rigorously enforced as an aid to keeping demonstrations a vehicle-free zone.

Lawyers

The most knowledgeable and, therefore, the most threatening people were lawyers. They rarely played any part in the negotiation process; the only exception being when the 11th Hour Committee challenged the police interpretation of the Sessional Order on essentially legalistic grounds, which might have been written by lawyers (see p. 67). Where they increasingly intruded into public order operations was in the provision of "legal observers". These were people who attended marches and wore brightly coloured tabards adorned with the legend "legal observer". If and when an arrest was made, "legal observers" usually hurried to the scene, possibly taking photographs or videotaping the arrest and seeking information from the suspect and arresting officers. They then arranged for solicitors to attend the relevant police station to advise the arrested person. As such, they challenged police control of the situation at its most precarious moments. Arrests were rarely "tidy" and officers found it threatening to have all that they said and did recorded as they struggled with a suspect.

Police had not settled on a way of countering the threat that "legal observers" posed. Three provisional strategies could be seen in operation. First was denial of their status. The view here was that "legal observers" had no status beyond that of any other participant in the march. They were not stewards and would not, therefore, be afforded any privileges or responsibilities by the police. Police accused some protest organizers of issuing the tabards haphazardly to anyone who was willing to wear them. It was suggested privately that many of the "legal observers" had little or no legal training. Because they enjoyed no recognized status they were required to remain with the body of the march and, if they left it, they were to be instructed to return. In the event of their obstructing arresting officers in any way, then they too were to be arrested – but this did not arise. Officers were told that they were not obliged to provide them with any information about the reason for the arrest or to which station the person was being taken. This was, therefore, a strategy that tended towards confrontation.

Secondly, plans were made on some operations, where it was thought likely that arrests would be made, to defuse the threat from "legal observers". The principal means of achieving this was by mobilizing police-approved neutral referees, most notably members of lay visitor panels. Lay visitors are persons appointed to visit police stations and to check the welfare of people held in custody (Kemp & Morgan 1990). There are obvious restrictions on who can become a lay visitor and they are a body of people with whom the police have an opportunity to build a working relationship. They are, at least, a "known quantity", in stark contrast to the anonymous and probably antipathetic "legal observers". Thus, if arrests were expected, police asked that lay visitors should attend the respective charge centres to vouch for the propriety of police action and thus head off any challenge that might otherwise have been made.

Thirdly, on some operations attempts were made to incorporate "legal observers" into the police operation by according them special status. This was justified on the grounds that the police "have nothing to hide" and that they shared a common interest with the "legal observers" in protecting the civil rights of protestors and those who were arrested. On those relatively rare occasions where this strategy prevailed, junior officers were instructed to accord "legal observers" full co-operation; that is, to tell them the name and number of the arresting officer, the reason for the arrest and the charge centre to which the person was being taken. On one occasion, the senior officer in command (not an officer with much public order experience) suggested that "legal observers" should be invited to sit in the Special Operations Room. This caused some consternation amongst members of the Public Order Branch and the suggestion was dropped. It was considered fortunate that the "legal observers" failed to turn up to the march.

Politicians
Public order in general, and protest in particular, are indisputably political events and politicians sometimes filled the rôle of "challengers". They made demands on the police or refused to comply with police directions.

Politicians were amongst that group of VIPs most difficult to control, especially during ceremonial occasions. For example, whereas the public who attend ceremonials were regarded as compliant and "no hassle", the same could not be said of some of the major participants. Royalty were notoriously "prickly"; the military were sometimes inattentive to police priorities; and MPs and peers were renowned for jealously guarding their right of unimpeded access to the Palace of Westminster. Consequently, officers on duty occasionally found themselves confronted by an angry motorist insisting upon contravening traffic directions, or a pedestrian intent on ignoring restrictions, only to discover that the "motorist" or "pedestrian" was an MP. Officers were warned not to demand identification from MPs whom they failed to recognize, but to accept the word of Honourable Members. This, of course, appeared to most police officers as a recipe for disaster since anyone, including a terrorist, might claim such a privilege and obtain access to restricted areas. Equally, official vehicles sometimes suddenly appeared in the wrong place. This had its humorous side: during the 1992 State Opening of Parliament an official limousine was driven along the ceremonial route towards Parliament Square just as the Brigade of Guards were returning to their barracks. The car was hurriedly ushered off the route and a senior officer angrily enquired why it was being driven along Whitehall, only to be told that it was conveying the Prime Minister's lunch! It was reputedly the case that, after ceremonials, a pile of complaints from MPs and other VIPs was regularly received complaining of their treatment by police officers merely doing as they had been instructed. However, officers could afford to be relatively phlegmatic about such potential "grief", since arrangements were usually approved by the Whips' Office at the Palace of Westminster or the Lord Chamberlain's Office at Buckingham Palace, making all but exceptional police actions "fire-proof".

More seriously, perhaps, politicians could present the police with political obstacles to the organizing of marchers or exert pressure for a particularly hazardous course of action to be followed. It has already been seen that police felt compelled to persuade members of the Lambeth Council to allow the use of Brockwell Park for the second anti poll tax march (see p. 63); on the occasion of the "anniversary" anti poll tax march they resisted quite overt political pressure to ban the march entirely (see pp. 63–4); and when the Anti-Election Alliance protested, they felt obliged to ignore the Department of the Environment's refusal to grant permission for protestors to use Trafalgar Square (see p. 65).

However, the most routine pressure that politicians brought to bear on the police was through the Sessional Order (see p. 66). If the Sessional Order was not strictly complied with, senior officers expected serious in-the-job trouble. Thus, when the 11th Hour Committee marched in protest at the expiry of the UN ultimatum on Iraq and the commencement of the subsequent bombing campaign (see pp. 66–8), the police knew that they were running a considerable risk in allowing protestors access to Parliament Square at all. They sought to defuse any potential complaint by drawing the casuistical distinction between "marching along the highway" and "walking along the footpath". When the same protestors attempted to obstruct the main vehicle entrance to the Palace of Westminster on a subsequent occasion, they were immediately arrested, since police felt duty-bound, under the terms of the Sessional Order, to ensure unimpeded access of members and peers to the Palace.

The Sessional Order created "a ditch" in which the police felt expected to "die". It will be recalled how anxious the police were to prevent miners and their supporters flooding into Parliament Square after the demonstration against pit closures (see pp. 70–75). Detailed contingency plans were drawn up to "defend Westminster" should the segregation of the march and rally fail to materialize. If a large, but non-violent, crowd accumulated in Parliament Square, plans were made to keep them away from the immediate vicinity of the Palace of Westminster itself. Throughout this process, senior officers genuinely saw themselves potentially in the position of literally standing between democracy and anarchy. This was the position in which they claimed they were placed during the "battle of Westminster Bridge" when a breakaway march of students attempted to invade Parliament Square (see p. 17). On the occasion of a subsequent march by the National Union of Students, detailed plans were also made to prevent any invasion of Parliament Square (see p. 137).

Upholding parliamentary rights also imposed contradictory demands on the policing of political protest. Whereas the Sessional Order required the imposition of stringent restrictions on demonstrations, parliamentarians were equally jealous of the rights of constituents to lobby their MPs. The police could not, therefore, have simply created a sterile zone around the Palace of Westminster during a demonstration, but were obliged to allow constituents access to the Palace. The threat, of course, was that several thousand "constituents" might simultaneously demand to lobby their MPs. If demonstrators attempted to protest in Parliament Square, the police expected to be criticized for, on the one hand, failing to enforce the Sessional Order and, on the other, obstructing constituents.

Parliament Square was not the only politically sensitive location. Downing Street was another, although it was readily defended because gates have been placed across its entrance. However, if petitions were to be delivered, the police restricted the number of protestors allowed in the "petition party" to six and insisted that the envelope containing the petition be inspected for security purposes. Efforts were also made to ensure that any accompanying march did not stop opposite Downing Street. Ideally, the petition party was detached from the front of the march, escorted into Downing Street and then returned to join the rear of the march. This was done to minimize any attempt to blockade the entrance to Downing Street. It was justified to negotiators as allowing everyone in a march a clear view of the petition being presented as the march filed past.

Similar arrangements were made for the delivery of petitions to diplomatic premises, for they too were regarded as sensitive because the police had a legal duty to protect them and maintain their dignity. Throughout the anti Gulf war protests, police took extensive measures to ensure that the American embassy was fully protected (see p. 139). This extended to risking possible confrontation with one group of demonstrators who tried to burn an American flag outside the embassy. The flag was snatched from them and extinguished by a high-ranking officer on the grounds that it was an affront to the embassy. South Africa House had posed a continuing problem to the police for several years prior to this research, for it had been the site of persistent protest by the City of London Anti-Apartheid Group (CLAAG), a group with whom the police had repeatedly come into conflict. The embassy also fronts on to Trafalgar Square, the preferred location for many demonstrations, and therefore was regarded by police as a potential target for any protest group. The Indian High Commission was also the object of several passionate protests by various émigré groups from the subcontinent. It too received extensive protection, as did the Turkish embassy following several violent protests by members of the Kurdish community. Not all diplomatic premises were regarded as equally sensitive. On one occasion, the Iranian embassy objected to the police escorting a single representative of a protest group to the embassy to deliver a letter of protest. The reply of the officer in charge was that the embassy should be informed that Britain was a democracy. However, he might have been encouraged in his robust rejection of this diplomatic complaint by his impending retirement!

The media

Accounts of relations between the media and the police have tended to portray a supportive, even cosy relationship (Chibnall 1977, 1979, Hall et al. 1978, Ericson et al. 1987, 1989, 1991, D. Waddington 1992). This is not how the relationship is perceived by senior officers in command of public order operations. On the contrary, the media are seen as a threat that has two prongs: first, camera personnel are physically difficult to control in the immediate vicinity of a demonstration, and secondly the media are the ultimate "challengers", able to offer a version of events authoritatively at variance with that of the police. Relations between police and the media have become strained in recent years, with allegations made at the time of the year-long Wapping dispute that press personnel were obstructed, threatened and attacked by officers as they reported violent encounters on the picket-line. The Metropolitan Police Press Bureau has produced a training video film that tries to present both perspectives in order to encourage mutual appreciation, thereby implicitly according police–press relations the formal status of "a problem".

Under the guise of "freedom of the press", camera personnel – both photographic and video – claimed the right to move freely around a demonstration. On larger or more high-profile demonstrations, this amounted to literally a swarm of camera personnel transgressing the boundaries that the police sought to impose upon "the ground" as they sought the best vantage point (see pp. 150–51). Police control was thus compromised. First, camera personnel might be exposed to risk of injury from passing traffic and, since police were responsible for traffic management in the immediate vicinity of a march, responsibility for any accident might be "down to" them. Secondly, the desire of camera personnel to obtain a "good shot" sometimes impeded the progress of a march. Protestors also had a vested interest in receiving publicity for their grievances and tended, therefore, to co-operate with the demands of the press rather than with the possibly competing demands of the police. Thirdly, the freedom to move behind police cordons was thought to be open to exploitation by militant factions. Many of these groups published newspapers (for example, the SWP published *Socialist Worker*) and activists might have acquired press passes in their guise as journalists. These journalists were thought able to move behind police cordons, overhear police radio transmissions and then return to their colleagues to inform them of police dispositions, deployments and plans. Finally, the press could reveal police wrongdoing. The police believed strongly in a version of "sod's law": any provocative remark, poorly executed or ill-judged arrest would almost certainly be recorded by the media. During the anti Gulf war marches, briefings by senior officers repeatedly drew to the attention of their subordinates the propaganda advantage that would accrue to Iraq if there were scenes of violent disorder on the streets of London.

There was very little the police could do physically to control the press on marches, but sometimes the opportunity arose for the provision of facilities that also afforded such control. During the final anti poll tax demonstration, the press were given privileged access to the area at the foot of Nelson's Column. This gave them an unparalleled overview of the march as it passed through Trafalgar Square, but kept them securely out of the way of any disorder that might have erupted. Static demonstrations afforded greater opportunity to place the press in specially demarcated "pens" constructed from metal barriers. This gave them a privileged perspective on events, but also kept them securely contained in the event of trouble. The location of the pen sometimes received close attention. During an election meeting held by the British National Party (see pp. 113–14), the position of the pen was thought to be unfortunate should riot-control officers be deployed to disperse counter-demonstrators gathered outside the hall. In such an eventuality, riot police would have rushed towards and then past the press pen, and the images that would then have been portrayed in the media might have been less than flattering to the police.

Wherever they are located, the press are able to put a construction on events that might conflict with police interests. Police attempted to counter this potential through the employment of professional Area Press and Publicity Officers (APPOs). Their task was to supply the press with information and arrange interviews. On large or potentially difficult demonstrations, an APPO frequently accompanied the officer designated as "Silver". My research paid scant attention to the work of the APPO, which probably deserves much closer scrutiny. Normally, the relationship between the APPO and senior officers was unproblematic, but occasionally rôle conflict was experienced. This arose when an APPO sought to extend to the media facilities that provided comprehensive coverage of the event but conflicted with senior officers' desires to maintain control over space. In the election meeting referred to immediately above, a conflict arose because the APPO wanted the press to be allowed into the meeting, but the senior officer (for reasons to be explained later, see p. 126) wanted to deny access to anyone.

The rôle of the APPO represents a policy of controlling the media through incorporation. This was taken even further on some operations. During two anti-racist marches in southeast London a reporter from the local press was invited to attend the briefing and given a privileged insight into the policing operation, being escorted throughout by a sergeant. After the first operation a police commander confessed that he had been disappointed with the treatment the police received in the subsequent report, and so a different newspaper was given the opportunity to attend the second operation in the hope that the report would prove more favourable.

Community relations

Not all third parties represented a threat to be controlled. Allies were sometimes to be found in the most unlikely quarters. For example, in recent years police have been officially encouraged to develop contacts with those in the communities that they police. One means of doing so is through consultative committees. These committees were envisaged as containing police powers by requiring the police to listen, and be responsive, to the views of local community representatives. Morgan's research (Morgan & Maggs 1984, 1985a, 1985b, Morgan 1989) suggests that these committees have had far less impact than was envisaged and to a large extent have been appropriated by the police, who tend to dominate the agenda. My research suggests that appropriation might have spread beyond the confines of the committees themselves.

During the first of the two BNP election meetings described previously (see pp. 113–14), the police encountered a problem when counter-demonstrators demanded access to what should have been a *public* meeting. The police wanted to restrict access, fearing that otherwise there would be disorder inside the hall, which would provoke still further disorder outside. However, the BNP organizer had overestimated support and seats remained unfilled inside the hall, which made it difficult for the police commander to maintain that there were no seats available for the public. The officer in charge happened to encounter a small group of local councillors who also sat on the consultative committee and acted as lay visitors, who were observing events from the periphery. Unbidden they expressed hostility to both the BNP and their opponents. The officer explained his difficulty. The leading councillor suggested that he and his colleagues should enter the hall by a side entrance and remove surplus seating. Since the hall had a general proscription on standing during meetings, this would in effect deny the opportunity for further access. This done, the most vociferous counter-demonstrators who were demanding access were informed that there were no seats available.

Similarly, community policing also provides opportunities for, as well as restrictions of, police action. It was noticeable that, during a succession of anti-racist marches and one neo-fascist march held in southeast London, the police used the contacts they had established with ethnic minority communities to minimize the potential for disorder. Senior officers were clearly familiar with ethnic minority leaders and the complexities of local political rivalries. During the planning of one such march, the local chief superintendent interceded between two rival ethnic minority groups who were disputing "ownership" of the forthcoming march. He negotiated a truce that enabled the march to go ahead as planned. For each of the anti-racist marches the relevant briefing was attended by members of the local ethnic minority community, to reassure them of police good faith. This was normally regarded with some apprehension by ordinary police officers, some of whom expressed their opposition openly and forcefully. However, on the occasion of the second anti poll tax march to Brockwell Park the police invited a member of Lambeth Council, who incidentally was a black person, and he earned the applause of the police at the briefing when he sought reassurance that officers would be adequately fed!

An important function of community liaison officers (CLO) is in supplying relevant information and intelligence to their superiors. The CLO normally attended the planning meetings for Notting Hill Carnival, giving an update on what was occurring on "the ground". Police also began consulting the community relations officer assigned to maintain contact with gay and lesbian groups for much the same purpose. He was far better informed about the likely support for a forthcoming march than were other officers because of his contacts.

Through all these means police were able to employ structures instituted for one purpose for their own, quite different, objective – control.

Conclusions

The desire of police officers to maintain control over their essentially precarious working environment is a persistent theme in the literature on routine policing. In this chapter I have argued that it is also a feature of public order policing. Cognitive order is maintained by stereotyping protestors as either "genuine" or "the opposition". Police seek to protect themselves against various third parties who might threaten their interests, just as they cultivate those who might assist them.

CHAPTER 6

Remote control

Introduction

Previous chapters have suggested that the command of politically charged public order events by senior officers is remarkably similar to routine policing by the lower ranks. Police aims are largely achieved through informal means in conditions of low visibility. However, there are two obvious respects in which public order policing diverges from routine patrol work. First, the event itself will be highly visible. Demonstrators will be doing all in their power to ensure that they enjoy maximum visibility. Secondly, senior officers will be unable to exercise as much control over the policing operation as can a lone officer dealing with an incident on the street. A public order operation will involve many subordinate officers, sometimes amounting to hundreds. Senior officers command the operation, or some part of it, but they do not directly police the event themselves by their own actions.

If senior officers are to ensure that trouble is avoided, they must effectively control the actions of their subordinates and that must be achieved by *remote* control. How officers in command of public order operations exert control will be discussed in this chapter. The main weapons in their armoury are planning and briefing. Instead of following the planning process sequentially, I will consider how senior officers exert control over others who are progressively more remote from them.

128

Major and minor operations

How command was exerted over the operation depended hugely upon whether the operation was major or minor. Sensitive events – be they ceremonials, large-scale entertainment, or potentially problematic protest demonstrations – received quite distinct treatment from smaller, less problematic protest demonstrations. Minor operations were left to a chief inspector or, possibly, a superintendent to command alone. Such planning as there was occurred in private, possibly after brief consultation with colleagues in the Public Order Branch or Special Events Office, but were organized at area or divisional level. Planning amounted to little more than deciding which serials of officers were to accompany which side of the march, and who were to act as the mobile reserve, if any. The "operation order", designating personnel, call-signs and duties, was a cursory document printed on flimsy computer printout. The briefing of junior officers normally occurred when the officers were being fed immediately prior to the commencement of the operation. It took place either in a noisy canteen or in a small smoke-filled annexe, and consisted of either all the officers on the operation or just their inspectors and sergeants. The control room for the operation was usually housed on board the control van that led the march. The officer in command of the operation was usually physically present at the scene and in a position directly to instruct subordinates.

The position was quite different for a major operation, which took on a distinctly paramilitary character. The officer in overall command, designated "Gold" for the operation, headed a command team consisting of a forward ground commander, "Silver", and various "Bronze", or sector, commanders, who had particular territorial or functional responsibilities. On very large or highly sensitive operations there was even a tier of "sub-Bronzes" who assisted sector commanders. For example, the 1992–3 New Year's Eve celebration was divided into six territorial sectors and subdivided into 14 subsectors, plus a reserves co-ordinator and traffic commander. Specialized support services, from civilian "barrier crews", who erected crowd control barriers, to terrestrial and airborne closed-circuit television, were often available. A series of strategy meetings and strategy briefings were held to plan the policing operation. The "operation order" was a properly printed document containing considerable detail regarding the duties of officers. The briefing was normally held in the briefing room at Scotland Yard some days prior to the operation. Senior officers gave the "Gold" and "Silver" briefings respectively, and on very large operations

129

each sector commander also separately briefed the officers under their particular command. Almost invariably such a briefing was restricted to serial inspectors only. Radio communications were controlled from the Special Operations Room at Scotland Yard – a large room in which operators sat at computer terminals as they communicated with officers using several separate radio channels. The "Gold" commander usually sat on the "bridge" in the Special Operations Room – an arc of consoles – looking at closed-circuit television screens and communicating with sub-commanders via the Controller – the senior officer in charge of the Special Operations Room.

Major and minor operations had quite distinct characteristics. Table 6.1 shows that the level of overall command displays a distinctly ∪-shaped distribution, a distribution that is repeated in the number of sub-commanders (including "Silver") deployed (see Table 6.2).

In other words, operations tended to be regarded either as major, whereupon they received the attention of the most senior officers, or as minor and were entrusted to a junior officer. The bias of this research to the larger and more problematic operations is confirmed by the fact that the "operation order" was compiled by the Public Order Branch for 58 of the 78 operations and control was located at the Special Operations Room for 48 of them.

This division between major and minor operations is itself a reflection of the "potential", as it is called, of an event – that is, the potential for trouble. But herein lies a paradox: it is the most sensitive events, where the likelihood of trouble is greatest, where the senior officers in command had least direct control over the implementation of the operation. "Gold" was obliged to rely upon his "Silver" and "Bronzes", for they were "on the ground" and in a position both to appraise the situation and to take appropriate action. If he was to control the operation, he must effectively control his sub-commanders.

Table 6.1 Command level of observed marches.

Command level				
DAC	Commander	C/Supt	Supt	C/Insp
31	16	8	10	17

Table 6.2 Number of sub-commanders per operation.

Number of sub-commanders						
6+	5	4	3	2	1	0
36	11	3	3	7	2	19

Controlling sub-commanders

How, then, did officers in command of major operations seek to control their sub-commanders, so that the latter acted in ways of which the former would approve? It is naïve to imagine that this could have been achieved by the communication of directives issued by radio. The Special Operations Room would quickly have been overwhelmed if all decisions had to be referred to Gold. Moreover, decision-making in public order operations was like decision-making in routine policing: it was context-specific and discretionary (Manning 1977, 1988, P. Waddington 1993a).

For example, during the 1991 Notting Hill Carnival a sector commander discovered that there were plans to hold a "pay party" in a derelict house near Portobello Green. The premises were inspected by local authority health inspectors who declared that it would be dangerous if used for such a purpose. The sub-commander decided to bar access to the house by nailing boarding over the doors and windows. The problem confronting the officer was how to board up the premises without causing a confrontation with revellers. He formulated a plan for first closing the short street in which the house was located; bringing a local authority lorry transporting the workmen and materials into the road; effecting the boarding-up; and re-opening the road. As a precaution, he asked for TSG officers to be placed on heightened readiness and for additional officers in ordinary uniform to assemble in a nearby sterile area. When everything was in place, the operation commenced and was concluded smoothly. Throughout the operation "Gold" and "Silver" were kept informed. However, they were wholly reliant upon the judgement of their sector commander as to the nature of threat (the "pay party" in this house), the appropriate solution, and the type of operation needed to achieve the desired end. He was "on the ground" and able to assess the situation in a way that was unavailable to his superiors despite the banks of closed-circuit television at their disposal. (For a comparable example see P. Waddington 1991.)

Experience and command

The first mechanism for establishing control over sub-commanders was to select officers who shared a common perspective. Like routine policing, it was firmly believed that public order policing could not be done according to "the book". Again like routine policing, public order policing was regarded as experiential – it could not be taught; learning must be acquired through experience. During a planning meeting for the policing of the New

131

Year's Eve celebrations in Trafalgar Square, inexperienced officers were repeatedly advised to "wait and see" before making suggestions about the operation, since they could not appreciate the context without having experienced it. Newcomers to the Notting Hill Carnival were warned that they could have no comprehension of the noise and density of the crowds. Appropriate policing of protest marches depends upon its particular context.

The discretionary, experiential and context-specific nature of public order policing condemned senior officers to trust their subordinates to act in ways that were appropriate to the circumstances. However, trust entailed senior officers in effect ceding control and placing responsibility for the avoidance of trouble in the hands of others. Some measure of control was restored by investing trust in officers who had a "track record" for having acted appropriately in the past. This created a small circle of officers with such experience who were known personally to each other and shared a common culture. Most of them had spent long periods serving in central London where public order is a routine demand. The two most senior officers in central London at the time spoke of how they had worked together so often on public order operations that each would know what the other would do before he did it. Certain officers were identified as part of that fraternity even when they had been posted away from central London, and their services would sometimes be sought.

It became the source of some friction between the Public Order Branch at Scotland Yard and the outer London areas when the former sought to recruit named individuals rather than accepting whoever was allocated by area headquarters. The force policy of creating a "cadre" of senior officers throughout the force area formally trained in commanding public order operations was also thought likely to threaten this informal network. Those within the fraternity repeatedly complained that, whereas "cadre" status was valued by others because it enhanced their curriculum vitae, few of those seeking "cadre" status were committed to, or suitable for, public order command. The proposal that in order to retain "cadre" status officers should frequently command public order operations was seen as a threat, for it entailed that unknown individuals of unproven experience would be seeking to take command of operations in central London (where protest is concentrated). This was regarded as a recipe for trouble and there were several occasions when senior officers rejected suggested sub-commanders on the grounds that they wanted someone they knew and could trust.

The public order fraternity was not, and could not be, hermetically sealed. There were two routes in. The preferred route was by apprenticeship. Junior officers were invited to command the policing of small unproblematic marches. Their success in avoiding problems and a general reputation for competence, often disseminated by much lower-ranking officers who were able to observe their performance from the control van, would make them eligible for progressively larger and more problematic operations. In addition, officers were informally appraised by how they conducted themselves during very large operations when they acted as "sub-Bronzes" in command of a sub-sector under the direction of a more experienced "Bronze" commander.

The second means of gaining access to the fraternity was when officers were posted to positions that virtually carried an automatic involvement in public order operations. These officers were obliged to "win their spurs". To cushion them, steps were usually taken to assign more experienced subordinates to their command team. Again, the reputation of the senior officer often depended upon how his nominal subordinates appraised his command decisions.

"Good" public order commanders were perceived as having a number of important personal qualities. Because public order policing was seen as experiential, "intellectual" officers were regarded as lacking in necessary "commonsense". One senior officer was felt by his superiors not to "have the public order touch" and others, including subordinates, were instructed to "keep an eye on him".

The principal valued quality was the capacity to remain calm. Officers who panicked, over-reacted or were too headstrong were seen as a liability. Such officers might show commitment, but this itself was regarded in some instances as unhealthy. One officer was repeatedly criticized by his colleagues during this research for his "excitable" nature. For example, during one anti Gulf war march I was accompanying the "Silver" commander as he walked through Hyde Park. There was an alarming radio message from the officer in question, reporting a gathering of 50 "skinheads" at Marble Arch – the implication being that the "skinheads" were intent on disrupting the assembly or attacking protestors. The "Silver" commander diverted towards Marble Arch, wearily predicting that we would find a small group of anti Gulf war protestors trying to cross the road – he was correct! Calmness is, of course, at a premium if and when disruption or disorder occur. Rash or reckless over-reaction can create both on-the-job and in-the-job trouble for the officer concerned and his or her superiors.

In addition to calmness, senior officers were valued for their decisiveness. They were expected to "stand no nonsense" and "get a grip" both of the demonstrators and, equally important, of the police operation. Their experience enabled them to assess the particularities of any given event speedily and accurately. Decisiveness meant that they gave clear instructions to subordinates so that there was little room for error. They should be "on top" of the policing operation: knowing deployments and serial numbers, and various other details of the operation by heart. I was told by one senior officer that one could identify a competent public order commander by the fact that he would have devised some method for reducing the information contained on the voluminous operational order so as to fit on a sheet that could be carried inside his cap.

Ideally, they must also be brave and "up front". "Silver" commanders who "took a back seat" and were noticeable for their absence were despised by their colleagues. This was the cause of some rôle confusion. Notionally, the "Silver" commander should not have been too much to the fore; he should instruct his "Bronze" commanders and not deploy serials of officers directly. One of the criticisms of the Metcalfe report (1991) into the Trafalgar Square riot was that there was precisely this confusion of command when "Silver" appeared on the scene. This echoed criticism of the policing of disorder outside the News International newspaper printing plant on 24 January 1987, when it was alleged that a Deputy Assistant Commissioner countermanded an order given by the Commander acting as "Gold" (Police Complaints Authority press release, 14 February 1990). The "good Silver" should be clearly present, identifying problems, but then advising his "Bronze" commanders as to the action they should take, rather than taking action directly himself. It was a precarious line to tread, especially in the potentially confused circumstances of a public order operation.

Wilson criticized many critics of the police for their adherence to a "good man" theory of policing (Wilson 1968). In reality, police officers themselves are the firmest adherents of such a theory: senior officers seek the best people they can find as sub-commanders.

Ownership and control

Having selected trusted sub-commanders, the next form of control that senior officers could exert was to create a shared perspective and common set of priorities. The mechanism for this was the series of strategy meetings and strategy briefings held prior to any major event. The planning of major operations, especially those regarded as having "potential", was remarkably similar for ceremonials, celebrations and political protests. The major variable was the amount of time available for planning. Ceremonials and most celebrations were either repeated annually at set times or planned by organizers on a long-term basis. This allowed for reflection and deliberations which contributed to senior officers feeling "comfortable" with the operation. The notification of political protests varied from months to days (see p. 70).

It was more or less openly acknowledged by senior officers that, where the potential for trouble was high, the operation must be done, and be seen to be done, properly. A self-conscious appraisal of how the operation would appear to any subsequent inquiry frequently accompanied discussion during these meetings. The corporate approach to planning of major operations was recommended by the debrief report into the anti poll tax riot (Metcalfe 1991), but was also attributed by many to the need to "guard the back" of the senior officer in command. A contrast was drawn by many experienced senior officers between the pre and post poll tax riot eras. Before the riot, I was repeatedly told, senior officers would plan the operation more or less alone, perhaps in consultation with a few trusted colleagues. "Bronze" commanders would find themselves told what their rôle was, in much the same way as were their subordinates. The problem with this was that, when a disaster occurred, as it did during the first anti poll tax march, then responsibility was borne entirely by the senior officer in command. I cannot confirm whether this is an accurate description of the situation before the anti poll tax riot, but I can say that it portrayed procedures significantly different from those I witnessed during the nearly three years that followed. On these occasions the Bronze commanders were routinely involved in the detailed planning of operations.

In the strategy meetings that I observed, the command team discussed the situation and any options that might need consideration. The total manpower needed was agreed upon and also the division of subsectors. Sometimes there was an element of bargaining about the number of officers required and the size of sectors and location of sector boundaries. Depending on the size and sensitivity of the operation, there might have been several such meetings. Notting Hill Carnival, for instance, merited eight, plus two "training days" when sector commanders were presented with various contingencies during an exercise mounted by the staff of the Public Order Training Centre. Generally, the more sensitive the operations the more numerous the meetings.

The pattern of strategy meetings and strategy briefings evolved during the period of observation was designed to encourage as much "ownership" by "Bronze" commanders of the agreed strategy as possible. Their views were systematically sought, issues were discussed, and over the period planning was gradually devolved to an increasing extent. The aim, ostensibly, was to ensure that officers nearest the site of action would have thought about the operation beforehand and be aware of the overall strategy and how their sector or function related to all the others. It also meant that they had a strong incentive to ensure that, if difficulties started to arise, they were dealt with effectively, because they shared corporate responsibility. Although this approach was dismissed by some of the "old hands" in the public order fraternity as "planning by committee", most senior officers who expressed a view about it were positive. They welcomed the "ownership" they were given.

"What if . . . ?"

Much of the discussion at strategy meetings concerned organizational matters, such as calculating the number of officers needed and whether they should accompany a march or line the route (that is, stand at intervals along the footpath). The creation and reinforcement of a common perspective and set of priorities were achieved when discussion turned to the "What ifs?". This referred to hypothetical contingencies the response to which was agreed. In many cases this rapidly became a standard list that was enunciated rather than genuinely discussed. It would typically take the form of listing various possibilities that might arise at different stages of a march. For example, "disorder at the assembly", "sit-down *en route*", "disorder *en route*", and "disorder at the rally". The typical list of preferred responses was to contain troublesome people and groups, encourage marchers to continue with their march, and then arrest those committing offences as necessary and at the convenience of the police. Sit-down demonstrators were to be left and the march encouraged to go past them, on the assumption that, in the absence of a police response, the sit-downers would quickly become bored and uncomfortable and re-commence the march. Nevertheless, the repeated recitation of these contingencies reinforced the philosophy that precipitate action was to be avoided. Officers were not to rush in and make arrests or seek to disperse the protestors. They were to wait and, after deliberation, take whatever action was necessary. In central London, where this approach was most highly developed, there was a clear proscription against dispersing unruly or violent crowds. This arose from the experience of the anti poll tax riot, when rioters were dispersed from Trafalgar Square throughout the West End, where they were able to create mayhem. By articulating preferred alternatives, sub-commanders were not simply presented with a proscription, but were offered guidance as to what action would be appropriate.

Occasionally, specific contingencies might need to be considered. Hence, detailed plans were made in the event that the second anti poll tax demonstration attempted to turn northwards at Camberwell Green along Walworth Road, from where the march had been excluded by the conditions imposed under the 1986 Act (see pp. 61-2). Reserves were strategically positioned out of sight of the marchers to block the junction in such an event. Likewise, detailed plans were made to accommodate any concerted attempt by marchers on the final anti poll tax march to occupy Trafalgar Square. Plans were laid for the cordon of officers lining the southern side of the Square to retreat until supported by a second cordon. If that joint cordon came under serious pressure, it would divide on command, allowing demonstrators on to the Square, where they would then be contained. On the occasion of a large student demonstration, it was feared that there might be a repeat of the attempt to march to Parliament in breach of the Sessional Order, where a confrontation akin to the "battle of Westminster Bridge" (see p. 17) might ensue. Detailed plans were laid to retreat, allowing any breakaway march to become fully divorced from the main march, and then to block the Embankment and redirect the breakaway marchers across a bridge over the Thames on which they were to be contained. Similarly, a detailed evacuation plan for the New Year's Eve celebrations in Trafalgar Square was devised, which allocated tasks to each of the serials involved in the operation.

What this consideration of "What ifs" could not hope to achieve was an exhaustive set of options to be employed for a comprehensive list of contingencies. Senior officers were well aware of the unpredictability of public order operations. This unpredictability was vividly exemplified by an incident at the 1991 Remembrance Day service in Whitehall, when VVIPs and detachments of military and veterans' organizations gathered in Whitehall to honour the war dead. Just as the service was about to commence, there was a disturbance at the northern end of Whitehall and a cloud of smoke rose above the crowd. I accompanied the "Silver" commander to the scene, where we found a young man lying in the gutter suffering quite severe burns, being attended to by ambulance personnel. Apparently, he ran down Whitehall towards the Cenotaph where the service was being held, and as he did so he poured flammable liquid over himself and ignited it. He leapt the crowd control barriers that demarcated the ceremonial area before being tackled by several officers, who brought him to the ground and extinguished the flames, suffering burns themselves. Had they not responded promptly to this wholly unforeseen contingency, then the man would have been amongst the ranks of veterans within moments. It is in such circumstances that the senior officers must trust and rely upon their subordinates.

Exercises and "team building"

A development of the "What if?" contingency planning was the holding of simulated exercises. They were uncommon and employed only for very major operations. They were a regular feature of preparations for the Notting Hill Carnival, but were also used in the build-up to the final anti poll tax march. Essentially, the process was the same in each case: it involved staff from the Public Order Training Centre posing various contingencies to the sector command teams for them to respond to in "real time". There was an air of unreality about such exercises, not least because the simulations tended to be rather more dramatic than the real thing. Notting Hill command teams jokingly remarked that such exercises invariably concluded with Armageddon and the carnival being terminated in disorder. There was also little opportunity for sector commanders and sub-commanders to simulate direct intervention on their own part, for example by checking out a reported incident that they happened to be near. The value of these exercises for senior officers was that, however unreal it might have been as a simulation, it allowed for "team building". That is, by confronting hypothetical contingencies new members of the command team had an opportunity to assimilate the style and philosophy of their colleagues.

Vulnerable premises

A variation on the theme of "What ifs?" was the protection of vulnerable premises. This was something specific to the policing of political protest and highlights its political context. Police attempted to identify any premises that might have been specially vulnerable to attack by protestors and took steps to protect them. Thus, during marches for foreign nationalist groups not only the embassy buildings were protected, but also airline offices and banks on or near the route of the march. If police failed to appreciate the vulnerability of premises, they hurriedly deployed mobile reserves to correct their oversight. For example, when anti-vivisectionist protestors began jeering and angrily gesticulating at Boots chemist shops, mobile reserves were rushed to the scene to prevent any attempted invasion of, or damage to, the shop. Other similar premises along the remainder of the route were quickly identified and protection provided.

Nevertheless, the concept "vulnerable premises" refers not just to the vulnerability of particular locations to attack, but also to their political significance. They mark the "ditches" in which the police felt compelled "to die", if necessary. It was an indication of the seriousness with which these buildings were regarded that police officers under specific command were dedicated to their protection. If they were damaged or invaded, then there would be trouble, because the occupiers had the power to cause trouble.

Downing Street and the Palace of Westminster were routinely provided with such protection for major operations. This often amounted to an entire serial of officers (a total of 21 people) being posted to each location, usually to spend their time idly waiting for something to happen. The Palace of Westminster also received protection from any river-borne assault by Thames Division police boats, which deterred small craft from approaching the terrace too closely. When the protest concerned some specific aspect of government policy, then additional serials were posted to protect government departments. For example, the Department of Education received this protection for each of the National Union of Students protests and the Department of Trade and Industry was specially protected during the miners' protest against pit closures.

Amongst the most sensitive premises were foreign embassies, for whose protection and the maintenance of their dignity the British government was responsible under international treaty. Throughout the protests against the Gulf war the Metropolitan Police went to the most extraordinary lengths to protect the American embassy in Grosvenor Square. It was designated as a separate sector for all but the smallest and least problematic protest marches. Up to 10 mounted officers were held on standby at the rear of the embassy. TSG and level II shield-trained officers were deployed. The contingency plan was for officers in ordinary uniform to cordon off the front of the embassies and, if they came under sustained attack, riot-equipped TSG officers were to deploy and the officers in ordinary uniform were to withdraw, equip themselves with riot gear and redeploy in defence of the embassy. In fact, the principal protests against the Gulf war paid no heed to the embassy and so the officers and the contingency plan were not needed. Not all embassies received this level of treatment, although any embassy that was the target of protest was specially protected. Usually, the police negotiated a route that took marchers past the embassy, but did not permit them to stand and protest outside it.

Authority levels

Deciding what should be done in the event of a contingency arising still left unresolved the question of *who* should do it. Another means of extending control was to authorize only specified commanders to take the required action. The setting of "authority levels" revealed the perceived likelihood of in-the-job trouble following the use of particular tactics and personnel. Thus, the deployment of shield serials and mounted officers against disorderly crowds was almost entirely reserved for "Gold" and "Silver". Occasionally, there was quite vigorous discussion of the command level at which any given authority should be set. There was, for example, a protracted discussion of whether the three separate "Silver" commanders responsible for the sectors of the final anti poll tax march should have authority to deploy shields and mounted officers. "Gold"'s initial disinclination to yield such authority was a reflection of the sensitivity with which that particular operation was viewed. As we see shortly, on some operations authority to make an arrest was reserved for middle-ranking officers because it was feared that their subordinates might not act with the tact and sensitivity that the occasion demanded (see pp. 177–8). The least sensitive occasions were those small unproblematic marches that were placed under the sole command of a chief inspector or superintendent.

Controlling junior officers

Ensuring that a small group of sub-commanders shared a common perspective and set of priorities was relatively easy compared with achieving any measure of control over hundreds and possibly thousands of junior officers deployed in serials. Senior officers were conscious of the possibility that some imprudent action by a junior officer could be the spark that ignited a riot. They were equally aware of their tenuous control over the actions of such officers. The literature on policing generally indicates the rift there is between "street cops" and "management cops" (Reuss-Ianni & Ianni 1983) and the virtual independence of the occupational subculture of the lower ranks (Holdaway 1983).

Over-policing

One way in which senior officers exerted control over their junior colleagues was by determining the number of them posted to any operation. One of the first tasks in planning any operation was to decide upon the number of officers required for it. The principal task for which police officers were required was to escort a march through the traffic-congested streets of central London. Officers usually walked alongside marchers to provide protection from cars and ill-disposed opponents, to demarcate the boundaries of the march, to prevent marchers from straggling across the road disrupting traffic, and to be available to intervene in the event of disorder. Obviously, the larger a march, the more officers were required to accompany it, and so some marches became major operations purely as a result of the number of the demonstrators they attracted.

If a march was so large that "aid" from other force areas was needed, senior officers found themselves under a constraint to make an early assessment of the size of the policing operation. Under nationally agreed arrangements, police officers were entitled to receive at least 28 days' notice of any change to their rostered duties. An officer who was re-rostered with less than 28 days' notice was entitled to overtime pay, and if notice was less than 8 days the officer received both overtime and a day off in lieu. This imposed costs upon the Metropolitan Police that senior officers tried to avoid. There was, therefore, a strong incentive to beat the 28-day deadline and to allocate an adequate, or more than adequate, number of officers to the operation, since this was less costly than adding additional manpower after the deadline had passed.

In addition, the avoidance of trouble turned this incentive to over-police into a strong imperative, since it encouraged senior officers to err on the side of caution. Caution dictated that planning should rest on the maximum estimate of protestors likely to attend the event. If police assumed a lower number and a much larger protest then took place with untoward consequences, the police expected to be criticized. The principal source of estimates as to the size of a march was the organizer of the protest, but organizers were notorious for optimistically overestimating support for their cause. Thus, the incentives all acted towards allocating more officers to the operation than were needed. Even if it was appreciated later in the planning process that the numbers of protestors likely to attend were fewer than first thought, the tendency was to retain the large number of officers initially allocated "just in case".

A similar imperative arose from recurrent operations such as the Notting Hill Carnival. Many senior officers said that the carnival was trapped into its massive size because a serious attempt to reduce it would risk the possibility that any disorder would be attributed to such an attempt. It would be, in their view, "a brave man" who took such a course of action. Moreover,

141

the process of debriefing was unintentionally geared to highlighting problems, which tended to encourage the allocation of additional officers. It was more difficult to identify aspects of the operation that were over-supplied with resources, since, first the absence of any difficulties was less apparent than the occurrence of difficulties, and, secondly, success was readily attributable to the presence of officers. Over-supply could have been tested only by reducing resources and awaiting the consequences. When those consequences were considered dire, few senior officers were willing voluntarily to expose themselves to such a risk.

There were budgetary pressures to reduce the scale of policing opera-tions, but once a disaster had occurred – such as the anti poll tax riot – those budgetary pressures were in effect countered by the "just in case" rule that police apply to a wide range of policing possibilities (Ekblom & Heal 1982, P. Waddington 1993a). Both organizational and political pres-sures thus combine to make over-policing a chronic feature of public order operations.

"The Home Beat from Barnet"
A source of repeated complaint amongst senior officers was the poor qual-ity of junior officers assigned by other areas to public order duty in central London (and also to the Notting Hill Carnival). These officers were perceived as not having the same incentive to avoid trouble as those in command of the operations. Senior officers feared that junior ranks "switched off" (or, perhaps more accurately, never switched on). At cer-emonials there was the perceived danger that junior ranks regarded the operation as a "nice day out, up town" and were insufficiently attentive to security considerations. During demonstrations, officers accompanying the march were often characterized as plodding along with their "mind in neutral", like "mobile traffic cones". Serials were found to be slow in dis-embarking from their buses and unresponsive to the need for urgency if an incident occurred.

Senior officers felt that they had few sanctions against poor perform-ance. They wrote to areas that supplied conspicuously poor serials, but expected little support. They imagined that public order operations in cen-tral London were regarded throughout the rest of the Metropolitan Police as an unwelcome drain on local resources. Outer London areas were thought to have little vested interest in assigning their best officers to serve the interests of central London. As a result, the stereotypical officer dis-patched to public order duties in the centre was the "Home Beat from

Barnet" – that is, a long-serving officer with little ambition, whose normal duties were community policing in a leafy suburb.

Not all lower-ranking officers were viewed with such disdain. Individual serials were sometimes congratulated, either informally or formally, by senior officers for the quality of their performance. For example, the officers who prevented the "human fireball" from reaching the assembled ranks of ex-service personnel at the 1991 Service of Remembrance (see pp. 137-8) were all formally thanked and recommended for commendations. More generally, senior officers regarded the TSG as much more professional, competent and interested in public order duties than were other officers. They were given the more difficult and sensitive tasks to perform because senior officers felt that they could be relied on.

Senior officers also tried to control the quality of junior ranks allocated to the operation by attempting to stipulate minimum levels of training for serials engaged on particular duties. At Notting Hill Carnival, for example, the attempt was made to ensure that some serials were composed entirely of level II shield–trained officers. These were officers who had received extended public order training but were not public order specialists like the TSG. Their value to the operation was that, being better trained, they should have known what action to take in support of shield serials, if shields were deployed. They would, for example, appreciate the need to follow shield serials to secure "the ground" that the shields had "won". Two problems arose: first, areas reported the gravest difficulty in recruiting sufficient level II officers to staff the required number of dedicated serials; secondly, a dispute arose over whether these officers should bring their riot equipment with them. It was not intended to deploy them in riot equipment at the carnival, but if serious disorder erupted elsewhere in London the force mobilization plan required that these officers should have ready access to their riot equipment. On the other hand, if they brought their equipment and disorder broke out in the carnival, senior officers feared that, instead of remaining in ordinary uniform and performing the rôle assigned to them, some or all of the level II serials would return to the holding centre and don their equipment. This is just how tenuous senior officers believed was their control over subordinates.

Another reason for worrying about the control that superiors were able to exert over subordinates arose in the aftermath of the anti poll tax riot. There was vociferous criticism of commanders, voiced not least in the force newspaper *The Job*. They were accused of incompetence in dealing with the riot. This re-awoke complaints that ineffective command had contributed to the death of PC Keith Blakelock, who was savagely hacked to death during the Broadwater Farm riot of 1985 (*Police*, November 1985). Some senior officers responsible for the two subsequent anti poll tax marches remarked repeatedly how important it was for them to be *seen* by their subordinates to "get it right". If they were not seen in this light, it was feared those subordinates might act on their own initiative and senior officers would lose control entirely.

Briefing

How, then, did senior officers try to control the behaviour of their subordinates? The answer was by briefing them thoroughly. Virtually all senior officers laid considerable emphasis on the need for thorough briefings. Almost as many were deeply pessimistic about their actual value.

For major operations, briefing was approached quite systematically. Serial inspectors (that is, inspectors who supervise each of the serials of officers deployed on the operation) were usually summoned to the briefing room at Scotland Yard some days before the event. Here they were addressed by "Gold", who provided an overview of the strategy, and "Silver", who explained in greater detail how that strategy was to be achieved. These senior officers spoke to a script written by the Public Order Branch and approved beforehand. Senior officers varied in their willingness to extemporize around this agreed script.

The briefing normally commenced with a brief explanation of the nature of the event. If it was a protest march, then the protest group was identified and its cause explained. Any previous experience of the group was usually made known, and a Special Branch assessment was occasionally given or read out. Sub-commanders were introduced and invited to stand up so that they could be identified.

Apart from details regarding specific postings and duties, what was noticeable about briefings was the exhortations made by senior officers. One of the most important was to encourage those present to brief their subordinates properly. A period of half an hour or so was normally included in the "operation order" to allow a briefing to be given by the serial inspector to the serial after the last individual had been collected from his or her home station. Senior officers pleaded for this time to be used properly for the purpose of briefing. The audience were repeatedly told that considerable effort had gone into the planning of the operation and that this would come to nought if they failed to play their part. Appeals were made to their professionalism and how their subordinates deserved to be properly briefed. However, senior officers felt that the odds were stacked against them. They repeatedly complained about serial inspectors failing to attend briefings and sending sergeants in their place. Some senior officers insisted that only inspectors able to attend the briefing should be assigned to the operation and when, as still happened, sergeants attended as surrogates, the sergeants were instructed that it was they who were to brief the remainder of the serial, not the inspector. Whether these, or any other, instructions or exhortations had any effect was a matter of speculation for senior officers. A few senior officers tried to cajole serial inspectors with threats that they would ask officers at random what their task was and how it fitted into the whole operation, but I witnessed no occasion when the threat was carried out.

The limited effectiveness of briefing as a means of determining behaviour could be gauged by the frequency with which serials defied the proscription on parking coaches in certain streets in the vicinity of "feeding centres". They were instructed to park them in reserved parking bays at specified locations and warned that coaches would receive no special treatment from traffic wardens if parked elsewhere. Still the streets in question were frequently littered with police vehicles illegally parked. Equally common was the arrival of serials, some or all of whom were improperly dressed. For example, officers were repeatedly instructed to wear black epaulettes on their reflective jackets, but a consistently high proportion failed to do so, including many supervising officers. Indeed, on one New Year's Eve operation a superintendent was reprimanded by the "Silver" commander for not being dressed in accordance with the "operation order".

Senior officers somewhat fatalistically recognized that most serials were interested only in what affected them directly and paid little heed to other aspects of the operation. In their own eyes they seemed condemned to impotent frustration at their limited ability to direct the actions of those whom they notionally commanded.

The chronically poor performance of ordinary serials would seem to reflect a paradox that lies at the heart of public order policing. Individual initiative is a positive threat to the concerted action needed in public order operations, and the style of command tends to exclude it. Moreover, few operations offered much opportunity to display initiative, since most protestors trudged compliantly, even willingly, along the agreed route, posing no threat. If the operation went "pear-shaped", it usually did so rapidly and unexpectedly. This required immediate action on the part of those nearest the scene, but they were often left waiting to be told what to do.

Specialists

The problem of controlling other police officers was not restricted to the lower ranks who escorted marches. Specialists also presented a problem, for they possessed the additional resource of their specialist knowledge and priorities. One group whom senior officers found irritatingly difficult to control was the force firearms unit, SO19. These officers provided armed support at ceremonials, where their task included the removal and protection of VVIPs in the event of terrorist attack. This posed senior officers with a dilemma: on the one hand, SO19 needed to be readily available to intervene immediately if an attack commenced, but on the other hand they should not be so conspicuous that they drew attention to themselves and detracted from the ceremonial itself. SO19 officers understandably placed more emphasis upon their interventionist rôle, which resulted in senior officers responsible for the whole operation repeatedly trying to restrain them and complaining at their limited success in so doing.

Controlling non-police personnel

The previous chapter discussed how police perceived and related to third parties. There were also third parties that needed to be integrated within the policing operation itself. A simple, but important, example was the participation of other emergency services. Blaring sirens in the vicinity of a crowd were discouraged by police, for fear that a siren might have been misinterpreted as evidence of a confrontation between police and other members of the crowd, when in fact there was none. Police tried to co-opt the other emergency services by inviting them to supply liaison officers in the control room. Through this channel, police commanders tried to have instructions passed to the emergency services to cease sounding their sirens in the vicinity of the event. However, commanders had difficulty enough silencing police sirens and had even less success in silencing other emergency services.

The limited success with which the police exerted control resulted from their dependence on those other emergency services. They were obliged to balance achieving compliance with their own priorities against alienating such groups. St John Ambulance Brigade, who provide volunteer first aid and ambulance facilities at virtually all ceremonial and many other events, were notoriously difficult to control. Being a volunteer organization, their own senior personnel were believed to find it difficult to impose discipline. Thus, it was a repeated source of complaint that at ceremonials some St John's personnel, particularly young cadets, passed into restricted areas without security passes. It was alleged that on one occasion a group of St John personnel carried a stretcher into a restricted area in order to obtain a privileged position as spectators until ushered out by a senior officer.

Conclusions

On the face of it, major public order operations are impressive organizational structures. There is an almost paramilitary command structure, with an "operation order" detailing the duties of all those employed and a detailed briefing to all officers down to those of quite junior rank. However, beneath the organizational veneer lies a reality of the precarious hold on command by senior officers. Paradoxically, it is the smaller, less problematic minor operations that allow senior officers more direct control because there they can intervene directly and are not reliant upon a chain of command that may prove tenuous.

CHAPTER 7

Commanding the ground

Introduction

What happens on the picket-line or during a demonstration captures most public attention. This is the "stage" on which police and protestors alike perform. But it is a performance that usually receives attention only when disorder erupts. The image of riot-police battling with demonstrators is quite misleading. Rarely was there disorder or even disruption, even in this collection of operations biased towards the biggest and most problematic. By and large, demonstrators assembled at the agreed location, proceeded along the agreed route, held their rally and dispersed peacefully. Such problems as there were usually related to traffic congestion. For the police, public order was a recipe for boredom, rather than the exhilaration of battle. As with other aspects of public order policing, what is fascinating is how the police subtly extended maximum control over the event, rather than how they confronted demonstrators.

Taking the ground

The phrase "taking the ground" has been erroneously and misleadingly applied to aggressive actions by riot police (Jefferson 1990). This usage confuses "taking the ground" with "fighting for the ground" (P. Waddington 1993b). Commanding officers tried to achieve the former so as to avoid the latter. This they achieved by transforming otherwise public space into "police property". Barriers or tape demarcated areas in which the public, demonstrators, spectators and other nominated categories of person were allowed. This was passively imposed because the police aimed to arrive long before those attending the event. Upon arrival, demonstrators, spectators or revellers found themselves channelled into occupying areas reserved for them. The provision of reserved space was both a service and a control, for in occupying it people were thereby contained. At ceremonials and festivities this could be done overtly (see p. 45), but for demonstrations police took the ground by stealth, to avoid accusations of using oppressive measures.

The main way in which the ground was taken was through the negotiation of a "standard route" that presented as few problems as possible. If marches had proceeded along Oxford Street and Regent Street, the traffic congestion created would have been enormous. The route from Hyde Park to Trafalgar Square, via Park Lane, Piccadilly and the Haymarket, was much more easily managed. The necessary traffic diversions had long been formulated and were readily implemented with few alterations to account for roadworks and other temporary problems. Marches following this route found that, after passing the junction with St James's Street, they were directed from the nearside of Piccadilly to the offside, so that traffic could pass by on the nearside and thus continue to circulate. As the marchers diverted to the centre of the road, they thus complied with the police agenda.

Police also attempted to enlist the organizer of the protest to assist them in ensuring that the assembly conformed to police priorities. For example, a favoured location for assembling large protest marches was the Victoria Embankment, near the Embankment tube station. This station is an intersection of four underground train lines – Circle, District, Northern and Bakerloo. Obviously, many protestors alighted at the Embankment station, but this caused congestion, both in the station and on the footpath immediately outside. Organizers were often asked not to refer to the Embankment station in publicity, but to instruct marchers to alight at Temple station so that they could join the rear of the march in an orderly fashion. A large march terminating in Hyde Park (such as the TUC march against pit closures) posed the reverse problem of protestors all heading for the nearby Marble Arch station and causing congestion there. Again, organizers were asked to direct protestors to alternative stations in the vicinity – Hyde Park, Bond Street, Green Park, Knightsbridge, and Lancaster Gate. Police officers would no doubt claim, quite justifiably, that they did this in the interests of the protestors themselves. Congestion was inconvenient and potentially hazardous, but its avoidance involved appropriating organizers to achieve police priorities.

Assembling a large number of protestors on one carriageway of a heavily used road like the Victoria Embankment may appear odd at first, for it is surely a recipe for traffic disruption. However, it afforded the police extensive control over the assembly. First, in order for the road to be used as an assembly point, it must be closed to traffic, and that occurred at the discretion of the police. They decided when there were sufficient marchers present to close the carriageway to traffic and assemble the march. Secondly, an abiding preoccupation of the police was to ensure that the bona fide organizer retained control of the demonstration, for it was with this person and the group he or she represented that negotiations had been conducted and agreement reached. One of the principal ways in which the organizer controlled the march was to decide who led it, which implied leading it along the route that had been agreed with police. What the police feared most was that another, possibly militant, faction would "take the head of the march" and lead it astray. Assembling on the highway helped avert such a possibility. Police were aware that they were about to close the carriageway to traffic and were, therefore, able to arrange for those designated by the organizer to head the march to position themselves at the head of the march as soon as the traffic ceased to flow. In addition, since a carriageway is an elongated rectangle, once the head of the march was in place, other marchers were encouraged to fall into line behind. Finally, because the march proceeded along the carriageway, groups were physically prevented from inserting themselves at the front by barriers and cordons of police lining the footpath. Groups congregating at intersections and other vulnerable points were viewed suspiciously by the police and ushered to join the march at the rear.

When a march assembled not on a roadway but in an open space like a park, alternative means were used to control the head of the march. Demonstrators typically milled about haphazardly. Police then approached the organizer and agreed a time for forming up the march. The head of the march was then positioned at the exit from the park, so that the railings prevented others from inserting themselves at the front. At Hyde Park, the police typically created a V-shape with barriers, which funnelled marchers to the desired width as they approached the exit. By inserting the head of the march into the funnel the police were likewise able to deter any attempt by militant factions to "take the head of the march".

As marches proceeded, the police retained control of "the ground" through which they passed by the careful direction of traffic. On the grounds of minimizing traffic disruption and congestion, the police contained a march between moving walls of steel. The march was kept to its allotted carriageway, or lanes of the carriageway, by traffic passing alongside it. Ahead of the march, traffic division officers halted traffic at intersections to allow it to pass. Smaller marches were escorted by a team of five or six police motorcyclists, who went just ahead of it to prevent traffic turning out of or into intersecting roads. Larger marches were preceded by a large van from which traffic direction signs and cones were off-loaded to mark the route. Immediately behind the march the crew of another van collected the signs and cones. This, in effect, contained the march within a hermetically sealed traffic-free zone.

Traffic could be used as a physical barrier to deter marchers from diverting from the agreed route. For example, the organizers of one modest-sized march from Hyde Park to Trafalgar Square had been insistent on proceeding along Oxford Street. Officers were unsure of how successfully they had persuaded the organizers to accept the "standard route". As a safeguard, traffic division officers were instructed to halt the traffic in Marble Arch as near to the line of the march as possible and to pack vehicles as closely together as they could, so as to form a physical barrier to prevent any attempted diversion.

Police controlled physical space in other ways. For example, the route of a large and/or problematic march was invariably surveyed some days prior to the actual event. Skips containing rubble and other debris were removed. The police sometimes even had their own skip lorry available with which to accomplish this if all else failed. Building and demolition sites were visited in an attempt, not always successful, to persuade contractors to close entrances and remove supplies of materials from the highway. If a march was particularly problematic, as was the final anti poll tax march, then shopkeepers along the route were visited and advised to close their premises and draw window shutters.

On the day of the march, police usually surveyed the route again and noted any unexpected changes. For example, on the morning of one anti Gulf war march, senior commanders were informed that a large tower crane had been erected in a street along the route. It did not obstruct the progress of the march, but they feared that it might be climbed by protestors and used to hang banners on. Steps were hastily taken to surround the offending crane with crowd control barriers, and a serial of mobile reserve officers were deployed to the location to deter any such behaviour. It was common to find that roadworks had commenced along the route of a march and police often liaised with the workmen to ensure that they completed their work or that the site was properly protected by mobile reserves by the time the march arrived. Ironically, one of the threats that needed repeatedly to be removed during the period of this research was the "no parking" signs that the Metropolitan Police had liberally strewn around Whitehall as part of the additional security arrangements installed following the Provisional IRA mortar bomb attack on Downing Street. To prevent their theft, the police had used waist-high signs with a steel shaft and heavy base. These were regarded as particularly effective weapons and were temporarily replaced by the more common lighter yellow plastic cones for the duration of any protest march.

The degree of sensitivity with which any march was regarded could be gauged from the number of senior police officers found "walking the route". The aim here was to detect any small threats that might need removal; for example a crate full of empty milk bottles in a doorway might need to be removed to prevent the bottles being used as ammunition. Street traders were warned of the imminent arrival of a march so that they could cover up their stalls or put away goods that might be stolen or damaged by passing demonstrators. Troops on ceremonial guard duty were warned of the arrival of the march and their commanding officers advised to bring guards indoors to prevent them being exposed to abuse. It is instructive, perhaps, that the commonly used argot to describe a route that had been surveyed and from which all problems had been removed was that it was "clean".

Negotiating at the scene

However much negotiating had been done prior to the event, there were always issues to be resolved at the scene. Of course, the senior officer in command of the policing operation had his copy of the "route form" to refer to if necessary, but, as in prior negotiation, the preference of commanding officers was to resolve issues amicably, provided they did not obstruct police aims.

Negotiating at the scene presented different contingencies, one of which was that the organizer was not alone, but had the support of other demonstrators. This could, with skill, be turned to the advantage of the police. In a studied performance of "spurious friendliness", some senior officers greeted the organizer warmly. From several yards away they called his or her first name, strode towards the organizer hand outstretched and a broad grin on their face. "How nice to meet you again", or something like it, was said. They were consciously aware of the message that they were sending to other demonstrators: it was that the relationship between the police and protestors was not antagonistic, that the police were not a threat, and that they were reasonable people who would facilitate the reasonable demands of the protestors.

Occasionally, the opportunity arose to "brief" the stewards. It was eagerly taken; stewards were able to help or significantly obstruct the police in the achievement of their aims. Just as in prior negotiations, emphasis was given to the protest being the responsibility of the protestors themselves: the police would not intervene unless invited to do so, or in the event of some external attack, or because marchers were behaving in a manner that the police could not ignore. In the latter eventuality, stewards were told that the police would seek to enlist their help before acting on their own authority. The theme of safety was also emphasized: stewards were asked to pay attention to small children and advised that they should be kept away from passing traffic. The message the police, more or less consciously, conveyed was that their mission was to protect and facilitate the march, not to confront it.

"Neat and tidy"

In Chapter 4, reference was made (see pp. 87–9) to how police try to keep the march compact by controlling the speed of their own control van that preceded the head of the march. They tried to keep the march "neat and tidy". This achieved a number of goals. First, if gaps appeared in a march there was a tendency for drivers of vehicles to push their way through the march. Grossly inconsiderate, not to say downright dangerous, behaviour was frequently shown by motorists to demonstrators. Secondly, a march that became divided into several sections was less easily controlled than one that remained a single entity. For example, rear sections might run to catch up their colleagues at the front. A running crowd was regarded by police as a threat, since they feared that it might get out of control. Thirdly, if gaps appeared, factions could easily divert from the agreed route. Fourthly, a straggling march simply took longer to cross intersections and disrupted traffic crossing its path for longer, causing motorists frustration and annoyance, and sometimes threatening disorder.

153

It was not only the marchers whom senior officers tried to keep neat and tidy, but also the police who accompanied them. Senior commanders frequently detached themselves from the march and took a position, for example on a traffic island, from which they could see the march as a whole, or a substantial portion of it. They became agitated if escorting police officers were unevenly spaced along the length of the march. If this occurred, steps were often taken to rectify the spacing. This usually amounted to nothing more than asking individual officers to speed up or slow down as necessary for the adjustment. On large marches, additional serials were sometimes summoned to fill the gaps. Why were senior officers so concerned that escorting officers should be spaced uniformly? The answers given to this question were, first, that police officers "like things neat and tidy". As a disciplined uniformed service, they should make as good an impression on bystanders as possible and this involved distinguishing themselves from the disorganized crowd of protestors in both their appearance and behaviour. Secondly, it was hoped that officers would monitor the behaviour of the crowd in their immediate vicinity, for example listening for any suggestions that a faction was about to initiate some action. This sounds plausible, and on occasion officers did report overhearing something that caused them alarm. However, this purpose was strangely inconsistent with the stereotype of escorting officers, most of whom allegedly had their "brains in neutral". Moreover, the more militant factions were also thought to give escorting officers a "hard time" by engaging them in badinage and making offensive remarks. To defeat this, sergeants and inspectors were advised to circulate escorting officers so that they did not remain with the same factions for too long. Not only does such a policy seem designed to defeat the "winding up" of officers, it would also seem to have defeated any intelligence-gathering function. Another justification for even spacing was to keep protestors within the body of the march and deter them from spreading across the carriageway and the footpath. Finally, in the event of any disruption or disorder, it was thought that if officers were near at hand they could intervene quickly. Unfortunately, it was a common complaint of senior officers that escorting serials remained largely oblivious to anything that was going on around them.

An alternative interpretation of why spacing was regarded as so important is that its purpose was symbolic: police officers escorting a march defined its boundaries and, if large sections of it were unescorted, the boundaries became indistinct. Bounding the march was important for maintaining control over it; knowing where the march began and ended defined the scope of police responsibility. This was one reason for confining marches to the carriageway, where they were distinct from other pedestrians. Protestors who spilled on to the footpath and mingled with bystanders blurred that distinction.

Factions

Police commanders were also very attentive to the location of factions within a march. The position of "the opposition" was carefully monitored throughout. As marches assembled, the position of Socialist Workers' Party and Class War banners were noted. If they were near the front of the march, concern increased; if they were to the rear, apprehension was reduced. As such factions approached sensitive locations along the route of the march, radio messages were broadcast giving their exact location. The density of escorting officers was routinely increased alongside those sections of the march heavily populated by "the opposition". In all of this the factions themselves facilitated the police. When a march was organized by an umbrella group, such as the Campaign to Stop War in the Gulf, factions seemed to express their distinctiveness by grouping together in a solid phalanx and often maintaining a small distance from others around them. In achieving their distinctiveness, they aided the police who were monitoring them.

"Insurance"

Police are notorious pessimists: they always fear the worst and therefore they planned for it by way of "insurance". This has led Jefferson (1990) to suppose that "planning for the worst case scenario" is a step in the self-fulfilling prophecy that leads, seemingly inexorably, to actual disorder. This is an erroneous conclusion, based upon reliance on retrospective analysis of those few incidents where disorder has erupted. The null hypothesis is not tested by considering a sample (and a very small one at that) consisting only of occasions where disorder occurs. The reality is, as the previous chapter made plain, that police habitually plan for the worst-case scenario, especially for major operations, yet few of these end in disorder (P. Waddington 1993b).

Jefferson also contends that the presence of public order specialists, like the TSG, adds to the potential for disorder because such squads are allegedly more aggressive than their non-specialist counterparts. These non-random observations, biased towards the larger and more problematic demonstrations, show that TSG officers were deployed quite frequently. Of the 70 operations for which data are available in the files, TSG officers were deployed on 48 of them. They comprised the sole mobile reserve on 23 occasions, and the mean number of TSG serials deployed was 3.66, amounting to an average of 16.64 per cent of the total foot duty serials deployed on these operations. However, officers were deployed in protective equipment on only two of these occasions, one of which was during a full-blown riot – the anti poll tax riot in Trafalgar Square (see pp. 52–3) – and the other during serious disorder outside Brixton prison, again in connection with an anti poll tax demonstration (see p. 63). Officers were allowed to don their protective equipment in readiness for disorder on just three occasions, but were not actually deployed. The first was the final anti poll tax march (see p. 64), the second was a march by anarchists opposed to the holding of a general election (see pp. 65–6), and the third was after intelligence reports were received that an anti-racist march in south London was to be attacked by the extreme right wing (see pp. 168–71). For the most part, TSG officers remained on standby, attired in ordinary uniform, sitting in their personnel carriers.

Mounted officers were deployed much less frequently. On 43 of the 78 occasions for which information is available, there was no mounted contingent. On five occasions there were up to 10 mounted officers deployed, but on another 15 operations there were between 11 and 20, and on 15 more there were in excess of 20 mounted officers. However, apart from the anti poll tax riot, these officers were not deployed in a riot-control capacity. Although the police frequently had the iron fist available, it was normally enclosed within a velvet glove.

What the Jefferson hypothesis fails to take into account is the dual nature of trouble. If trouble was restricted to that arising on the job, then there would be little impediment to the iron fist being openly displayed. It might then be true that it becomes a self-fulfilling prophecy (although experience in countries where the iron fist is routinely displayed does not support such a conclusion; see Jeffery 1991). However, in Britain trouble is not so restricted, and the avoidance of in-the-job trouble compelled police to be circumspect about their deployment of mobile reserves and other coercive resources. If they were not, they left themselves vulnerable to accusations of "provocative policing". Thus, whether or not the display of overtly coercive policing methods was actually self-fulfilling, the police avoided

156

such methods for fear that it might prove to be so or that they would be blamed for any disorder that arose.

Normally, this circumspection amounted to keeping such resources discreetly out of sight. A conspicuous example of this was to be found at the Notting Hill Carnival. For the 1991 carnival there were 18 serials of TSG officers, plus their "medic" support, and 12 mounted officers all available for immediate deployment. In addition, baton gunners and a full firearms team were held on reserve, available for deployment in the event of serious disorder – as ferrous "a fist" as one could imagine. However, the police went to enormous lengths to ensure that this reserve capability was not seen by carnival-goers. Officers were held out of sight in school buildings converted to "holding centres". They were strictly forbidden from leaving the confines of the "holding centre" in their public order equipment without authorization. They were conveyed to and from the centre in personnel carriers and at times when few people were in the carnival area. Many carnival-goers might have been dimly aware that the police had such a presence, but few would have seen them.

In much more minor operations than this, mobile reserves – which are only rarely equipped with riot gear – were still kept out of sight. They normally "shadowed" marches from a distance, driving in their personnel carriers along a parallel route, ready to intervene if called upon, but safely out of sight. Even so, where riot equipment was available, officers were rarely allowed even to put on protective clothing, lest they were seen.

However, there is a price to be paid for circumspection of this kind, which created a dilemma between avoiding in-the-job trouble, on the one hand, and on-the-job trouble, on the other. Tactical effectiveness is clearly compromised if reserves are far from the scene of any potential or actual disorder and they need a long time to don suitable equipment. It was a source of severe criticism from within the Metropolitan Police that, at the anti poll tax riot, reserve officers were not authorized to don their protective equipment earlier and that as a consequence they were delayed in making their intervention. It was alleged that some officers did not have time fully to equip themselves and suffered injury as a result (see p. 54).

Clearly, where there is a strong anticipation of disorder, there will be less incentive to compromise tactical effectiveness in order to avoid charges of provocation. Even so, senior officers were always attentive to achieving an appropriate balance between these competing considerations. This is illustrated by considering three occasions when police *were* unusually prepared to be "up front" in their deployment of reserves. The first was on the occasion of a small march along the length of Park Lane on 1 August 1992, the day on which the new annual registration letter for motor vehicles was issued. The group in question were environmentalists protesting about motor cars. They proposed to tow the shell of a car from the southern exit of Hyde Park to the northern entrance – a distance of a few hundred yards – and then to demolish it. Police feared that the group might be associated with militant environmentalist organizations and that they might stage some form of direct action. There were several showrooms for quality cars in Park Lane and many of them were planning champagne receptions for their clients to celebrate this landmark in the motoring calendar. Police were anxious to prevent any invasion of these showrooms by the protestors. The problem was to provide mobile reserves (TSG officers in ordinary uniform) that would be able to intervene sufficiently promptly, while not being provocative. If police were seen to be conspicuously present outside each of the showrooms, then this might provoke precisely the reaction from the protestors that the senior officers sought to avoid. The solution decided upon was to station three personnel carriers at important intersections along Park Lane. This ensured that the carriers were nearby and yet not associated with the showrooms as such. In the event they were not needed and the march concluded without incident.

The second example was during the Anti-Election Alliance, to which reference has previously been made (see pp. 65–6). Although police had gone to some lengths to accommodate this anarchist group, they still feared that some disruption, if not violent disorder, would erupt. How could reserves be readily to hand and properly equipped without appearing provocative or oppressive? The officer in charge of the mobile reserves proposed that his officers should be fully equipped in their "baby-gro" flame-retardant overalls, but that they should wear their normal duty anoraks and flat caps, instead of riot helmets. In the event of disorder, the reserves would need only to slip off their anoraks and exchange their riot helmets for their flat caps. At the same time, anyone catching sight of them would assume that they were wearing their ordinary uniforms. When he made this proposal at a strategy meeting, his compromise was greeted by spontaneous applause from his colleagues and cries of "brilliant!".

The third example was when the balance between on-the-job and in-the-job trouble tipped decisively in favour of the former. This was the case when the final anti poll tax demonstration was held. It will be recalled from the discussion in Chapter 3 (see p. 64) that police resisted strong political pressure to ban the march. By going out on a limb they were courting severe in-the-job trouble if there was any on-the-job trouble. Accordingly, they invested in enormous resources by way of "insurance". A total of nearly 5000 police were on duty, including 44 serials of mobile reserves, of whom 12 were level I TSG and 14 level II shield-trained officers. In addition, there were 48 mounted officers. Not only was this force assembled and the "worst-case scenario" systematically planned for during a one-day exercise (see p. 138), the iron fist was more openly displayed than on any other operation. Serials of TSG, fully equipped in riot gear, were parked all around Trafalgar Square, albeit out of sight of the marchers as they passed through the Square. Mounted officers were similarly equipped and distributed. Intelligence reports after the march suggested that individual members of militant factions were observed "spotting" in the area and, having seen the level of police preparedness, had dissuaded their colleagues from "coming out to play". Whether this is accurate or not cannot be ascertained from my observations. It tends to conform to the stereotyping of "the opposition" discussed earlier (see pp. 112–14). What is clear is that this was regarded as a quite exceptional operation in which police were able to be much less circumspect than would normally be possible.

When "the wheel comes off"

The notion that disorder is often initiated by some otherwise minor incident is one that enjoys wide academic and popular currency (D. Waddington et al. 1987, 1989). I have argued elsewhere (P. Waddington 1991) that the concept of "precipitating incidents" or "flashpoints" is neither analytically useful nor empirically testable. Explaining why violence and disorder erupt when and where they do requires a much more comprehensive database than has so far been available for analysis.

Lay theories of disorder

Operational police officers cannot await the deliberations of academic analysts. They need some comprehension of why events occur as they do and rely on commonsense knowledge to provide it. Senior officers made reference to three "lay theories" of disorder. First was a version of the "precipitating incident" model: they attributed disorder to some more or less random concatenation of unpredictable circumstances. Many were prepared to concede that disorder might be sparked by an injudicious or ham-fisted arrest or other police intervention. Just as often, they envisaged that it could be sparked by the intervention of bystanders or some genuine misunderstanding between police and protestors. Secondly, there was a belief that some protestors actively sought to be provocative in order to prompt such injudicious or ham-fisted intervention. Thirdly, disorder was seen as resulting from the deliberate activities of militant extremists – "the opposition". Whether "the opposition" decided to "come out and play" was believed to rest on entirely opportunistic factors, principally their assessment of the relative strength of police to "the opposition". This explained why "the opposition" were frequent attenders at demonstrations but participated in violence only infrequently. What is interesting about all three "lay theories" is that they perceived the outbreak of disorder to be more or less uncontrollable. Injudicious action by a subordinate, a provoked over-reaction, or a deliberately intended attack by extremists were all difficult to anticipate and control. This placed police commanders in a position of some helplessness and explains why they invested so much in trying to exert extensive control over the event.

Non-precipitating "precipitating incidents"

This perceived unpredictability of disorder also meant that police commanders were tremendously sensitive to events that might be harbingers of trouble. Although the vast majority of operations concluded without incident, tension had a habit of oscillating quite significantly. There was no lack of potential precipitating incidents. Considering only the anti Gulf war marches, there were many occasions when tension rose and trouble seemed imminent but did not materialize.

One source of tension lay in indications of malign intent on the part of demonstrators. The circulation of leaflets giving advice on what to do once arrested, and overheard remarks about how a left-wing banner was to be "defended", were interpreted on one march as preparation for confrontation. More serious, perhaps, was the discovery of weapons. One supporter of an anti Gulf war march was found to be in possession of a replica firearm.

Hostile bystanders who jeered at marches as they passed also raised tension. Football supporters having a pre-match drink in a pub came out to hurl abuse at a passing anti Gulf war march. TSG personnel carriers were dispatched to the scene and parked between the two groups, and the football supporters returned to their drinking. Bystanders waving American and/or Union flags at an anti Gulf war march were dissuaded from doing so by police accompanying the march. On another occasion, an organized group of counter-demonstrators, supportive of the war, assembled in Trafalgar

Square. Police were deployed to the scene and instructed to "relocate" the group, which they did without incident. Newspaper sellers attached to the protest and protestors handing out leaflets sometimes became embroiled in heated verbal confrontations with bystanders. Isolated individuals occasionally shouted abuse at marches, provoking a response. Police intervention in the incidents that I witnessed amounted to no more than telling individuals concerned to "move on". There was one occasion when a person threw a flour-bomb at an anti Gulf war march and was arrested. When he reappeared at a later march he was detained until the march had passed. It was a regular feature of the anti Gulf war marches that the whereabouts of identified right-wing counter-demonstrators was carefully monitored and mobile reserves redeployed accordingly.

Provocative actions by protestors were often ignored, but sometimes not. For example, as one march passed the American embassy and a man at its head turned and signalled others to stop, he found himself being propelled along the route by a couple of officers who released him once the march had continued past the embassy. Another provocative act was the burning of an American flag outside the American embassy, referred to earlier (see p. 139). Neither event sparked disorder.

Occasionally, disputes amongst marchers also caused tension to increase and prompted a police response. It was not uncommon for different factions to jeer speakers with whom they disagreed at anti Gulf war rallies. A contingency that was frequently planned for was to defeat any attempt by militants to seize the platform and incite the crowd. On several occasions police deployed around the margins of a rally, ready to intervene if such disagreements became heated. At one anti Gulf war march, two rallies were established, expressing mutual hostility, and police formed a cordon between them so as to prevent hostility turning to violence.

Banners were also a source of internal dissension on marches, as well as posing a problem for police. On one anti Gulf war march, a pro-Iraq (as opposed to anti-war) banner was unfurled at the assembly and was greeted with protests from other demonstrators. The pro-Iraqi faction replied with accusations that their critics were "collaborators". Tempers were rising and police intervened to escort the pro-Iraqi faction to the rear of the march and advised them to furl up their banner as it was causing a breach of the peace. Preparations were made to "take out" this group if they attempted to march with the banner, but they evidently decided against doing so and appeared to leave the assembly before the march commenced. A similar incident occurred a few weeks later when a militant left-wing faction

161

unfurled a banner announcing a sit-down demonstration in Parliament Square (see p. 108). Stewards asked police to assist them in removing the group associated with the banner from the march. The police view was that the organizers were embarrassed by the presence of such a hard-left group. The police applied pressure by warning the banner carriers that they were inciting a breach of the Sessional Order. TSG officers were redeployed close to the march, but there was evident reluctance on the part of the police to become involved in a mêlée. Eventually, it was decided to "stand down" the TSG and the stewards agreed to allow the faction to remain on the march.

Another potential source of friction, according to police, was the much more mundane problem of latecomers pushing in to the march ahead of those who had waited for some time for the march to set off. For this reason, the police often kept a march waiting until the tide of late arrivals had dwindled, usually, if not always, with the agreement of the organizer.

I witnessed only one incident where police made an arrest on their own initiative (see p. 57). However, police sometimes insisted on adherence with the "route form" conditions and threatened not to allow the march to proceed otherwise. On one occasion, a march of Muslims was held up until the organizer convinced supporters to remove hoods and masks as stipulated by the "route form". However, no action was taken against several individual marchers who pulled scarves across the lower half of their faces.

Any of the incidents described above could have qualified as a "flashpoint" had they been followed by disorder. Because disorder did not erupt they never became candidates. This highlights the essentially retrospective nature of the notion of precipitating incidents, for incidents qualify as precipitants only if they are followed by disorder. Hence, the theory is circular and unfalsifiable.

Losing it

Only once during the anti Gulf war protests did serious disorder seem at all likely. This was not when spontaneous marches breached the Sessional Order, or the Socialist Workers' Party marched past the American embassy. It was when a much larger crowd of protestors than expected overwhelmed police preparations on 12 January 1991 – three days before the UN ultimatum to Iraq was due to expire.

On arrival at Hyde Park, where the march was assembling, the "Silver" commander became alarmed at the unexpectedly large gathering and the absence of any apparent organization. There was no sign of the march having a discernible shape and protestors were milling around aimlessly. At one stage, a small group of protestors started to walk at their own initiative south along a major footpath in the park, the Broadwalk. This prompted a large number of others to follow them. This movement was stopped only by the crew of the control van, who drove down the Broadwalk, intercepted this incipient march and advised them over the public address system that this was not the official march, which would be commencing from Reformers' Tree.

Shortly afterwards, the commencement of the march was signalled by the more or less concerted movement of several large banners. However, the march was still not properly formed up and was certainly not "neat and tidy". Protestors swept irresistibly down the Broadwalk and left the park through several separate gateways. Officers positioned to escort the march were overwhelmed by the number and disorganization of the protestors. They quickly became lost in the milling throng.

Thousands of protestors swarmed across Park Lane and headed towards Hyde Park Corner. The "Silver" commander raced ahead of them into Piccadilly. As his entourage strode quickly towards Piccadilly Circus he busily tried to mobilize resources. Groups of officers encountered *en route* were instructed to form cordons to try and impose some discipline on the marchers. However, they were too few to have much impact. Desperate efforts were made to deploy mobile reserves, but this was impeded by problems with radio communication that always seem to arise when the situation became at all difficult.

Traffic officers started marking the route along Piccadilly and around Piccadilly Circus with traffic cones and signs in accordance with the prearranged traffic management plan. The crowd spread onward, chanting their opposition to the war. But when protestors encountered the cones, they began to keep within these confines. Traffic officers started directing traffic along the nearside of Piccadilly as had been planned. This was viewed with apprehension by members of the "Silver command team", who feared that motorists would be attacked as they tried to push their way through the crowd. On the contrary, the passage of traffic served simply to marshall the crowd into a more organized entity and it marched meekly around Piccadilly Circus and down the Haymarket and flooded into Trafalgar Square to hear the speeches.

There was no disorder, no damage, and no arrests. Yet the police felt that they had "lost it". They were not in control; anything might have happened; and the fact that it did not was due not to anything they had done, but entirely to the good nature of the protestors.

On only one other occasion that I witnessed was there the same sense that the police had "lost it". This time disorder did result. This was the march to Brixton prison that followed the second anti poll tax demonstration (see p. 63). As word was received by police at the prison that 2000–3000 marchers were leaving Brockwell Park *en route* for the prison, it became immediately evident that the arrangements to accommodate an expected picket of 150 were wholly inadequate. A barrier lorry was hastily summoned and barriers placed along the centre of Brixton Hill, where it passed the entrance to the prison. The unrehearsed aim was to halt the march in Brixton Hill, allowing northbound traffic to continue running and thus provide a moving steel barricade between the protestors and the prison. TSG reserves were also summoned to park their carriers in the prison car park out of sight of the protestors, so as to form a further barrier between the protestors and the prison, should they attempt to "storm" it. As the march neared the prison, tension became almost palpable. I was accompanying the reserves co-ordinator and was dispatched to his vehicle to collect riot shields and helmets; I stacked these strategically near the entrance to the prison. Officers in ordinary uniform deployed in a cordon across the entrance to the prison were now busily removing anything that might be used as ammunition. They were tossing loosened paving slabs into an adjacent yard surrounded by a fence.

When the protestors arrived at the prison, the police had hoped to persuade the head of the march to pass by the entrance, allowing those at the tail of the march sight of the prison and thus a focus for their protest. Unfortunately, those at the head of the march stopped and, increasingly frustrated, those at the rear moved forward. This had two consequences. First, it quickly caused the closure of Brixton Hill as protestors blocked both sides of the road. Secondly, protestors began occupying an area of open ground directly opposite the entrance to the prison. Commanders now began to fear that those on the open ground might start to arm themselves with stones and other missiles, so serials of officers in ordinary uniform were deployed into the area to deter them. Placard sticks, cans and bottles now began to be thrown by those assembled on the roadway. Police responded by deploying ordinary uniformed serials to the rear of the crowd to deter this. Soon, however, there were scuffles and arrests. Protestors were being dragged from the crowd. One woman protestor was carried from the crowd bleeding from a head wound and a police officer was also injured.

The decision was made to disperse the crowd. The reserves co-ordinator stepped into the road with a loudhailer and instructed the protestors to disperse, warning that officers with shields would be deployed if they refused. His repeated instructions and warnings were greeted with derisive jeers and catcalls. TSG officers approached the rear of the crowd nearest the entrance to the prison at a walk. Protestors were told to leave and then pushed with shields. There were scuffles and arrests. Quickly the crowd began to retreat, pursued by police. Soon there was a running battle northwards along Brixton Hill towards the centre of Brixton itself. Sporadic disorder and violence continued for another hour and a half. Some petrol bombs were thrown and officers were authorized to don their flame-retardant overalls. Gradually the police operation was scaled down and serials finally dismissed around midnight.

It is foolhardy to generalize on the basis of just two examples, but it is consistent with the general theme of this book that what police feared most was not disorder or violence per se, but the loss of control. Intervention, which was normally so strongly resisted, was precipitated by a compulsion to reassert control – "to get a grip". Police were unable to intervene on 12 January 1991 because they could not mobilize an effective response soon enough. There was no disorder, but what might have occurred if, instead of traffic division officers placing cones and signs along the route, reserve serials had been deployed to impose a "neat and tidy" march? The disorder that occurred outside Brixton prison when the crowd came to a halt was not particularly severe compared with other occasions that I witnessed, but the police felt compelled to "do something". Why? First, to "get a grip" on events that were rapidly slipping from their control. Secondly, because they had no room for manoeuvre. They could not allow the protestors any closer to the prison – this was a "ditch" in which they felt compelled to "die".

"The meat in the sandwich"

Support for the contention that police fear loss of control more than violence comes from those occasions when significant violence erupted but the police retained control. These were all confrontations between neo-fascist racist organizations and anti-fascist militants. As mentioned in Chapter 1 (see pp. 17–18), the task of keeping neo-fascists and their opponents apart has long been a problem for the Metropolitan Police. It was at one such confrontation in Lewisham in 1977 that riot shields were first deployed operationally (P. Waddington 1991), and at Southall in 1979 Blair Peach was killed during a police baton charge (Dummett 1980a, 1980b). Because it has been the tactic of neo-fascists to provoke a violent reaction from their opponents, the police have historically found themselves in effect defending them, which prompts accusations of partiality in favour of the right against the left.

An occasion for such a confrontation occurs annually on the afternoon following the Service of Remembrance at the Cenotaph in Whitehall when the National Front stage their own service of remembrance. This annual march was normally opposed by anti-fascist groups and in 1992 that opposition was quite violent. On this occasion leaflets had been circulated and picked up by police suggesting that the march would be fiercely resisted. As the time for the commencement of the march approached, police officers were scouting the area looking for groups of anti-fascists and the helicopter was scrutinizing the scene from above. Before the Front had assembled, a large contingent of their opponents had gathered near the entrance to Westminster City Hall in Victoria Street, along which the Front planned to march. The counter-demonstrators had been surrounded by TSG officers, who were containing them at this location using personnel carriers pulled across the footpath as additional barriers. The police plan was for counter-demonstrators to be contained but also given the opportunity to voice their opposition to the National Front.

The National Front arranged their march so that supporters gathered at the assembly point only a few minutes prior to setting off. When the Front arrived, there was a brief discussion about whether they should take an alternative route, but it was mutually agreed that the Front would stick to their original plan. One small adjustment was made and that was to march on the offside of Victoria Street, furthest away from the counter-demonstrators, and to keep traffic flowing on the nearside as a "moving wall of steel".

The march commenced and turned into Victoria Street. Immediately it was greeted by jeers, catcalls and abuse shouted by opponents still some distance away. The helicopter clattered above as the police escorted the marchers towards the gauntlet. As the march came within range, there was a surge from the anti-fascists and the cordon buckled. Additional officers rushed to provide reinforcement. This was followed by a hail of placard sticks, cans and bottles thrown low and hard at around head height. Police escorting the marchers were ducking and dodging the missiles and one officer caught a bottle with all the alacrity of a cricket fielder. A woman officer was less fortunate and sustained a cut to the face. There were now scuffles between police and counter-demonstrators and a few arrests. Within a few minutes the march had passed and was safely out of range. However, police kept the counter-demonstrators contained, refusing to allow them to leave until the Front had concluded its ceremony at the Cenotaph. There was no way that the police would allow a confrontation around the Cenotaph on the day when its significance as a national shrine was most apparent.

The Front, having concluded their brief service, were instructed not to return along Victoria Street as they had intended, but to proceed further along Whitehall and disperse in Horse Guards Avenue. A problem then arose because their coaches had been told to collect them in Victoria and there was no means of communicating the change of venue to the coach drivers. Police sent traffic officers to see if they could identify the coaches, but the Front could provide only the haziest description of the coaches for the officers to work on. Then the control room announced that "Gold" had instructed that the containment of the anti-fascist contingent should be relaxed, allowing them to leave in the direction of Victoria and away from Whitehall. This offered little satisfaction to the officers in Horse Guards Avenue still trying to disperse the Front. It was anticipated that the anti-fascists would use the Underground to circumvent police cordons. With the coaches still nowhere in sight and the Front members becoming increasingly agitated, the police agreed to the proposal that they should divide into small groups and make their own way across St James's Park back to their pick-up point. The problem was how to convey their flags and banners. It was decided that these would be loaded into a police van and deposited at the pick-up point. There were severe misgivings about this degree of police co-operation, for it might appear that the police were actively assisting the Front. It was felt, however, that there was little alternative, since groups of young men walking across St James's Park with furled flags and banners would advertise their identity and make them targets for attack.

This example underscores the dilemmas between protecting the right of groups to proclaim their beliefs, however offensive they might be, and being seen to be partial towards neo-fascists in so doing. The presence of a so-called British National Party (BNP) "bookshop" in the south London borough of Welling provided an opportunity to examine the process in reverse. This bookshop became an increasing focus for anti-racist protest during 1992, especially in the wake of a number of racially motivated attacks in the area, including at least two murders. Now it was the anti-fascists whose march the police had to protect from their neo-fascist opponents.

As it happened, the most violent confrontation took place the day before the Victoria confrontation described above. A young Asian, Roghit Duggal, had been stabbed to death, allegedly out of racist motives (although the police privately doubted this). The route of the protest march was from open ground near Shooters Hill police station towards the centre of Eltham. This took the marchers past the spot where Roghit Duggal had been murdered. The march then looped through the shopping centre of Eltham to cross its own path at the crossroads before terminating in a park near a pub with neo-fascist associations. The police had liaised closely with the organizers of the march, meeting frequently in the weeks preceding it and inviting representatives to the police briefing so as to reassure them of police impartiality.

The likelihood of some sort of attack by neo-fascist sympathizers was regarded as distinctly likely, and a major operation was mounted along the lines discussed in the previous chapter. Intelligence reports received the day before the march suggested that neo-fascists planned to attack the march, possibly taking the form of a "hit and run" on the vulnerable rear section. There were also rumours circulating amongst the marchers that there would be a right-wing counter-demonstration in Eltham High Street. Early reports from police scouting the area identified small groups of neo-fascist sympathizers in the vicinity. In view of this, it was decided on the day of the march that TSG officers should now be placed on a higher state of readiness, "kitted up" in their riot gear. It was also decided to deploy the helicopter, despite its being seen as potentially provocative.

As the march set off, the helicopter was circling a few hundred yards ahead and its crew, working in collaboration with intelligence officers on the ground, were identifying groups of apparent neo-fascists. TSG carriers were deployed to each of these sightings, but reported that as they approached the groups ran away into side-streets and alleyways.

The march halted at the scene of the murder to lay a wreath and a minute's silence was observed in memory of the murdered boy. Police were particularly vigilant at this point, for they felt that the march was now especially vulnerable to attack. However, helicopter and intelligence reports were indicating that the neo-fascists were gathering in the High Street, mingling with shoppers.

Mobile reserve officers in ordinary uniform were now deployed in strength around the crossroads. As the march approached, so the neo-fascists began jeering, whistling, chanting and gesturing. Marchers began replying in kind and the police commander appealed to them to keep marching. A few missiles, mainly coins, were thrown and plainclothes intelligence officers in the crowd identified some of the throwers, who were later arrested. Having now declared themselves, the police were able to contain the neo-fascist groups on three of the four corners with the aid of fixed pedestrian control barriers behind which the neo-fascists were held. However, suddenly a burly man broke through one such cordon and viciously attacked a press photographer. Police officers wrestled him to the ground and he was arrested. Then another man broke through the now depleted cordon and committed a similar attack; he too was arrested. In this confusion, the group of neo-fascists on the corner from which these attacks were launched were able to break out of the cordons containing them and move a crucial few yards around the corner into a position that left them closer to the march when it passed through the crossroads for a second time.

As the march looped around the shopping centre, plans were being made for the second passage of the march through the crossroads. Additional officers were deployed and carriers were positioned to separate the two groups. Mounted officers that had been initially deployed near the park were brought forward in case they were needed, although the officer in charge of the mounted section was hesitant about their use in a crowded shopping street. Traffic officers were now controlling the traffic flow through the crossroads manually, and it was decided that traffic flowing in the opposite direction to the march should be delayed until the march approached the crossroads and then released to provide a "moving wall of steel".

As these plans were being hastily laid, a further problem emerged. On one corner was a church whose bells suddenly began ringing. The possibility that a wedding was about to be held in the midst of this mayhem was too awful to contemplate. A junior officer was dispatched to the church to discover details. He returned to explain that the bell-ringers were only practising and he had convinced them to cease for a short time so that police could hear their radios.

A more substantial problem was that shoppers continued to mingle with the neo-fascist groups on the corners. Officers on the containment cordons found themselves being asked by women and children, elderly people and others who quite evidently did not belong to the counter-demonstration if they could pass through the cordons. Individual counter-demonstrators took advantage of these breaks in the cordons also to pass through them and escape. Senior officers expressed exasperation that their subordinates seemed incapable of acting more selectively. The result was that groups were recombining in side-streets and making their way towards the park where the rally was due to be held.

The march passed through the crossroads for a second time, with much jeering, shouting and gesturing from both sides, but little overt violence. The strong police presence that had now been assembled kept them securely apart.

The original plan had been to keep the neo-fascists contained at the cross-roads until the marchers had reached the park and held their rally. However, with roving bands of neo-fascists now spotted by the helicopter moving through back streets parallel to the direction of the march, it was decided instead to reinforce the escorting serials and attempt to keep counter-demonstrators at a distance. TSG carriers were buzzing around the march dispersing groups of opponents. Unfortunately, their efforts were hindered by the temporary absence of the helicopter, which needed to refuel.

The march proceeded to the park without further incident, but as it approached its destination reports were received of an attack on the "mar-shals". This caused some perplexity, but, because of the weight of radio traffic, the police commander was unable to obtain clarification. Soon all was revealed as the pick-up truck carrying the marchers' public address equipment drove rapidly from the park and those on board shouted that they had been attacked by neo-fascists. The police commander ran to the scene and began deploying a cordon, warning neo-fascists to disperse or be liable to arrest. Then, as the march entered the park, some of the marchers broke away to confront the now retreating neo-fascists. Another cordon had now to be established, although officers accompanying the march were frustratingly slow to respond to instructions. Senior officers later specu-lated that serials had been more preoccupied with finding their own coaches than with what was occurring around them. Mounted officers were also deployed, but, misunderstanding what they had been told, faced the marchers rather than the neo-fascists; they were quickly instructed to turn around amid fears that they had unwittingly antagonized the marchers.

As cordons were established it was decided to move the neo-fascists away across the park. It was then realized that there was a soccer match in progress between two exclusively black teams. The neo-fascists needed to be steered around this soccer match amid overheard suggestions from the neo-fascists that they should attack the soccer players.

When the rally concluded, the police asked the marchers how they wished to depart. Police officers had been deployed throughout the after-noon to guard the location where their vehicles had been parked. The problem lay in marchers returning to this place. The organizer expressed a desire for the marchers to return *en masse* under police protection, but, as this was being arranged, marchers themselves drifted away. The helicopter continued to circle the area reporting the movement of the neo-fascists and departing marchers, and TSG carriers were deployed to locations where there was felt to be a danger of the two groups coming into contact. Shortly afterwards, the two groups had evidently dispersed and the police operation was concluded.

The striking feature of these two events was their similarity. Following the spirit of *Beatty* v. *Gillbanks*, the police were prepared to protect the march against opponents who sought by force to prevent it. Equally striking was that on neither occasion was there any sense that the police had lost control. Although there was significant violence and a clear confrontation between opposing groups, the police were relatively comfortable. They knew what their task was and how they would achieve it and had ample resources. Plans needed to be formulated *in situ* because unforeseen problems arose, such as the decision to allow anti-fascists to leave the containment in Victoria Street and the escape of sufficient neo-fascists to pose a continuing threat to the Eltham march, but this did not threaten continued control by the police because it was of a type that the police had anticipated. The police also had room for manoeuvre. In Whitehall, the Front was told that they could not return along Victoria Street; at Eltham the march was stopped for several minutes prior to re-passing through the crossroads so that the police operation could be fully implemented, and police and organizers had a contingency plan to terminate the march at a bus depot away from the park if it became necessary. In other words, neither march was a "ditch" in which the police felt compelled "to die", in sharp contrast to Brixton prison where they felt their "backs were against the wall".

Thus, it seems that it is loss of control by the police that prompts serious confrontation between police and others, not violence itself. Violence that can be contained is preferable to non-violent behaviour that threatens to "get out of hand".

Conclusions

The problem of describing incidents in which serious violence and disorder erupted is that it gives a wholly unrepresentative picture of the policing of political protest. The vast majority of marches had all the appearance of routine. This was because the police achieved extensive and uncontested control over the event. Police control was achieved not by heavy-handed methods, which were regarded as counter-productive, but by the subtle mechanisms of "taking the ground", negotiating with organizers so as to enlist their help and maintaining a discreet presence of "insurance". It was when police perceived that they were losing control that they were prompted to take interventionist action that threatened confrontation.

CHAPTER 8

Institutionalizing dissent

Introduction

Previous chapters have absorbed us in the minutiae of the routine policing of public order: the motives of police commanders have been exposed; the process of negotiation between police and protest organizers has been dissected; the planning for and command of public order operations have been examined. In this chapter, I will widen the analytical perspective to consider the rôle of the police in the process of "institutionalization".

Institutionalization and the police

It has become something of a sociological cliché that the absence of significant social unrest in developed industrial societies is attributable to the institutionalization of class conflict and incorporation of the working class. Historically the effectiveness of incorporation has been most evident in that cauldron of class conflict – strikes. As Taft & Ross (1979) document, the period from the mid-nineteenth century to the mid-1930s was tumultuous for American industrial relations. Full-scale battles between troops and public and private police forces, on the one hand, and pickets, on the other, frequently left many dead and injured. In one incident in 1913 an armoured train was used to attack strikers living in tents, firing over 200 shots in the process. The workers were not defeated by these methods nor was conflict suppressed. It was the New Deal and specifically the Wagner Act of 1935, supplemented by the Taft–Hartley Act of 1947, that quelled what had become endemic violence. It did so by providing mechanisms for the expression of grievances, independent arbitration and channels for influencing government policy.

Britain witnessed a less bloody, but essentially similar process (for a general discussion see Critchley 1970). From 1898, when two strikers and two others were shot dead by troops, to the 1980s there was, according to Geary (1985), a transition from "stoning and shooting" to "pushing and shoving" on the picket-line. Conflict between workers and management was diverted into collective bargaining between unions and employers, on the one hand, and into parliamentary channels through the Labour Party, on the other. As these alternative institutional channels opened up, there was less incentive for workers to resort to violent confrontation and no benefit to the Establishment in suppression that might serve only to arouse sympathy for the nascent labour movement. There was, therefore, a common interest in "cooling" the potential for confrontation on the picket-line. Until, that is, the election of Mrs Thatcher, when a more confrontational stance towards the unions was reintroduced and police soon found themselves battling with strikers on the picket-lines.

As the miners' strike and the Wapping dispute showed, confrontation is expensive. The police (and through them the state) may triumph, but the legitimacy of their authority may be weakened. Institutionalization is less costly, because the common interest in "cooling it" allows extensive control to be extended surreptitiously, apparently by agreement.

Institutionalization of social movements

Institutionalization has profound implications for the development of social movements. On the one hand, it offers to the movement the prospect of exerting influence at little cost. As Eisinger (1973) notes, the authorities in effect issue a "licence to protest" by their unwillingness or inability to use violence. As Finer (1966) observed, influence is more effectively wielded by lobbying quietly before a decision is taken, rather than protesting noisily after it has been taken. On the other hand, this is not free of cost. Indeed, Piven & Cloward (1977) regard it as so costly that social movements should resist institutionalization, for exerting influence in the "corridors of power" entails a willingness to compromise fundamental beliefs. Likewise, institutionalized social movements can take advantage of favourable tax arrangements for charitable bodies. But charitable status is also a potent weapon in the state's armoury, for it is an effective non-coercive method of constraining the movement's activities with the "rules of the game" (McCarthy et al. 1991).

174

The police can likewise reduce the costs of participation in a social movement by accommodating those willing to compromise and reciprocate. As we have seen, the TUC, NUM, students and the CND-based Campaign to Stop War in the Gulf received consideration and assistance from the police because they "played the game". The police virtually planned the NUM protest against pit closures, down to the provision of coach parking facilities, because the NUM were prepared to accept the police goal of separating their Hyde Park march from the lobby of Parliament. Indeed, almost any of the protests described hitherto could be treated as examples of institutionalization.

Institutionalization does not exist *sui generis*, but is a process of reciprocation. The police feel comfortable with trade unions and other organizations because they have built up an established relationship of reciprocity over a number of years. New social movements have had no such opportunity and, if they indulge in novel forms of social protest, police may have difficulty in deciding what "ground rules" should apply. A characteristic of "new social movements" is their predominantly middle-class base. For the police, this means dealing with articulate and knowledgeable people who may be less receptive to control.

One such social movement is gay rights and AIDS activism. Not only is it a relatively new social movement, it pursues an aim that is anathema to the masculine culture of the police (Policy Studies Institute 1983). The movement covers the spectrum from "Stonewall", which aims to exert influence through emphasizing the respectable face of homosexuality, through the Lesbian and Gay Coalition, which has employed traditional methods of protest about anti-gay legislation, to "OutRage!" and "ACT-UP", whose confrontational methods and civil disobedience seem unlikely to endear them to the police (Watney 1990, Carter 1992). How, then, did police respond to protests from these various groups? What does their response tell us about the process of institutionalization?

"Gay Pride"

A simplistic explanation of police–protestor conflict is to attribute it to antipathy: police officers are mainly politically conservative, therefore they dislike and oppose radical left-wing groups (Hewitt 1982). If there is any movement that the police could be expected to oppose on these grounds, it is gay rights and AIDS activism. So how did the police relate to the respectable end of the gay rights spectrum?

175

The most acceptable of the protest organizations with which the police routinely had contact was probably "Gay Pride". This organization restricted itself almost entirely to arranging an annual festival of gay culture, which included a march through central London. This march and its associated planning were observed during both 1991 and 1992. In 1991 the march proceeded from Victoria Embankment to Trafalgar Square, along Whitehall, past the Palace of Westminster and on to Kennington Park, south of the River Thames, where the festival was held until late evening. In 1992 the event had become so popular that Kennington Park could no longer accommodate it and the festival was relocated in Brockwell Park, further to the south. This alternative location was deemed too far to walk to from central London and so the march terminated at Hyde Park and marchers went by public transport to the festival. Organizers resisted attempts to hold the march elsewhere than central London, suggesting that an important element of the event was the high-profile public affirmation of sexual preference.

"Gay Pride" had a long-established working relationship with the police. Although organizers changed annually, the culture of the organization was accommodating. The police felt that they could "do business" with this group, because it was a well-organized group who could be trusted to deliver on their side of the bargain. Negotiations were relaxed and amicable, the police earning the thanks of the organizers amongst the acknowledgements listed in the festival brochure that was produced for both events. This was not to say that the police genuinely liked the organizers or approved of the organization – in private, most officers were openly homophobic. When one junior officer was invited by the organizers to join them at the festival for an off-duty drink, she was anxious to reassure colleagues that she would not be attending. Hands used to shake those of gay representatives were often theatrically wiped once the organizers had departed. Yet these sentiments were not allowed to impede the business of organizing a peaceful event.

The principal concerns of police were organizational. These focused on the presence of vehicles connected with the march and, in 1992, arrangements for the transfer of marchers to the festival. The organizers had secured the concession of having a number of floats following the march some years previously. This, of course, breached the effective prohibition that the police attempted to impose on vehicles. These floats were mainly tableaux depicting homosexual themes. For example, as part of the 1991 march one float depicted a homosexual wedding. Participants dressed up in costume, often extravagantly cross-dressing. The organizers sought to

176

integrate these floats into the body of the march, whereas the police, resisting any further concessions, tried to separate them from the rest of the march. The police wanted to be rid of the floats entirely, but the power of precedent was used against them: they had allowed floats in the past and floats were permitted at the Notting Hill Carnival. Hence, the police adamantly insisted that the floats should follow at the rear of the march. They arranged for traffic division officers to escort floats from a marshalling area to the assembly on Victoria Embankment, so that they could be viewed by revellers while they awaited the commencement of the march. Like other such concessions, this also ensured that the police retained complete control over the location of these floats. Continued resistance to further integration of the floats as part of the march was accepted with good grace by organizers during both negotiations. In 1992, accepting defeat, the organizer smiled and remarked "I have to try".

The problems of transferring 30 000 or more marchers across London in 1992 to the festival posed enormous logistical problems. The police collaborated with the organizers in seeking a solution. One suggestion involved hiring trains and organizing a shuttle service from Victoria station to Herne Hill station. Metropolitan Police liaised with British Transport Police to assess the viability of what was, for them, an acceptable plan. Unfortunately, British Railways informed the police that engineering work on the line would prevent such an arrangement. Again, police collaborated with the organizers to arrange for coaches to be used as a shuttle service and to ensure protection for marchers who made their own way, many of whom felt vulnerable to attack.

The marches themselves were regarded as unproblematic. The only difficulty concerned the limits of decency. A new commander was felt by his subordinates to be in danger of taking too hard a line with regard to public displays of affection between gay couples. He was "talked around" to accepting the existing tolerant policy, and eventually agreed that any intervention by police should be through stewards and arrests should be made only on the authority of an inspector after a complaint from an identified member of the public who was willing to act as a witness. This was regarded as such a stringent set of requirements as in effect to rule out police intervention except in the most exceptional circumstances.

The problem for senior officers was thought to lie in the attitudes of their subordinates. The briefing of junior officers concentrated upon the need to display tolerance to a section of the population of whom they might personally disapprove. Senior officers made no attempt to disguise their own disapproval of homosexuality, but presented the tolerant policing of the march as a challenge to their subordinates' professionalism. Another concern lay in subordinates' fear of AIDS, and a section of the briefing consisted of reassurance from occupational health specialists about the minimal risks of contracting HIV and what protective measures should be taken in the event that first aid needed to be rendered to any of the marchers.

Clearly, the policing of "Gay Pride", though undoubtedly distasteful to many officers, was indistinguishable from the policing of other comparable events. Indeed, the concession that "Gay Pride" had won in having floats accompanying the march might be regarded as displaying significantly more tolerance than was usually forthcoming.

Mainstream protest

Gay rights and AIDS awareness have also been pursued by mainstream protest organizations. An annual march was organized under the title "Reach Out and Touch with Flowers", and the Lesbian and Gay Coalition organized a large demonstration to oppose legislation thought to be anti-gay. Neither march caused anxiety, apart from the need to reassure officers that they were unlikely to catch AIDS from marchers. It is not worth dwelling on these two marches, since the policing of them conformed entirely to the general pattern of policing other protest marches.

Both "Gay Pride" and these mainstream protest organizations were already more or less securely institutionalized, at least in so far as the police were concerned. The establishment of a liaison officer in response to the allegation that the Metropolitan Police had been indifferent to attacks on gay men served to strengthen their institutionalization still further. However, there were groups on the militant fringe of the gay rights movement that were not at all institutionalized at the commencement of this research.

"OutRage!"

The group that was perceived as distinctly problematic by the police was "OutRage!". This was regarded as a radical militant group whose participation in marches organized by others occasioned the same kind of attention that was otherwise reserved for the Socialist Workers' Party and Class War. For the police they were the gay equivalent of "the opposition". They had an established reputation for committing acts of civil disobedience, such as their much-publicized "Kiss-in" at Piccadilly Circus to protest at proposed changes in the law. They had also been to the fore of a campaign to convince the Metropolitan Police to recognize attacks on gay men as a serious problem. Officers also spoke of a demonstration in Trafalgar Square during the evening rush hour in which protestors had waved placards containing obscenities.

On the other hand, Tatchell (1992a) has argued that the ideology of the group is conventionally civil rights oriented. The group claim that full civil rights should be extended to homosexuals as they have been to other minorities. Their programme is to make common cause with other minority groups also seeking their civil rights. Gamson (1989), on the other hand, points to a contradiction between these aspirations and the tactics employed, which tend to reaffirm the separation of gay men and lesbians from wider constituencies. The type of protest that is preferred is the "Kiss-in", in which the stereotype of the homosexual is reflected back at bystanders in an exaggerated form designed to shock conventional opinion. These "stunts", as activists called them, were often performed as high-profile media events so as to reach as wide an audience as possible. For police, this was a protest group that was highly problematic, since it was difficult to control. Intervention and suppression risked accusations of homophobia, while failure to intervene risked contrary accusations of favouritism.

A more direct threat to police interests occurred during the State Opening of Parliament on 31 October 1991. State Openings were regarded by the police as ceremonial events, in which context political protest was illegitimate since it detracted from the dignity of the occasion. State Openings do, however, have hybrid characteristics, since they mark the commencement of the parliamentary session and could, therefore, be considered to have political connotations. Police were always sensitive to the possibility that this ceremonial would be disrupted by political protest. "OutRage!" was identified from the outset as a group that might engage in such activity. When a group of "OutRage!" supporters were observed near Churchill's statue, mobile reserves were hastily deployed to the scene and, as the protestors were about to unfurl banners that they had wrapped around their bodies, police swiftly intervened to escort them away (see Garfield 1991). "OutRage!" did not, in the police view, "play the game" and were, therefore, regarded with the utmost suspicion.

Breaching the Sessional Order

As the date of the general election neared, the leading personality of "Out-Rage!" approached the police to discuss plans to hold a march in breach of the Sessional Order. This was regarded as a singular departure: it was the first time that the group had made such an approach to the police. Given that the size of "OutRage!" demonstrations was usually very small by comparison with other protests that the Metropolitan Police routinely dealt with, the initial meeting consisted of a large number of officers and the rank of its chairman (a Commander) testified to the seriousness with which the group was viewed – "OutRage!" were trouble. The organizer – an articulate man, active in left-wing Labour Party politics – was precisely the type of person with whom the police least preferred to negotiate. In particular, he was sufficiently knowledgeable about the Sessional Order to challenge the view that it forbade demonstrations within the Sessional Area. He pointed out that it prohibited *disorderly* gatherings and *obstruction* of free access to the Palace of Westminster, and that the proposed protest would satisfy neither criterion. Police were acutely aware of the limitations of the Sessional Order, just as they were aware of the trouble that resulted from any breach of parliamentarians' expectations. However, they insisted that, given the record of "OutRage!" demonstrations, police were entitled to apprehend that the march might be disorderly and therefore it would not be permitted within the Sessional Area.

The purpose of the demonstration was discussed at length and the police attempted, unsuccessfully, to persuade the organizer that the aims of the group could be achieved by less confrontational methods. Eventually, it was accepted that the march would take place, but that once it reached the Sessional Area it would be halted and anyone attempting to proceed would be arrested. The police could not be seen to conspire with the organizers to breach the Sessional Order and, therefore, would agree only to a route from the assembly point to the edge of the Sessional Area, which for these purposes was near Leicester Square underground station.

Police planning followed the usual pattern, save that a superintendent was appointed for what would otherwise have been a minor operation and TSG officers were to be deployed to make the arrests. Interestingly enough, given Jefferson's censorious views about squads like the TSG (Jefferson 1990), they were selected because senior officers felt that they could be trusted to act in a highly professional manner while making arrests. Other officers were expected to be less proficient and more likely to get into needless confrontation. Care was also taken over the grounds upon which arrests were to be made. After consultation with the Solicitors' Department, it was decided that "Commissioner's Directions" were "not worth a light" and so it was agreed to use common law powers to prevent a breach of the peace to make arrests and to charge demonstrators with obstruction of the police and/or of the highway.

On the day of the march, the police arrived outside Bow Street police station just as the marchers were beginning to assemble. The superintendent met briefly with the organizer to finalize arrangements. Then, as the march was about to commence, the crew of the control van were asked to broadcast a prepared warning regarding the Sessional Area over the PA system. Officers had confidently expected that this warning would be drowned out by whistles blown by the crowd and had arranged for a video crew to film the scene. Whistling did commence, but the protest organizer quickly quietened the noise and instructed marchers to listen to the police. The warning given, the march set off. It did not take long to reach Leicester Square underground station. There was, as so often, a moment of tension that could have proved to have been a "flashpoint" had disorder occurred. As the march neared the station, there was a scuffle on the footpath; officers were struggling with a man, and press photographers, who were present in abundance, rushed to the scene. Marchers, evidently thinking that one of their number had been arrested, refused to continue. The officer in command dispatched a subordinate to discover what had happened. It turned out to have been the arrest of a busker by officers wholly unconnected with the march. This was communicated to the organizer and the demonstration proceeded.

As the march reached the boundary of the Sessional Area, the control van stopped and the warning to marchers was re-issued. Moreover, the organizer stepped on to the footplate of the police control van heading the march and instructed all protestors who wished to avoid arrest to leave the march and stand on the footpath. This a number of them did. The march then proceeded around the corner and into the Sessional Area. The commanding officer instructed the control van to proceed until all the marchers had passed the boundary into the Sessional Area before halting. Again, a warning was given and marchers were instructed to disperse. At this, the marchers lay down in the road, as they said they would. There were a number of celebrities on the march and they were at the front holding a large banner. The police commander instructed TSG officers to make arrests from the rear of the sit-down towards the front so as to allow the celebrities maximum exposure to the news media. TSG officers went to each protestor in turn and, in a carefully rehearsed operation, repeated the warning, asked if the person understood the warning, asked them to move and when they refused arrested them. All of this was filmed by a police video crew. The arrested protestors were taken to personnel carriers and thence to charge centres.

The question now arose about what further action should be taken. Initially, it had been thought likely that all those arrested would be charged. However, the co-operation shown by the organizer was now thought to justify less severe action and all those arrested were released without charge. Police were gratified to receive the thanks of the organizer, some celebrities, and other protestors for their handling of the event. This gratitude was repeated in a magazine article by one of the celebrities that police displayed with a mixture of incredulity and pride when next I visited the Special Events office.

Truce

There then commenced a period during which "OutRage!" engaged in various protests as part of their campaign to make gay rights an election issue. During this period their relationship with the police steadily improved and police preparedness was reduced to the point where "OutRage!" demonstrations increasingly came to acquire the characteristics of institutionalized protest.

One such protest was held at four military statues in central London to protest at legal prohibitions on homosexuality in the military. They claimed that the famous military figures honoured by these statues were closet homosexuals. Negotiations were amicably conducted. The protestors compromised on their intention of hanging feather boas and other decorative items on the statues in return for police arranging that they could get near enough to ensure that press photographs showed them and their placards close to the statues. This involved the police negotiating access to some of the statues that were technically located on Ministry of Defence land.

Another demonstration involved holding a "bonk-in" at Piccadilly Circus, followed by a lobby of Parliament. The protestors constructed a model house and the "bonk-in" consisted of male protestors winking extravagantly at each other, exchanging outsized business cards, entering the "house" in pairs, dropping their trousers and simulating vigorous sexual activity. The whole enterprise was extremely light-hearted and, although the officer in charge kept a close eye on the proceedings to ensure that decency was maintained, no attempt was made to restrain the protest. On the contrary, the complaints of a few bystanders were ignored and building workers near the scene were instructed to stop taunting the protestors.

The lobby of Parliament did cause some problems, mainly because of the sensitivities of parliamentarians. The protestors were allowed to proceed from Piccadilly to the Palace of Westminster as small groups escorted by officers. Inevitably they coalesced as they went, and so, on arrival at Parliament Square, the fiction that a march, albeit on the footpath, had been prevented was maintained by the police holding the body of protestors in Whitehall and allowing them to cross to the Palace of Westminster in small groups. Not only did protestors agree to this, a steward was left to organize it, rather than the police taking responsibility.

There were problems outside Parliament because some protestors wished to turn the lobby queue into a protest assembly. They were instructed not to carry placards or to make speeches, and when one or two of them behaved provocatively they were "turfed out" of the queue and told to leave. On the other hand, members of a trade union who were planning to hold an organized lobby, and who objected to the presence of the "OutRage!" demonstrators, were brusquely told by the officer in command that the "OutRage!" protestors had as much right to lobby their MPs as did the trade unionists. When the trade union organizer claimed priority for his members in the lobby queue, it was denied. This caused considerable personal friction between the trade union organizer and the senior police officer. Eventually, the "OutRage!" lobby was concluded without further incident and the protestors dispersed.

During this period of truce, lasting several weeks, the police established a good working relationship, as they saw it, with the "OutRage!" negotiators. They soon took the view that "OutRage!" could be trusted to do what had been agreed. "OutRage!" threatened neither on-the-job nor in-the-job trouble and so "What if?" preparations were gradually scaled down.

Breakdown

Following the general election and the re-election of a Conservative government, the State Opening of Parliament took place on 6 May 1992. Just as at the previous State Opening, it was feared that "OutRage!" might seek to protest and steps were taken to maintain surveillance of the area to identify any gathering of activists. On the morning of the operation, the Deputy Assistant Commissioner revealed that "OutRage!" had asked for copies of the Commissioner's Directions for the event, which suggested that they intended to take some action. A little later, a press release was discovered to have been issued in which a police officer was named as having warned the group against protesting and accusing the police of suppressing freedom of speech. It now seemed inevitable to the police that "OutRage!" would seek to disrupt the occasion by staging a protest that would detract from its ceremonial dignity.

Almost immediately the operation commenced members of "OutRage!" were identified as gathering near the Palace of Westminster. A sub-commander spoke to them and was told that they intended no disorder, only a passive demonstration. Immediately plans were laid to increase the police presence at that location and to bring mobile reserves of TSG officers closer to the scene to act as an arrest squad, if necessary. Shortly afterwards, the leader of "OutRage!" approached the sector commander in Parliament Square and explained that they were intending to do no more than hold placards. The sector commander forcefully replied that such a protest would not be permitted since it was inappropriate to the occasion. The "OutRage!" leader argued that their proposed action was entirely appropriate since the Queen's Speech contained no proposals to repeal homophobic legislation. He accused police of wishing to stifle freedom of speech and asserted that the protest would not contravene the Commissioner's Directions since it would be neither disorderly nor obstructive. The sector commander repeatedly reaffirmed that the protest would not be permitted and that, since "OutRage!" had demonstrated a willingness to break the law in the past, they would be treated accordingly. The "OutRage!" leader pointed to how the breaching of the Sessional Order had been arranged in collaboration with the police and that a good working relationship had emerged in the weeks since that event. "OutRage!" had scrupulously kept their word and would do so on this occasion, given the chance.

"OutRage!" were not given the chance. As the royal procession approached, TSG officers moved into position just to their rear and, as the first banners were unfurled, so the protestors were arrested and taken away – some being carried after they refused to walk. A second, smaller demonstration, a few minutes later, was dealt with similarly. The protestors were not charged, for the police purpose had been to maintain the dignity of the event by removing the protestors, but the leader of "OutRage!" was reported to have been most unhappy at being arrested.

"OutRage!" had encountered the trouble that ceremonials posed for the police. Whereas the police were prepared to be tolerant and accommodating towards what they regarded as bona fide protest demonstrations, the threat of in-the-job trouble resulting from an unopposed protest during the

State Opening excluded a tolerant response. Claiming that military heroes were closet homosexuals might antagonize individuals, but that was within the rules of the game governing legitimate political protest; disrupting a state occasion was not. Even if it destroyed the amicable working relationship the police had developed with "OutRage!", this was a price worth paying so far as the police were concerned.

Conflict

The police seemed not to realize the implications of this confrontation in Parliament Square for their relationship with "OutRage!", possibly because the State Opening was not regarded as a protest-related, still less an "OutRage!"-related, operation. It was a ceremonial occasion and therefore subject to quite different ground rules. Thus, when the "OutRage!" negotiators approached the police regarding a march to conclude the campaign they had waged throughout the election period, the police assumed that they were continuing the pre State Opening relationship.

There was, indeed, no evidence that the relationship had changed. The meeting between police and the negotiator for the group was very amicable. Police officers were relaxed, they and the negotiator laughed at each other's jokes and quips, and the negotiator told the police of his future personal plans. Three points were negotiated. First, the assembly place: "OutRage!" wished to assemble at Piccadilly Circus - a location of symbolic significance for homosexuals, it was claimed. Police were unhappy about such a gathering at a crowded Saturday lunchtime. The negotiator agreed to discuss an alternative with the group, but, when "OutRage!" insisted, the police relented and the march assembled around the Eros statue. Secondly, a petition was to be handed in to Downing Street. The police stipulated their usual requirements that the march should keep moving and the petition be conveyed by no more than six people. The organizer felt that marchers would want to halt temporarily and the police indicated that they would not make an issue of it. Thirdly, "OutRage!" proposed that the rally should be held in The Broadway outside New Scotland Yard. The police insisted that this was an unsuitable location and proposed instead holding the rally in Caxton Street, directly opposite the Yard, which they would close for the purpose. The negotiator indicated that this would not be a high-profile event: the media were not invited, there would be no "stunts" and the number of marchers would probably not exceed 150. The police, too, regarded it as a minor operation that could safely be entrusted to a chief inspector, albeit someone with considerable public order experience. The negotiator happily signed the legal notification form, despite the fact that he said he was not the true organizer of the event.

Anxiety started to be felt amongst police two days before the march. The police had seen an announcement of the march in the magazine *Time Out*, which lists such events. The announcement mentioned concluding the protest with a gathering at the Queen Victoria Memorial, which forms the hub of a roundabout directly in front of the public face of Buckingham Palace – known to police as "the wedding cake". The royal palaces are "ditches" in which the police would "die", if necessary. Protest demonstrations are simply not allowed in any royal park other than Hyde Park, and certainly not in the immediate vicinity of the residence of the Head of State. For "OutRage!" to propose such a thing was "naughty", and the claim by the negotiator that it had been mentioned during the earlier meeting with police was regarded as bordering on "bad faith". Still the initial response was not one of confrontation: when they spoke on the telephone the negotiator was simply informed by the officer handling negotiations that permission was needed from the Department of National Heritage to assemble in the park, knowing that it would be refused. Police were puzzled; hitherto "OutRage!" had "played the game". What had impressed police most during the preceding weeks was that "OutRage!" had not been duplicitous – they could be trusted to do as had been agreed.

At a negotiating meeting the day before the march the issue of the "wedding cake" was raised by the "OutRage!" representative and he assured the police that participants in the march intended simply to go there in small groups and hold a picnic and "have fun", not to demonstrate. The assurance was repeated when the chief inspector in charge of the policing of the march arrived, and there was little further discussion of the matter. The majority of the meeting was concerned with making the usual arrangements for a march. The good faith of the negotiator was enhanced in police eyes when he freely discussed the gay political scene, identified extremist groups that he feared were attempting to hijack the movement and suggested that the police should be wary of them. After the meeting was concluded the chief inspector was reassured by his colleagues, who had greater experience of "OutRage!" demonstrations, that the group had always been trustworthy in the past and that, while they might be "a bloody nuisance", they were not violent.

However, the precaution had been taken of inviting an inspector from the Royal Parks Police to attend this meeting as an observer. The royal parks, being privately owned, are under the jurisdiction of this force and subject to by-laws. The inspector explained that the "wedding cake" would be sealed off throughout the day, because it was felt that any attempt to police a demonstration in the middle of a traffic roundabout would be too hazardous. "What about the picnic?", he was asked. Only small groups would be allowed and they would be kept to Green Park, preferably as far from the palace as possible. The Metropolitan Police officers thought it would be difficult to enforce this, since large organized groups of tourists frequently picnic in the park. However, the police still did not regard this march as particularly problematic. Manning levels were not increased and no charge centre was designated.

All officers on this march were briefed together in the canteen after they had finished their meal. Particular attention was paid to the possibility that marchers might attempt some demonstration at the "wedding cake". They were told that no one would be allowed on the "wedding cake" itself and that anyone attending a picnic should be encouraged to go into Green Park. The inspector from the Royal Parks Police then explained the by-laws governing the park and pointed to a general "catch-all" offence with which any demonstrators could be charged if necessary. On the other hand, the chief inspector giving the briefing emphasized that it would be a "fun day" and the demonstrators could be expected to be "festive, colourful and noisy" and that officers should "laugh with them, not at them". If the march stopped while the petition was delivered to Downing Street, officers should not "get upset".

The assembly proceeded at first without incident. A member of the public complained to police that such a demonstration should not be allowed, but was told that everyone ought to be tolerant of the opinions of others. The petition party was identified and arrangements made for them to deliver the petition. Arrangements were also agreed for the forming up of the march.

However, the chief inspector overheard, apparently by sheer chance, the leader of the group referring to the Queen Victoria Memorial. The leader was taken aside by the chief inspector and told that the march would terminate in Caxton Street as agreed, that the memorial was closed to the public and that no demonstration would be permitted in the royal parks. If individuals and small groups wished to go to Green Park, then they would be allowed to do so, but there would be no large gathering. The leader of the group seemed reluctantly to accept this. Nevertheless, the chief inspector summoned the inspectors supervising serials deployed on the operation to the control van for a meeting. He told them of what had occurred, saying that they would need to respond quickly to any such eventuality. However, a sergeant with experience of the previous "OutRage!" protests added that "OutRage!" had always informed police in the past when they did anything likely to lead to arrest. He doubted if they wanted a confrontation with police.

The march formed up and commenced without incident, but it was immediately obvious that there were many more than the 150 demonstrators expected. The official count by a police officer suggested a figure around 450.

The route of the march led through Trafalgar Square and as it passed in front of the National Gallery a woman passer-by stood on the footpath making an obscene gesture towards the protestors. Two male demonstrators detached themselves from the march and stood in front of the woman kissing vigorously to the noisy approbation of their fellows. This brought the march to a halt. The chief inspector walked over to the scene and instructed the woman to cease her obscene gesture and told the two marchers to resume their participation in the march, which they did.

As the march turned into Whitehall, arrangements were made for the petition party to detach themselves from the march and go ahead to deliver the petition to Downing Street. However, as the march passed Horse Guards Avenue marchers suddenly broke away and ran *en masse* to the Downing Street gates, where they sat down in the roadway. The leader was approached by the chief inspector and told that this was in breach of their agreement. The leader assured the chief inspector that it would be only a brief demonstration. The escorting serials of police were standing around the perimeter of the sit-down and traffic division officers quickly diverted traffic away from Whitehall. Mobile reserves were summoned and a cordon was formed to prevent the march continuing along the "wrong side" of Whitehall when it recommenced.

The chief inspector now set about obtaining additional officers and making contingency plans. There were two sources of possible support. First was the TSG officers who constituted the "Commissioner's Football Reserve", who responded to soccer-related incidents in central London. Permission was granted for some of this reserve to act as an additional mobile reserve for the "OutRage!" march. Secondly, another march was taking place nearby. This had been expected to be larger than it turned out to be and so surplus officers could be redeployed. These officers were deployed to provide protection to the Palace of Westminster and New Scotland Yard, judged by the chief inspector to be the most vulnerable premises. The Royal Parks Police were also informed of developments. As the chief inspector explained, he was in no hurry for the sit-down demonstration to conclude, for it was allowing him time to make ad hoc arrangements.

Shortly afterwards the march recommenced and the protestors filed, as they were bidden, to the near-side of the road. They marched only a couple of hundred yards, however, for when they reached Parliament Square they staged another sit-down demonstration in the middle of one of the principal intersections. Again, the escorting police stood around the perimeter of the sit-down, while mobile reserves were deployed, this time to cordon the front of the Palace of Westminster. The chief inspector now found the negotiator, who had played no obvious part in the day's proceedings except as a participant. He drew his attention to the fact that he had signed the formal notification of the march and was the identified organizer who would be held responsible for the sit-downs. The negotiator quickly got to his feet and hurriedly spoke to the *de facto* leader of the group who was clearly orchestrating events. Shortly afterwards the march recommenced and proceeded into Victoria Street.

However, as the march proceeded reference was made over a hand-held loudhailer to a "party" to be held at the Queen Victoria Memorial. The chief inspector spoke to the negotiator and reaffirmed that the marchers would not be allowed to go to the memorial. Shortly afterwards the march came to a halt and the chief inspector was surrounded by the negotiator, the leader and two "legal observers". He repeated that the march would be terminated in Caxton Street and marchers prevented from continuing to the memorial. He added that the demonstrators had had a "good run" during the afternoon, but now it must cease. When challenged by the "legal observers" for the legal basis for his decision, he replied that he was relying on the park by-laws. The leader announced the chief inspector's decision to the remainder of the marchers and said that they would discuss it further in Caxton Street.

The chief inspector had now decided to be "firm" with the marchers. TSG officers were deployed to Caxton Street to cordon off the far end and prevent any movement towards the royal park. There was some confusion as the march entered Caxton Street and the cordons were not implemented as envisaged, but the march came to a halt. The leader asked other marchers what they should do. They replied that they should go to the memorial, there was a sudden surge and the crowd swept past officers supposedly cordoning off an alleyway leading to Victoria Street, but who seemed uncertain as to what they were expected to do. Officers were then dispatched to accompany the crowd as they walked and ran along Victoria Street and onwards in the general direction of the royal park. Accompanying officers were radioing reports as to the location and direction of travel of the crowd and the chief inspector was responding by establishing hastily arranged cordons to block their progress.

Eventually, the majority of the demonstrators were contained between two cordons of police in Buckingham Gate. There were some minor scuffles and I saw one man arrested, but the crowd was now almost entirely passive. The chief inspector arranged for small groups to be allowed to leave in the direction opposite to that of the memorial and the crowd appeared to disperse. However, it became clear within minutes that the crowd was coalescing again on the pavement opposite the Queen Victoria Memorial and Buckingham Palace beyond. Police were drafted into the area and cordons established around the perimeter of Queen's Gardens to prevent demonstrators getting any closer. By now soccer matches in the capital were concluding and officers deployed to them were being redeployed to the area outside Buckingham Palace. Soon a small army of police were assembled around the "wedding cake". The Central Command Complex was offering the additional assistance of another unit of TSG, but this was declined. At almost the same time the protestors made it plain to officers that they considered that they had achieved their aim and began to disperse. The police presence in the royal park was scaled down and reserves dispatched to a local police station.

At the debrief that followed the cessation of the police operation, there was general regret that the leader of the group had not been arrested and that the protestors had managed to escape the containment in Caxton Street. However, it was acknowledged that the event had been peaceful. Only two arrests were made throughout the afternoon. Perhaps most importantly of all, police made it clear that the relationship between themselves and "OutRage!" would henceforth be regarded as hostile.

Institutionalization

The events described above hardly qualify as a major battle – they merited only a few column inches in the national press – but they do, perhaps, suggest something about institutionalization that echoes politically more significant events.

The police are one part, but an important part, of the web of institutions that institutionalize conflict and dissent. They subtly adjust the costs and benefits of protest so as to channel protestors into accepting institutional restraints. For groups like "Gay Pride" the police will make concessions and offer favours in the hope of receiving reciprocation. Confrontation is costly for participants, who are liable to arrest and charge by the police and possible conviction by the courts. Accepting the "ground rules" avoids those costs. Even arrests can be made cost free if the police accept the goodwill of the protestors, as they did when "OutRage!" breached the Sessional Order.

However, "ground rules" do not simply require the abrogation of violence and disorder by protestors; they mean not causing the police trouble. "OutRage!" were neither violent nor disorderly, but they were troublesome. Breaching the Sessional Order, claiming that military heroes were closet homosexuals, and holding a "bonk-in" were not trouble. Trouble was caused when "OutRage!" attempted to protest – without violence or disorder – at a ceremonial occasion. A failure to protect the dignity of a state occasion threatened enormous in-the-job trouble and is not something the police could easily tolerate. Moreover, the attempt by "OutRage!" to protest at the "wedding cake" threatened yet more trouble. Had the march concluded at Caxton Street, the organization would not have endeared itself to the police, but it might not have ruptured the good working relationship that had been established. As the chief inspector expressed it, they had "had a good run". It was, however, the decision to proceed to the royal park that was the final straw. A measure of the importance with which this particular "ditch" is imbued can be gauged by the willingness of the force control complex to dispatch additional officers from soccer matches and to assign the Commissioner's Reserve. All this for 450 protestors, who no one imagined would prove violent, only "a bloody nuisance".

"OutRage!" also illustrates how precarious is institutionalization. As Eisinger (1973) and Lipsky (1968, 1970) both note, there is a delicate line to be trodden between attracting public attention by protest that is disruptive and potentially disorderly, and alienating the sympathy of those whose support is needed. The cost to the movement of remaining on the orderly side of that line is that it cannot force its issues on to the agenda. The cost to "OutRage!" of institutionalized protest was to abstain from protesting during a state occasion. This apparently proved too much. Militancy is, as Tarrow (1989) notes, the principal resource available to marginal groups.

Institutionalizing workers

Only social movements that have alternative resources would seem able to accept the bargain that institutionalization represents. The trade unions were able to accept it during the first half of this century because they could mobilize working-class support through the electoral system. Picketing could progressively rely on union solidarity to enforce the picket-line. Since the 1960s several influences have worked against continued institutionalization of the unions. First, the poor industrial record of Britain was attributed to the malign influence of trade unions, diminishing their legitimacy and leading to their eventual exclusion from Whitehall and even the desire of the Labour Party to distance itself from them. Secondly, the collapse of "smoke-stack industries" diminished the unions' traditional bedrock support and main source of leverage upon government. Thirdly, that same collapse has left many unions and their members facing the virtual oblivion of their industries. Facing such a threat is virtually the ultimate cost and leaves the movement with little to gain from continued institutionalization and, by the same token, little to lose from confrontation.

In these circumstances, although the scale of the policing operation was clearly exceptional, the policing of the miners' strike was entirely predictable. Senior officers in the coalfields faced the most enormous trouble. The extent of the on-the-job trouble was apparent from the initial confrontations at Ollerton colliery, where David Jones was killed in clashes between picketing strikers and working miners. The extent of in-the-job trouble was also apparent from statements made by government ministers. Central government interference in policing during the miners' strike was regarded by many as exceptional. However, Reiner (1990) suggests that Chief Constables are routinely subject to Home Office control to a far greater extent than had previously been supposed. Certainly, my observations of the Metropolitan Police confirm that they are extremely attentive to the political ramifications of public order operations. In the absence of any willingness by the NUM, at least in certain areas, to negotiate (Wright 1985, cf. Leonard 1985), the police resorted to the "insurance" of their coercive power.

Institutionalizing the community

It was argued in Chapter 1 that there is no reason *a priori* to suppose a continuity between community disorder and protest. If the miners' strike represents the furthest extremity of protest to be witnessed in recent years, it remains distinct from the "community disorders" that have intermittently rocked the inner-cities and "dump estates" of Britain. As resource mobilization theory maintains, the *sine qua non* of protest is *organization*, for protestors must assemble and proclaim a cause. Organizations are vulnerable to institutionalization, for, being engaged in instrumental activities, they are sensitive to the manipulation of costs and benefits. They can engage in negotiations with the police and other agencies of the state, and seek alternative means of achieving their aims.

The capacity for organization is not equally distributed, any more than are other sources of power. Part of the condition of powerlessness is the inability to organize to achieve collective aims by concerted action. As Campbell's journalistic treatment of the riots in Cardiff and Oxford and on Tyneside suggests (Campbell 1993), it is precisely this organization that is lacking amongst the "underclass". There may be grievances that would merit organized protest, but social deprivation and decay militate against it. People are condemned to impotent frustration until it is vented in rage. This, of course, invites only suppression, rather than negotiation.

In this connection, developments in the relationship between the police and the Afro-Caribbean community both give reason for hope but also illustrate some of the obstacles that remain. The mobilization of a movement to oppose racism in general, and racially motivated crime in particular, has given a focus for black anger. It has also enabled police to develop their rôle as impartial guardians of law and order. The holding of demonstrations that are vulnerable to attack from neo-fascist groups has allowed the police to present themselves as *protectors* of black rights.

However, "community disorders" have tended to arise not from such grievances, but from the imposition of low-level public order on the streets. The 1980 riot in St Paul's, Bristol, arose from a police raid on a café allegedly supplying illegal alcohol (Joshua & Wallace 1983); the 1981 Brixton riot occurred in the context of a "stop and search" operation targeted at street crime (Scarman 1981); the 1985 Handsworth riot was arguably sparked by an altercation over illegal parking (Dear 1986, Silverman 1986); in Cardiff, disorder erupted from a dispute between two food retailers; and in Blackbird Leys and on Tyneside it was measures taken against car theft that resulted in serious rioting (Campbell 1993). These are not formally organized activities capable of institutionalization, but are inherently rebellious rejections of authority.

Such rebelliousness traditionally lay at the heart of the Notting Hill Carnival. Attempts to impose control by the police resulted in confrontation. Since 1989 the police have supported attempts to transform the carnival into a commercially viable festival of Afro-Caribbean culture. In doing so they are repeating the experience of their predecessors who, 150 years previously, confronted similar problems with fairs (Cunningham 1977). The eventual solution lay not in suppression but in their incorporation as a respectable form of entertainment. It was commercialism that imposed discipline, not the police.

Herein, however, there lies a paradox: for the more that the Notting Hill Carnival adheres to the structure of a well-organized, safety-conscious cultural festival, the more it betrays its rebellious Caribbean origins. Spontaneity is the antithesis of control, but control is essential for the maintenance of order. The state, through its intermediaries – amongst whom are the police – has spent the past two centuries imposing control on public space. Leisure has been swept from the streets into private auditoria and stadia. It is doubtful whether this is a process that can readily be halted, still less reversed.

Policing and control

This discussion of institutionalization raises the issue of how policing relates to other forms of social control. It has become common for police researchers to distinguish between "policing" and the police, and to suggest that the public police are not the only means of "policing". Attention is sometimes drawn to the growth of so-called "private police" (Johnson 1992) as a means whereby order is maintained on privately owned property. Brogden & Shearing (1993) go so far as to recommend the widespread use of non-state "police" as a way of restoring community control over the police in a democratic South Africa. Interestingly, they cite the report of the "international panel regarding lawful control of demonstrations in the Republic of South Africa" (Heymann 1992) in support of their position. This report sought the maintenance of order through what it called the "safety triangle" in which local authorities, police and protest organizers work *together* to ensure peaceful protest. In other words, it echoed the preference of police in London for demonstrators to "police themselves".

Although the phrase "policing themselves" reflects the emphasis that the police give to non-coercive methods of order maintenance, it is misleading to take it too literally. Sociologists have long been aware that social control is largely achieved through unofficial means. Indeed, this was the central tenet of what was once called "consensus theory". "Policing" is diametrically opposed to such methods of social control, for the police are quintessentially *agents of the state*. "Private police" are not police at all, and what they provide is not *policing* but *security*. The public police intrude into social situations not as the agent of any particular party, but as impartial agents of the state, whereas private security staff are the agents of the party who pays them. That is why public order policing is such a sensitive policing task, for, when the state and its institutions are themselves party to a dispute, it is tempting for the police to be cast, and to cast themselves, in a partisan rôle.

Informal controls are a resource that the police use, but they are used as an *alternative* to policing methods. The Department of National Heritage helps to maintain order by imposing private contractual restrictions on protest meetings held on property for which it is responsible. The police *use* those restrictions to secure control of the demonstration, but that is not to say that the Department of National Heritage "polices" anyone or anything. Just as the police use traffic as a "moving wall of steel" to contain marchers, so they use informal methods of social control. It is when such mechanisms fail that the police resort to their own resources – the "insurance" of mobile reserves capable of imposing compliance by force.

The essential difference between policing in liberal democracies like Britain and in authoritarian regimes like apartheid South Africa is that in the former the police can rely upon those non-coercive methods of social control to a considerable extent and in the latter they do not. It is because social institutions in liberal democracies enjoy widespread legitimacy, even amongst those who oppose government policy, that policing can afford to be so low key. Equally, it is because the institutions of apartheid have always lacked any legitimacy that the police in South Africa have been obliged to impose order by brutal means (Jeffery 1991). In other words, the policing of public order must be seen as embedded within the social and political institutions of the society that is policed.

The importance of social and political institutions was repeatedly witnessed throughout this research in the self-restraint shown by all but the tiniest minority of protestors, however radical their cause. Policing was so low key because protestors willingly trudged from the assembly to the rally. They jeered and shouted abuse as they passed by government premises, but rarely posed any serious threat to them. What was most surprising was the repeated spectacle of militant left-wing and anarchist groups chanting the most blood-curdling slogans calling for the destruction of capitalist society, while meekly complying with police directions. Literally speaking, protestors cannot "police themselves", but they can and often did *control themselves*.

It was when the legitimacy of those social and political institutions was seriously disputed that restraint was relatively lacking (although still far from abandoned altogether). This arose most often in the context of opposition to racism and fascism. Fascism is excluded from legitimate social and political institutions to a degree that even revolutionary socialism is not. Self-restraint in the face of the spectre of neo-fascist groups openly propounding their views or holding election meetings is evidently regarded as a compromise with evil. When self-restraint was lacking, the police could no longer rely (at least not as exclusively) on enlisting informal methods of social control.

Conclusions

Institutionalization is a very effective method of controlling conflict, for dissident groups exchange their capacity to disrupt for the opportunity to exert modest influence on decision-making. However, it is a process not a condition: the pattern of industrial conflict and gay rights protest each illustrate, at their different level of analysis, the contingent and reversible nature of that process. At the same time, institutional imperatives to avoid trouble continue to act as an incentive for the police to institutionalize protest as much as possible.

CHAPTER 9

Power and public order policing

Introduction

Commentary on public order policing has been dominated by the analysis of riot and riot control. Inevitably, perhaps, this has created an image of policing that is aggressive, not to say violent, and oppressive. It has led commentators to fear for the health of "policing by consent" (Northam 1988) and for the future of democracy itself (Manwaring-White 1983, Jefferson 1990). These fears have been entertained on the iceberg principle: police battling with rioters and pickets is just the visible part of an iceberg of coercion.

The analysis contained in this book suggests that the policing of public order is more benign than its critics imagine. Confrontation and disorder are rare, arrests uncommon and most operations are characterized by boredom amongst police officers rather than the exhilaration of battle. The policing of public order is quite different from the policing of public disorder. The aim of the former is to avoid becoming embroiled in the latter. However, important issues regarding the rôle of the police in contemporary society remain just beneath the surface of this analysis. They centre on the concept of power.

Policing by consent

On the face of it, public order policing in contemporary Britain remains a triumph of "policing by consent". However, political protest is still largely conducted on terms determined by the police. In other words, their interests are served and in doing so the interests of protestors are, at least, compromised. Protest is emasculated and induced to conform to the avoidance of trouble. In police argot, protest organizers are "had over".

To what extent, then, can it be said that protestors *consent* to the restrictions placed upon them? Restraint is not coerced in any obvious way; the whole process is characterized by amicability and the deliberate avoidance of confrontation. Organizers are not compelled to follow the "standard routes", although almost all of them do so. Restriction and restraint have the appearance of being agreed to. Yet, in making that agreement, the odds are not stacked equally between the police and protestors. Police use their structural advantages, routine practices and interactional ploys to achieve their goals, and it is doubtful whether any protestor is aware of what they are doing. Ironically, radical groups that predominate amongst protesting organizations may have been imbued for so long with the demonology of the police as agents of the authoritarian state that they are mesmerized by the congenial face of policing that greets them. But the ultimate power of the police lies in the simple fact that protestors need them considerably more than the police need protestors.

Police power

The authoritarian state thesis fails to explain the policing of political protest because, surprisingly perhaps, it relies upon an impoverished conception of power. The only power that the police are thought to wield is legal and physical coercion. This corresponds to Lukes (1972) one-dimensional view of power: the overt use of power in head-to-head conflict. Police avoid head-to-head conflict, precisely because it is here that they are at their weakest, for confrontation threatens in-the-job trouble.

Far more potent weapons for achieving control lie in negotiating with organizers, both prior to the demonstration and at the scene, "taking the ground" and *not* making arrests. For, although these have a benign appearance, they remain an exercise of power – Lukes' second and third dimensions. The apparent helpfulness of police, who "organize it for them", prevents issues arising. Even a group like "OutRage!", whose knowledgeable and articulate leaders challenged the police interpretation of the Sessional Order, eventually succumbed to stage-managed arrests at the periphery of the Sessional Area and applauded the police for doing so. By such means are protest groups subverted, whereas a more aggressive adherence to the provisions of the 1986 Act by the police might lead organizers to seek legal advice and challenge arrangements favoured by the police.

198

In exercising power, what the police abstain from doing is as important as the actions they take. Proffering only the "standard route" in a helpful manner in effect rules out the alternative of protestors proceeding along Oxford Street. *Not* invoking the law, *not* making arrests for minor offences and *not* confronting do not surrender power but use it. The police retain the option of taking enforcement action, but choose not to do so because it would threaten their interests. As Lukes (1972) pointed out, this is the third dimension of power and possibly the most potent, for in abstaining from taking action the police exercise untrammelled power, because in most circumstances no one else is likely to know that the choice has been made.

The police reduce the costs of protest for protestors who "play the game". It is in reducing costs for protestors that the police most effectively exercise power, for they subtly invite demonstrators to emasculate the force of their protest.

Power and consent

Exercising power by reducing the costs of protest is not, of course, unconditional. Demonstrators who fundamentally challenge police interests, by pushing them into a "ditch" in which the police feel compelled to "die", will experience police coercion, as did "OutRage!" protestors at the State Opening of Parliament described in the previous chapter. The police force that organized the NUM demonstration against pit closures is the same force that defeated striking miners on the picket-line, and would do so again. This raises three crucial issues. First, does the accommodating stance of the police merely mask their truly coercive rôle? Secondly, is it proper that the police should obtain through such means what they could not achieve by the exercise of their legal powers? Finally, can a consensual approach coexist with paramilitarism?

As custodians of the state's monopoly of legitimate force (Bittner 1970, 1974), the police will resort to coercive measures if necessary. They are duty-bound to do so if public order is seriously threatened. However, there is surely a difference to be drawn between policing that seeks to retain the velvet glove and that which openly displays the mailed fist. The habit of some continental European police forces of openly displaying their equivalent of mobile reserves equipped in riot gear as a veiled threat is clearly more intimidatory than a style of policing that not only keeps mobile reserves hidden away, but also exercises the utmost caution in allowing them to don their protective equipment.

"Policing by consent" is still *policing*, and policing entails the potential ultimately to use coercive power. "Consent" cannot mean genuinely informed and unconstrained agreement, for that would imply the abrogation of police authority itself. What this, admittedly unhelpful, phrase points to is the ability of the police to wield power without overt coercion. Achieving their ends by "winning over" protest organizers may not be truly consensual, but is equally not coercive.

Although non-coercive, such an approach to policing may still infringe civil liberties. Police aims are, as we have repeatedly seen, more extensive than legal restrictions. The commanding officer who decides that too few demonstrators have attended a march to justify "bringing the streets of London to a halt" (see p. 102) is in effect preventing a march taking place that might otherwise have been permitted by law. Would civil liberties be better protected if the police were compelled simply to enforce the law? There are two reasons to doubt that this prescription would work. First, the scope of the common law is so extensive that, if the police were to enforce it strictly, then it would probably restrict the exercise of democratic freedoms far more than it is now (although not necessarily in the same ways). Secondly, if protestors disregarded the standards of *socially* acceptable behaviour, then it is likely that those whom they antagonize will cause the law to be changed so as to restrict civil rights more comprehensively. Thus, if marches did actually insist on proceeding along Oxford Street and Regent Street, with accompanying disruption to traffic, it is very probable that the businesses thereby affected would successfully lobby for a legal prohibition. The achievement of order by negotiation, no matter how unequal the parties, is surely preferable to the imposition of universal legal restraint.

Can this last? Some commentators have suggested that the development of paramilitary equipment and tactics encourages, if not compels, the police towards adopting a more confrontational style. It is implied that if such a capacity exists then it will be used, either operationally or politically. Jefferson (1990) argues that paramilitary methods will probably lead to self-fulfilling escalation. However, as I have argued at length elsewhere (P. Waddington 1993a), the probabilities suggest the contrary. "Planning for the worst-case scenario" and control of space and the crowd are an almost invariant accompaniment of major public order operations, yet very few result in disorder.

A wider argument is hinted at in a later article by Jefferson (1993), that a paramilitary approach to policing is a denial of democracy, for it seeks to repress popular opposition to government by coercive means. As Northam

(1988) argues, paramilitary methods are the means used to maintain the subjugation of a subject population, such as occurs under colonial regimes. This argument erroneously equates the organization and weaponry of policing with a relationship between state and citizen. First, there is no such empirical connection, for most continental European nations have quite explicit paramilitary police forces in almost every sense of the term and yet remain within the democratic fold. Access to protective equipment and various munitions for enforcing the dispersal or incapacitation of violent crowds is common to police forces throughout the world. If this disqualifies them from membership of the democratic club, then "democracy" is emptied of meaning. Secondly, although it is the aspiration of democratic government to rule by persuasion and not force, not everyone will be persuaded of the rightness of any given course of action. This may be a failure of the democratic ideal, but if, for example, political groups refuse to allow the expression of contrary opinions by their rivals, then the democratic rights of protest should surely be enforced. If that requires the use of forceful means, then so be it. Thirdly, this is to confuse the policing of *disorder* with the policing of public *order*.

Far from an accommodative approach to the maintenance of public order being incompatible with the development of paramilitary methods, they actually coexist and the latter reinforces the former. The police were able to resist political pressures to ban the third anti poll tax march because they mounted a paramilitary operation capable of containing any disorder that might have arisen (see pp. 63–4, 158–9). During that operation, they did not over-react to threats of disorder, because senior officers were "comfortable" that adequately equipped mobile reserves were readily available should they be needed. As argued in Chapter 7, it was when loss of control was threatened that the imperative to impose control was most keenly felt. Paramilitary planning and reserves equipped with the tactics and technology to impose control mean that loss of control is less of a threat. The irony of public order policing may be that, the more control the police exercise, the more freedom protestors can be allowed.

Power over the police

Whereas the police exercised power over protestors, others exercised power over them. It was the capacity to threaten or create in-the-job trouble that constrained police action. Again, this was power that was only infrequently exercised but was continually applied as police tried to avoid trouble. The mere possibility that MPs or Black Rod might have complained about the presence of banners and placards in Parliament Square was sufficient to compel the enforcement of restrictions that seemed to have little basis in law.

In so far as police acted in accordance with their anticipations of trouble, they translated *power structures* into individual *power relationships*. They also reproduced those power structures. Parliament, government, royalty and foreign embassies are part of the institutionalized power structure of contemporary Britain. The Cenotaph, military statues, royal parks and Trafalgar Square are all powerful symbols. Their power is reflected in the fact that the police are willing to "die in a ditch" to defend them. The police imagine that they have no choice in this. Their only room for manoeuvre lies in using guile in preference to force to achieve the aim that they feel compelled to accomplish. In achieving it, they thereby re-create the "ditches" in which future generations of police will no doubt feel equally compelled to "die". This power is structural, since no person need actually force or induce the police to do what they would otherwise prefer not to do. Power lies in the anticipation the police have of trouble.

As Lukes (1972) implies, power structures are the more potent the less power is actually wielded. When those in authority sought to influence police decisions, their power to do so itself became an issue. Thus, the pressure to ban the final anti poll tax march and the refusal to allow the Anti-Election Alliance to assemble in Trafalgar Square raised the issue of whether the exercise of power was reasonable or acceptable. Police resisted pressure to ban the anti poll tax march in part because they wished to retain the autonomy they had achieved. Brogden (1983) argues that the history of the police has been a struggle to achieve autonomy. If police autonomy were conceded on these occasions, they would henceforth face the threat that political figures could define the "ditches" in which the police might be obliged to "die". Allowing the Department of the Environment to "get away with" refusing the use of Trafalgar Square would have amounted to a change in the power structure within which the police operated, creating a new "ditch".

Thus, in exercising their power, police contribute to the reproduction of the power structure that also confines them. As Giddens (1979) has argued, it is through such mechanisms that social institutions are sustained by social action. Equally, the expectation that heavy-handed policing would evoke a critical response restrained police from confrontation. From where was this criticism expected to arise? This remained unclear, but it was repeatedly claimed (and with some trepidation) that, if certain courses of action were followed, "we will be criticized". I suspect, but cannot prove, that it was the very unpredictability of possible criticism, especially that voiced in the media, that proved so powerful. However, this too reproduces a commitment to liberal democratic values that are breached only with circumspection and usually not breached at all. So the power of public criticism to produce in-the-job trouble is not actually put to the test. Nevertheless, it remains a potent constraint.

Controlling police power

If police can be constrained by such institutional influences, there seems ample opportunity for extending democratic control of policing. Elected representatives would be in a position to cause police officers "grief" and thereby influence how they acted.

The argument for subjecting police to the control of elected representatives is constitutionally compelling. Senior officers may have defended the democratic rights of anti poll tax protestors and anarchists opposed to elections, but one is entitled to ask on what constitutional grounds they did so. The proper decision may have been made by improper means, for unelected officials do not have the constitutional competence to make such a decision (see Lustgarten 1986 for a fuller discussion).

There are two grounds on which to oppose this constitutionalist position. First, it assumes that police will suffer increased "grief" by direct political control. On the contrary, political responsibility might remove this burden from police shoulders. If elected representatives had decided that either or both of the marches mentioned above should have been banned and instructed the police to prevent them from marching, there would have been little or no in-the-job trouble from any disorder that subsequently occurred. The police would have been doing only as they were instructed to do and the "grief" would have rested with the elected representatives who instructed them. There would, correspondingly, be less incentive for the police to avoid confrontation, with the likelihood that democratic rights would be restricted. As this research illustrates, governments have little incentive to protect the democratic rights of their opponents.

I have suggested that police avoid confrontation because the consequences of doing otherwise are *uncertain*. The only thing that is certain, as they see it, is that they will be left "holding the baby". Uncertainty is a potent disincentive to action, and so police try to stay clear of anything that might have untoward consequences. The more certain the consequences of failing to act, the more inclined are the police to intervene. It is the near-certainty that MPs will complain about breaches of the Sessional Order (real or imagined) that encourages its strict enforcement. Control by elected representatives would replace uncertainty with certainty. The decisions of an elected body would amount to the creation of "ditches". Certainty digs "ditches" in which police (and democratic liberties) will "die".

Secondly, there can be few corners of sociology left in which such formalism receives so much credibility. Formal rules, procedures and organizational structures are notable for their impotence in the face of informal arrangements. Yet we are invited to believe that elected representatives will discharge their mandate sublimely immune to the kinds of influences with which political scientists have been familiar since the writings of Pareto, Sorel and Michels. If the police found their interests being threatened, they would use ploys to protect them. These would not be the same ploys as they now use in negotiations, but they would still retain control of information. If the police claimed to anticipate disorder, it would be a brave authority that refused to heed their warning. But whatever difference was made to the position of the police, democratic control would do nothing to change the position of protestors. They will remain isolated, marginal and powerless, because there would be precious little reason to protest if they were otherwise. The irony of constitutional propriety is that it might result in compromising further the democratic rights it seeks to uphold.

The constitutionalist retort to these objections is likely to be that democratic rights should be entrenched in statute. Critics of British public order law habitually note that, unlike most other countries, Britain does not possess a written constitution and Bill of Rights. They look wistfully to the United States, which entrenches democratic rights in its constitution. They ignore the recent history of the United States, which has seen civil rights protestors clubbed, gassed and shot. They pay little heed to the 1968 Democratic Party Convention in Chicago when Mayor Daley's politically controlled police clubbed and gassed anti Vietnam war protestors (Walker 1968). And they forget Kent State University where National Guardsmen opened fire on students protesting at the invasion of Cambodia (Lewis 1972). Nor were these singular events, for, as Gurr (1979) reports, during the 1960s the United States suffered the highest casualty rate in civil conflict of any Western industrial nation.

Public protest is a *political* phenomenon subject to political processes, which are not reducible to a set of principles capable of universal application. It would be a mistake to underestimate the impact of political culture on the police. Although rarely articulated as such, there was a widespread tacit commitment to liberal democratic values. Occasional references were made to the legitimate rights of protestors and the need to safeguard them. Although there was frequent disagreement with the causes espoused by protest groups, and even occasionally distaste for them, animosity was rarely displayed. This reflects a culture of rights that was much in evidence during the debates on the Public Order Bill, when there was repeated appeal to contending rights and freedoms by all parties. It is a culture that is reaffirmed by Home Office Circular 11/1987, which reminds the police:

> The right to assemble, demonstrate and protest peacefully within the law is fundamental to our democratic way of life. Senior police officers responsible for the policing of assemblies and demonstrations will no doubt continue to have regard to the need to protect these rights within the framework provided by the law. (Home Office 1987: para. 11)

The greatest animosity was directed not at protestors but at organizations like the London Marathon and "Pavarotti in the Park", who were seen as *illegitimately* disrupting London and commandeering police resources for commercial or self-serving interests. Indeed, one senior officer half-jokingly alluded to this difference of attitude when, after a prolonged and fraught planning meeting regarding "Pavarotti in the Park", he laughed and joked "but if you want 30 000 gays marching to Hyde Park - no problem!".

Again, as Lukes (1972) has argued, the greatest power resides in institutions whose existence is barely acknowledged, still less challenged. Protestors compliantly trudge from Hyde Park to Trafalgar Square, listen to speeches and peacefully disperse, in the main not because of anything specific the police do, but because that is what protest entails in contemporary Britain. What is truly remarkable is that radical leftist and anarchist groups remain as bounded by the tacit conventions of social protest as do mainstream organizations. Those conventions provide the taken-for-granted backdrop to the negotiation and policing of protest. They bind *both* the police and protestors, to the benefit of the established order.

Constitutionalists are mistaken in looking to formal rules to safeguard democratic rights, for rules can be evaded and subverted. Of course, this does mean that protestors will be reliant upon the "benevolent exercise of discretion by those in power" (Ewing & Gearty 1990: 94). A democratic political culture is a far more robust safeguard against the abuse of that power than are rules that the powerful must interpret and apply. Despite all the conjecture that Britain is "drifting into a law and order society", this research indicates that the interpretation and application of those rules by the police remain remarkably benign.

Research methods

Observation

The research methods used in this study were almost entirely observational. It therefore benefits from all the advantages of such an approach and suffers from all its drawbacks. Space does not permit a detailed discussion of the advantages and disadvantages of those methods, nor would it be appropriate. Here I will note only the direct impact of the research methods on this research.

Access was facilitated by the research that I had previously conducted on armed policing and riot-control methods (P. Waddington 1991). This gave me the opportunity to build a relationship of trust with police officers engaged in highly sensitive aspects of policing. However, I was not initially accommodated fully. I was permitted to witness a NUS march, the anti poll tax demonstration at Lambeth town hall and what became the anti poll tax riot, but only as it occurred on the street. I was not invited to the briefing, or to any preparatory meetings. I did, however, write a factual account of what I had witnessed during the riot and made it available to the police and was interviewed by the debriefing team. I cannot say whether it was this that prompted it, but shortly afterwards I was contacted by the superintendent in the Public Order Branch who announced that it had been decided that, if I was to obtain a comprehensive view of public order policing, I must observe it all, from the earliest contact with protest organizers, through the planning of the operation and its implementation. Henceforth I was informed of most meetings that were being held and invited to attend them. Occasionally I was not informed, usually because the operation was regarded as of no significance. Of course, not all meetings could be attended because of incompatible schedules. Whenever clashes occurred, I chose to attend those meetings and other activities relating to the larger and more problematic operations. For both these reasons my research is distinctly skewed towards the more problematic operations and under-represents "nothing jobs".

The greatest advantage of observational methods is their flexibility. When I commenced this research, I laboured under many of the same misapprehensions that have misled other researchers and commentators. I assumed that public order was a violent and exhilarating business. I was encouraged in this view by my initial exposure, since during the course of my previous research I had attended the 1987 Notting Hill Carnival and found myself in the midst of a riot. I was then invited to accompany officers on a major drugs raid on the Broadwater Farm in 1989. Although no disorder occurred, this was an operation bristling with paramilitarism in all its guises. My third exposure to public order policing was the anti poll tax riot in March 1990. It consequently took some considerable time for my preconceptions to dissipate.

It never occurred to me that the policing of ceremonials might be of such significance. It was only as I mixed with members of the public order fraternity that I became aware of the seriousness with which ceremonials were imbued. A methodology that did not allow for redefinition of the problem in the light of experience might have led this research seriously astray.

Although I hung around the Public Order Branch and 8 Area Special Events, and even shared the occasional beer with those who worked there, I hesitate to call this research an ethnography. Public order operations, certainly the major ones, are formally organized. It is in meetings and briefings, when senior officers come together, that the approach is formulated. Although much goes on in these meetings that is not formally recorded, they are formal occasions and I was only one of several taking detailed notes. Notes were transcribed on to a personal computer as soon after the event as possible, usually within a few hours, but occasionally the next day. However, there were other contacts that took place over the telephone or in private meetings to which I was not privy. The results of, at least some of, those contacts were reported to colleagues at subsequent formal meetings that I witnessed, but I cannot vouch for the veracity of those reports. Of course, whether accurate or not, the version disclosed to colleagues became the version that influenced their actions.

Although the formality of the settings in which I participated allowed me openly to record what was being said, I found it difficult, not to say impossible, to capture direct speech. Apart from the occasional phrase, I have avoided attributing direct speech to those whom I observed. I am filled with admiration for those ethnographers who are able to recover from memory lengthy passages of direct speech spoken some time previously.

During operations themselves I usually accompanied the most senior forward commander. On minor operations this was the senior officer in charge (usually a chief inspector or superintendent). On major operations I accompanied the "Silver" commander, in effect forming part of his entourage. I was supplied with a police radio, which was tuned to the "command channel" when more than one channel was being used. Apart from enabling me to listen to radio broadcasts, the possession of a "talking brooch", as the radio handset is known, proved invaluable in moving freely around the scene. Of course, even granted this amount of access to the policing operation did not allow me to witness *everything*. It is physically impossible to observe everything that occurs in a large and complex event like a public order operation. These observations were made from the perspective of commanders, not the lower ranks. This is a crucial perspective, since subordinates rarely did anything without being commanded to do so, or at the very least without the senior officer in charge being informed. Yet, this was a perspective that excluded the banter of the personnel carrier and other subterranean activities.

My scope of observation was limited even more by the fact that these observations took place in London, and mainly in central London. There is a simple reason for this: London, being the capital city, plays host to vastly more protests than anywhere else and those protests are concentrated within the central area. However, the Metropolitan Police cannot be assumed to be representative of other police forces in Britain. Indeed, officers responsible for the central area cannot be assumed to be representative of officers in the other areas. Their familiarity in dealing with public order operations suggests that they are not. The representativeness of this research will be gauged only by survey data.

Like all such observational research, this study suffers from the lack of transparency of the methods used. The reader is obliged to take my word for it that events happened in the way I have described them. It can also be justifiably described as impressionistic. I have used terms like "frequently", "often", "rarely" and so forth, without being able to quantify how often is "often", or how frequently is "frequently" or how rarely is "rarely". Impressions are both the advantage and the disadvantage of such observational methods. They benefit from the researcher coming to share the language, assumptions, beliefs and perspective – in short, the culture – of those whom he is researching. The commonplace comes to be known as it is known to participants, because in interacting with participants those commonplaces are the bedrock of understanding. It is difficult to quantify that which is so ubiquitous, since so often it is understood by all those present without being made explicit. For example, the antipathy felt for particular individuals or the ease with which a situation is regarded are not always conveyed in a manner that allows for quantification. However, this is a weakness with the chosen method; it limits its utility to that of a heuristic that I hope prompts others to use alternative methods to corroborate the conclusions I have arrived at.

Atkinson (1990) has recently argued that ethnographers use data as a means of persuasion. Examples are selected to illustrate the argument being presented, rather than to test or qualify it. Shipman (1988) also warns against "exampling" rather than sampling. I believe that these criticisms are well founded and seriously limit the value of ethnographic or observational research – including that reported in this book (P. Waddington 1992). Data can be used only in an illustrative fashion, otherwise the reader would be burdened by detailed descriptions of events as comprehensive as the fieldnotes from which they are drawn. The inherent unreliability of observational records disqualifies any attempt to use them for quantification. However, these criticisms do not *invalidate* observational methods, which have a place – limited though it may be – within the spectrum of research methods. Like any other research, observational or ethnographic studies should be approached with caution, and with an awareness of their strengths and weaknesses.

I also formally interviewed 44 of the officers most frequently involved in the negotiating, planning and command of public order operations. I decided against using extracts from those interviews to corroborate assertions made in describing events in this book, since that corroboration would be spurious. The selection of extracts from interviews is just as vulnerable to the charge of unreliability as are observational methods, and a non-random sample of this size could hardly be used to confer quantitative respectability on these data. I used the interviews instead to assist my own understanding of how senior officers approached their work.

One attempt was made to obtain quantified corroboration and that was through systematically recording information from files kept on public order operations. However, although this proved of some value, its value was limited by the incompleteness of the files themselves. For example, many files contain a copy of the "event message" compiled at the conclusion of any public order operation via the computerized message switching system. This lists information such as the official count of the demonstrators attending the protest, the number of arrests, and so forth. Unfortunately, not all files contained this copy and I was unable to track down all omissions. This explains why, when quantifying operations in the text, the number of operations referred to vary, because the amount of information contained in the files varied from one operation to another.

I had hoped to be able to compare files relating to the operations I observed with those that had taken place previously. It was again unfortunate that the information contained in the files about earlier operations proved to be so sketchy as to be of little value for this purpose.

One issue surrounding ethnographic or observational methods that has received less attention than it deserves is its ethics. The normal ethical standard is that subjects should exercise informed consent. Such a requirement is virtually impossible to satisfy in this type of research. Certainly, the Metropolitan Police needed to consent before access was granted, but, once the organization had done so, it was difficult, not to say impossible, for subordinates to object. Attending a meeting at the invitation of the senior officer chairing it was one thing, but having the informed consent of all other participants was probably something else. Of course, during the protracted period of observation, I sought to establish rapport with the people I observed and I became quite friendly with many of them, and still count some amongst my friends. But there were those who appeared only momentarily upon the scene and it would have been quite artificial, disruptive and inconvenient to all concerned if I had taken them aside and explained who I was and the research I was doing, and sought their individual informed consent. For most occasions my presence was not announced. My appearance and demeanour and the fact that I usually knew most of those present, with whom I exchanged the usual pleasantries of everyday life, probably encouraged strangers in the view that I was a police officer or, at least, an employee of the Metropolitan Police. Certainly, on operations I had little opportunity to secure the informed consent of the numerous officers deployed.

When attending meetings between police and protest organizers I was almost always formally introduced. This was equally invariably as part of the general introductions conducted by the police officer chairing the meeting. This introduction was normally accompanied by a very cryptic account of my research, such as "He's looking at us". Protest organizers were rarely asked explicitly whether they consented to my continued presence. Although one might argue that the organizer's continued participation in the meeting amounted to tacit consent, the same pressures were applied in this connection as I have argued applied in other aspects of the negotiating process. Social scientists should perhaps reflect more upon the extent to which any group of individuals can genuinely consent to the research that is being conducted upon them. There is an irony in the argument that, say, people who "consent" to being searched by the police do not truly *consent*, when it is based upon observations to which possibly neither the police officer nor the person he or she has stopped to search have genuinely consented.

My conceptualization of the policing of public order has a still more direct implication for the methodology employed. I have argued throughout this book that police seek to avoid in-the-job trouble by extending control and "guarding their backs". The presence of a researcher represents an obvious potential for trouble. How, then, did the police seek to control me and how did they "guard their backs" against the threat I represented? One method of control used by those in positions of power generally is incorporation and, by affording me such unprecedented access, the Metropolitan Police could be seen to have been incorporating me. I was being "won over" to their perspective, as they attempt to "win over" protest organizers. It was successful: the reality that I witnessed included all the "backstage" work of planning, preparation and briefing. I was privy to all the "what ifs?" and, therefore, contextualized what occurred on the street in ways that senior officers contextualized them. Protestors, spectators, revellers and bystanders confronted a different reality, one that is probably experienced differently because it is set in a different context. Even lower-ranking police officers had only the most limited knowledge of the "backstage" within which senior officers operated. So the analysis contained in this book is unapologetically partial: it is *a* perspective – I believe an important one – but only one amongst others.

If my conceptualization is correct and officers seek to "guard their backs", then it is at least conceivable that they sought to protect themselves against any damage I might do. Of course, one can only speculate about how things were done in my absence, but one senior officer did confide that my presence encouraged him and his colleagues to "get it right", that is, to plan operations in a way that would withstand scrutiny. This raises the prospect that by my presence I significantly enhanced the potential for in-the-job trouble, which was reflected in the attention paid to this considera-tion by those whom I observed – a self-confirming "researcher effect". This possibility should not be discounted, but equally there is the likelihood that it was offset by my value as a resource. Comments made from time to time suggested that I was also viewed as a kind of "insurance". If an opera-tion did "go pear-shaped", then there was an independent witness and con-temporaneous notes that would confirm the propriety of police action. Officers seemed genuinely proud of their professionalism and welcomed the opportunity to demonstrate their skills to an observer.

The Metropolitan Police imposed no formal requirement upon me to have this or any other manuscript vetted. I have nevertheless taken the opportunity to invite senior officers to read and comment on it. This was more than a courtesy, since I have attempted empathetically to understand their perspective. If that empathy was misplaced then I expected them to correct me.

Details of operations observed

National Union of Students' march, 15 February 1990
Observation of march and rally

Anti poll tax demonstration, Lambeth town hall, 29 March 1990
Observation of protest outside Lambeth town hall

Anti poll tax march and demonstration, 31 March 1990
Observations at Trafalgar Square, Hay-market and Piccadilly Circus

Notting Hill Carnival, August 1990
Observation of shield reserves

Muslims in Britain and Socialist Workers' Party marches, Saturday, 1 September 1990
Strategy meeting, Cannon Row, 29 August 1990
Briefing, Scotland Yard, 30 August 1990

Observation of marches, 1 September 1990

Hands Off the Middle East Committee march, 8 September 1990
Strategy meeting and briefing, Cannon Row, 6 September 1990
Observation of march, 8 September

Campaign Against War in the Gulf march, 15 September 1990
The meeting with organizer, New Scot-land Yard, 3 September 1990
Strategy meeting and briefing, New Scot-land Yard, 13 September 1990
Observation of the march, 15 September 1990

London branch of the All Britain Anti-Poll Tax Federation, Brockwell Park, followed by the Trafalgar Square Defence Cam-paign, march and rally, Brixton prison, 20 October 1990

Meeting with London Anti-poll Tax Federation, New Scotland Yard, 2 September 1990

Meeting with London Anti-poll Tax Federation, New Scotland Yard, 6 September 1990

Meeting with London Anti-poll Tax Federation, New Scotland Yard, 11 September 1990

Meeting with London Anti-poll Tax Federation and officials of Lambeth Council, New Scotland Yard, 17 September 1990

Strategy meeting, Brixton police station, 28 September 1990

Meeting with National Federation organizers, New Scotland Yard, 3 October 1990

Meeting, Assistant Commissioner, New Scotland Yard, 3 October 1990

Training at Public Order Training Centre, Hounslow, 8 October 1990

Strategy meeting, New Scotland Yard, 10 October 1990

Meeting with London Anti-poll Tax Federation, New Scotland Yard, 15 October 1990

Strategy meeting, Brixton, 15 October 1990

Briefing, New Scotland Yard, 18 October 1990

Meeting with London Anti-poll Tax Federation and Trafalgar Square Defence Campaign, New Scotland Yard, 19 October 1990

Observation of anti poll tax march, the Defence Campaign picket and march, 20 October 1990

Remembrance Sunday, 11 November 1990
Briefing, New Scotland Yard, 8 November 1990

Observations in Whitehall, 11 November 1990

Campaign to Stop War in the Gulf, Saturday, 24 November 1990
Strategy meeting, Cannon Row, 22 October 1990

Strategy meeting, Cannon Row, 19 November 1990

Meeting with organizer, New Scotland Yard, 5 November 1990

Briefing, New Scotland Yard, 21 November 1990

Observation of march and rally, 24 November 1990

Campaign to Stop War in the Gulf, Saturday, 12 January 1991
Strategy meeting, Cannon Row, 13 December 1990

Briefing, New Scotland Yard, 10 January 1991

Ad hoc meeting, New Scotland Yard, 10 January 1991

Observation of march and rally, 12 January 1991

Various events connected with the Gulf crisis, Tuesday, 15 January 1991
Informal discussion, New Scotland Yard, 10 January 1991

Briefing for senior officers, Cannon Row, 14 January 1991

Observation of events in Trafalgar Square, Whitehall and Parliament Square, 15 January 1991

Debrief, Cannon Row, 16 January 1991

Events following the outbreak of war in the Gulf
Strategy meeting, Cannon Row, 16 January, 1991.

Events in Westminster protesting at the outbreak of hostilities in the Gulf, 17 January, 1991
Strategy briefing, Cannon Row, 17 January 1991

Observation of events in Westminster, 17 January 1991

Campaign to Stop War in the Gulf march, 19 January 1991
Senior officers' briefing, Cannon Row, 18 January 1991

214

Observation of march and rally, 19 January 1991

Campaign to Stop War in the Gulf, march and rally, 26 January 1991
Briefing, New Scotland Yard, 25 January 1991
Observation of march and rally, 26 January 1991

Campaign to Stop War in the Gulf, march and rally, 2 February 1991
Strategy meeting, Cannon Row, 28 January 1991
Meeting with Campaign to Stop War in the Gulf and CND organizers, New Scotland Yard, 28 January 1991
Briefing, New Scotland Yard, 1 February 1991
Observation of march and rally, 2 February 1991

Anti-war protests in and around Trafalgar and Parliament Squares, 15 February 1991
Briefing, New Scotland Yard, 15 February 1991
Observation of events in Trafalgar Square, Whitehall and Parliament Square, 15 February 1991

Lesbian and Gay Coalition, march and rally, 16 February 1991
Briefing, New Scotland Yard, 15 February 1991
Observation of march, 16 February 1991

International Islamic Front march, Sunday, 24 February 1991
Briefing, New Scotland Yard, 22 February 1991
Observation of march, 24 February 1991

Campaign to Stop War in the Gulf, march and rally, 2 March 1991
Meeting with organizers from Campaign to Stop War in the Gulf, New Scotland Yard, 25 February 1991
Meeting with DOE officials, New Scotland

Yard, 25 February 1991
Meeting with "Internationalists" organizer, New Scotland Yard, 25 February 1991
Ad hoc meeting with officials from the DOE, New Scotland Yard, 25 February 1991
Briefing, New Scotland Yard, 1 March 1991
Observation of march and rally, 2 March 1991

Women's March for Peace, march and rally, 9 March 1991
Meeting with organizers from Campaign to Stop War in the Gulf, New Scotland Yard, 25 February 1991
Briefing, New Scotland Yard, 2 March 1991

All Britain Anti-poll Tax Federation, march and rally, 23 March 1991
Meeting, Assistant Commissioner, New Scotland Yard, 28 January 1991
Strategy meeting, Cannon Row, 6 February 1991
Meeting to plan presentation to public meeting, Cannon Row, 25 February 1991
Meeting with Anti-poll Tax organizers, New Scotland Yard, 8 March 1991
Public meeting on the Anti-poll Tax march, at Westminster City Council Town Hall, 11 March 1991
Strategy meeting, New Scotland Yard, 12 March 1991
Meeting with organizers, New Scotland Yard, 15 March 1991
Meeting with organizers, New Scotland Yard, 18 March 1991
Briefing, New Scotland Yard, 18 March 1991
Observation of Trafalgar Square, 23 March 1991
Debrief, Cannon Row, 8 April 1991

Iraqi People's Solidarity Committee march, 13 April 1991

215

Meeting with organizer, Cannon Row, 10 April 1991

Briefing and observation of march, 13 April 1991

Islamic Students' Association march and rally, 20 April 1991

Meeting with organizer, Cannon Row, 18 April 1991

Briefing and observation of march, 20 April 1991

National Anti-Vivisection Society, march and rally, 27 April 1991

Strategy meeting, Cannon Row, 18 March 1991

Strategy meeting, New Scotland Yard, 25 April 1991

Briefing, New Scotland Yard, 25 April 1991

Observation of march, 27 April 1991

British National Party, march and rally, Thamesmead, 25 May 1991

Strategy meeting, Plumstead police station, 16 May 1991

Strategy meeting, Plumstead police station, 23 May 1991

Trooping the Colour: HM the Queen's Birthday Parade, 15 June 1991

Strategy meeting, Cannon Row, 27 March 1991

Strategy meeting, Cannon Row, 25 April 1991

Trooping the Colour, 15 June 1991

Debrief, 26 June 1991

Gurdwara Siri Guru Singh Sabha, march and rally, 23 June 1991

Briefing and observation of march, 23 June 1991

"Gay Pride", march and rally, 29 June 1991

Strategy meeting, Brixton police station, 3 May 1991

Meeting with organizers, New Scotland Yard, 27 June 1991

Briefing, New Scotland Yard, 27 June 1991

Observation of march, 29 June 1991

Debrief, Kennington police station, 3 July 1991

Cancel the Debt, march and rally, Saturday, 13 July 1991

Meeting with organizer, New Scotland Yard, Wednesday, 19 June 1991

Meeting with organizer, New Scotland Yard, 11 July 1991

Briefing, New Scotland Yard, 11 July 1991

Observation of march, 13 July 1991

Pavarotti free concert, Hyde Park, 30 July 1991

Meeting, Cannon Row, 6 January 1991

Ad hoc meeting with Officials from DOE, New Scotland Yard, 25 February 1991

Meeting, Cannon Row, 18 April 1991

Meeting between Metropolitan Police, DOE, Fire Brigade and organizers, New Scotland Yard, 22 April 1991

Strategy meeting, Cannon Row, 23 May 1991

Strategy meeting, Cannon Row, 27 June 1991

Strategy meeting, Cannon Row, 9 July 1991

Strategy meeting, Cannon Row, 19 July 1991

Strategy meeting, Cannon Row, 23 July 1991

Meeting with DOE officials and other interested parties, Hyde Park police station, 25 July 1991

DOE debrief, DOE, Marsham Street, 19 September 1991

Notting Hill Carnival, 24–6 August 1991

Sector commanders' meeting, Notting Dale, 5 March 1991

Notting Hill Support Group meeting, Kensington and Chelsea town hall, 12 March 1991

Sector commanders' meeting, Notting Dale, 14 March 1991

Notting Hill Carnival "Seminar", Kensington and Chelsea town hall, 15 March 1991

Working party meeting, Notting Dale, 27 March 1991

Support Group meeting, Chelsea and Kensington town hall, 10 April 1991

Sector commanders' meeting, 17 April 1991

Working party meeting, Notting Dale, 24 April 1991

Pre-Support Group meeting, 7 May 1991

Support Group meeting, Kensington and Chelsea town hall, 8 May 1991

Sector commanders' meeting, Notting Dale, 15 May 1991

Strategy meeting, Notting Dale, 11 June 1991

Sector commanders' meeting, Notting Dale, 19 June 1991

Working party meeting, Notting Dale, 26 June 1991

"Training day", Public Order Training Centre, Hounslow, 5 July 1991

Strategy meeting, Notting Dale, 9 July 1991

Support Group, Kensington and Chelsea town hall, 10 July 1991

Training Day, Public Order Training Centre, Hounslow, 12 July 1991

Sector commanders' meeting, Notting Dale, 16 July 1991

Sector Three briefing, New Scotland Yard, 12 August 1991

Strategy meeting, 13 August 1991

Support Group, Kensington town hall, 14 August 1991

Sector commanders' meeting, 15 August 1991

Observation of "Panorama", Horniman's Pleasance, Saturday, 24 August 1991

Observation of Notting Hill Carnival, Sector Two, Sunday, 25 August 1991

Observation of Notting Hill Carnival, Sector Three, Monday, 26 August 1991

Support Group, Kensington and Chelsea town hall, 8 October 1991

Debrief, Imber Court, 6 November 1991

State Opening of Parliament, 31 October 1991

Strategy meeting, Cannon Row, 9 October 1991

Briefing, New Scotland Yard, 24 October 1991

State Opening of Parliament, 31 October 1991

Debrief, Cannon Row, 15 November 1991

Remembrance Sunday, 10 November 1991

Strategy meeting, Cannon Row, 5 September 1991.

Strategy briefing, Cannon Row, 9 October 1991

Briefing, New Scotland Yard, 7 November 1991

Observation of events in Whitehall and Victoria, 10 November 1991

Debrief, 19 November 1991

International Communist Party day of solidarity (cancelled)

Meeting with organizers, New Scotland Yard, 20 December 1991

Hackney Campaign for the Homeless, march and rally, Saturday, 21 December 1991

Briefing, Stoke Newington, 20 December 1991

Observation of march and rally, Hackney, 21 December 1991

New Year's Eve, Trafalgar Square, 31 December 1991–1 January 1992

Strategy meeting, Cannon Row, 5 September 1991

Strategy meeting, Cannon Row, 30 October 1991

Briefing, New Scotland Yard, 19 December 1991

New Year's Eve, 31 December 1991

Debrief, Cannon Row, 8 January 1992

Pakistan People's Party, picket at Pakistan High Commission, Sunday, 5 January 1992
Meeting with organizer, Cannon Row, 2 January 1992

State visit of the President of Portugal (cancelled)
Strategy meeting, Cannon Row, 7 January 1992

Iraqi People in UK, march and rally, 11 January 1992
Briefing and observation of march and rally, 11 January 1992

Piccadilly Hunt Club, Ban Hunting with Hounds, protest ride (cancelled)
Impromptu meeting with DOE officials, Hyde Park, 13 January 1992
Meeting with organizer, DOE store yard, Hyde Park, 17 January 1992

National Union of Students (London Branch), protest against the Asylum Bill, march and rally, 18 January 1992
Meeting with organizer, New Scotland Yard, 8 January 1992
Meeting with DOE, DOE store yard, Hyde Park, 13 January 1992
Briefing, New Scotland Yard, 13 January 1992
March and rally, 18 January 1992

Campaign for British Withdrawal From Ireland, march and rally, 25 January 1992
Meeting with organizers, New Scotland Yard, 18 December 1991
Informal strategy meeting, New Scotland Yard, 18 December 1991
Briefing, Highgate, 21 January 1992
March and rally, 25 January 1992

The Movement for the Defence of the Rights of the Peruvian People march, 1

February 1992
Meeting with organizer, New Scotland Yard, 27 January 1992
Briefing and observation of march, 1 February 1992

OutRage! march to breach Sessional Area, 6 February 1992
Meeting with organizer, Cannon Row, 27 January 1992
Informal strategy meeting, Cannon Row, 28 January 1992
Briefing and observation of march, 6 February 1992

National Union of Students, march and rally, 12 February 1992
Strategy meeting, Cannon Row, 7 January 1992
Meeting with organizer of the NUS Asylum Bill march, New Scotland Yard, 8 January 1992
Meeting with organizers, New Scotland Yard, 9 January 1992
Meeting with DOE, Hyde Park, 13 January 1992
Strategy briefing, Cannon Row, 14 January 1992
Strategy briefing, Cannon Row, 4 February 1992
Meeting with organizers, New Scotland Yard, 7 February 1992
Briefing, New Scotland Yard, 11 February 1992
March and rally, 12 February 1992

OutRage! protest at military statues, Westminster, 20 February 1992
Meeting with organizers, Cannon Row, 11 February 1992

The Rolan Adams Family Campaign/Anti-British National Party, march and rally, 22 February 1992
Strategy meeting, Plumstead police station, 17 January 1992
Strategy meeting, Morris Drummond section house, 20 February 1992

Briefing, Morris Drummond section house, 20 February 1992

Observation of march and rally, 22 February 1992

Unemployed Workers' Charter, march and rally, 29 February 1992
Meeting with organizer, New Scotland Yard, 27 January 1992
Meeting with organizer, New Scotland Yard, 25 February, 1992
Briefing and observation of march and rally, 29 February 1992

OutRage! Wendy House "bonk-in", 5 March 1992
Meeting with organizers, Cannon Row, 21 February 1992
Briefing and observation of "bonk-in" and lobby of Parliament, 5 March 1992

Kurdistan Front, march and rally, 14 March 1992
Meeting with organizer, Cannon Row, 12 March 1992
Briefing and observation of march and rally, 14 March 1992

Tibet Support Group, march and rally, 14 March 1992
Meeting with organizers, Cannon Row, 11 March 1992
Rally and march, 14 March 1992

Southern Sudanese Refugee Association, march and picket, 18 March 1992
Meeting with organizer, Cannon Row, 12 March 1992
Meeting with organizer, New Scotland Yard, 17 March 1992
Briefing and observation of march and rally, 18 March 1992

International Wildlife Federation, rally and march, 21 March 1992
Meeting with organizer, Cannon Row, 6 January 1992
Briefing and observation of march and

rally, 21 March 1992

Kurdistan Solidarity Committee, march and rally, 21 March 1992
Meeting with organizer, Cannon Row, 17 March 1992
Briefing and observation of march and rally, 21 March 1992

Islington Staff Representative Council, Save the NHS, Whittington Hospital, Islington, march to Congress House, 25 March 1992
Meeting with organizers, New Scotland Yard, 10 March 1992
Observation of march, 25 March 1992

Committee to Protest at the Massacre in Turkish Kurdistan, march and rally, 28 March 1992
Meeting with organizer, Cannon Row, 27 March 1992
Briefing and observation of march and rally, 28 March 1992

Anti-Election Alliance, rally and march, 4 April 1992
Meeting with organizers, Cannon Row, 26 February 1992
Meeting with organizers, Cannon Row, 21 March 1992
Strategy meeting, Cannon Row, 26 March 1992
Briefing, New Scotland Yard, 3 April 1992
Observation of march and rally, 4 April 1992

BNP election meeting, York Hall, Bethnal Green, 6 April 1992
Strategy meeting, Leman Street police station, 3 April 1992
Observation of march and election meeting, York Hall, Bethnal Green, 6 April 1992

Islamic Union of Iraqi Students, march and rally, 11 April 1992

219

Meeting with organizer, Cannon Row, 27 March 1992

Meeting with organizer, New Scotland Yard, 8 April 1992

Briefing and observation of march and rally, 11 April 1992

London Marathon, 12 April 1992
Meeting with organizers, New Scotland Yard, 16 November 1991

Strategy meeting, Eltham police station, 12 December 1991

Strategy briefing, Cannon Row, 12 March 1992

Briefing for regular police serials, Hendon training centre, 7 April 1992

Observation of the marathon from Special Operations Room, 12 April 1992

Islamic Union of Iraqi Students, march and rally, 18 April 1992
Meeting with organizer, Cannon Row, 16 January 1992

Meeting with organizer, Cannon Row, 8 April 1992

Meeting with organizer, Cannon Row, 15 April 1992

Briefing and observation of march and rally, 18 April 1992

Armenians, march and rally, 26 April 1992
Meeting with organizer, New Scotland Yard, 5 February 1992

Christians in Pakistan, march and rally, 4 May 1992
Meeting with organizer, New Scotland Yard, 8 April 1992

State Opening of Parliament, 6 May 1992
Strategy meeting, Cannon Row, 14 April 1992

State Opening of Parliament, 6 May 1992

Debrief, Cannon Row, 14 May 1992

National Forum for All African Organizations in Europe, march and rally, 30 May 1992

Meeting with organizer, New Scotland Yard, 12 March 1992

Meeting with organizer, Cannon Row, 27 May 1992

March and rally, 30 May 1992

Trooping the Colour: HM the Queen's Birthday Parade, 13 June 1992
Strategy meeting, Cannon Row, 31 March 1992

Strategy briefing, Cannon Row, 14 May 1992

Briefing, New Scotland Yard, 27 May 1992

Trooping the Colour, 13 June 1992

UK Sikhs Co-ordination Committee, rally and march, 14 June 1992
Meeting with organizer, New Scotland Yard, 18 May 1992

Strategy meeting, Cannon Row, 1 June 1992

Briefing, New Scotland Yard, 5 June 1992

Observation of rally and march, 14 June 1992

Muslim Iranian Students, march and rally, 20 June 1992
Meeting with organizer, New Scotland Yard, 4 June 1992

March and rally, 20 June 1992

International Civil Servants, march and picket (cancelled by organizer)
Meeting with organizers, New Scotland Yard, 18 June 1992

"Gay Pride", march and festival, 26 June 1992
Meeting with organizer, New Scotland Yard, 4 February 1992

Meeting with organizer, New Scotland Yard, 8 May 1992

Strategy meeting, New Scotland Yard, 15 May 1992

Meeting with organizer, New Scotland Yard, 5 June 1992

Meeting with organizer, New Scotland

Yard, 22 June 1992

Briefing, New Scotland Yard, 22 June 1992

Observation of march, 26 June 1992

National Music Day Parade, 28 June 1992

Meeting, DOE store yard, Hyde Park, 17 January 1992

International Federation of Tamils, march and rally, 25 July 1992

Meeting with organizers, Cannon Row, 22 July 1992

OutRage!, march and rally, 25 July 1992

Meeting with organizer, Cannon Row, 27 May 1992

Meeting with organizer, Cannon Row, 22 July 1992

Briefing, observation of march, and debrief, 25 July 1992

Reclaim the Streets, march and rally, 1 August 1992

Informal strategy meeting, Cannon Row, 26 July 1992

Informal strategy meeting, Cannon Row, 30 July 1992

Briefing and observation of march and rally, 1 August 1992

Reach Out and Touch, Brent HIV Centre, 23 August 1992

Meeting with organizer, New Scotland Yard, 4 June 1992

March and rally, 23 August 1992

BNP by-election meeting, York Hall, Bethnal Green, 24 August 1992

Observation of briefing, meeting and counter-demonstration, 24 August 1992.

Iraqi Muslims, march, 11 September 1992

Meeting with organizer, Cannon Row, 7 September 1992

Whose Earth? rally at Hyde Park, 15 September 1992

Meeting with organizer, Cannon Row, 17 March 1992

NUM march and rally in Hyde Park and rally in Central Hall and lobby of Parliament, 21 October 1992

Meeting with organizer, New Scotland Yard, 16 October 1992

Informal strategy meeting, New Scotland Yard, evening, 16 October 1992

Meeting with organizer, New Scotland Yard, 17 October 1992

Informal observations, New Scotland Yard, 19 October 1992

Strategy meeting, Cannon Row, 19 October 1992

Briefing, New Scotland Yard, 20 October 1992

March and rally, 21 October 1992

Debrief, New Scotland Yard, 21 October 1992

BNP AGM, 24 October 1992

Briefing, New Scotland Yard, 23 October 1992

Events on 24 October 1992

Society for the Protection of the Unborn Child, protest "chain", 24 October 1992

Strategy meeting, New Scotland Yard, 9 September 1992

Trades Union Congress, march and rally, 25 October 1992

Meeting with organizers, New Scotland Yard, 19 October 1992

Strategy meeting, New Scotland Yard, 22 October 1992

Briefing, New Scotland Yard, 23 October 1992

March and rally, 25 October 1992

Debrief, New Scotland Yard, 25 October 1992

Dr Ambedkar Memorial Committee, rally and march, 25 October 1992

Meeting with organizers, New Scotland Yard, 19 October 1992

Lesbian and Gay Coalition, march and rally, 31 October 1992
Meeting with organizers, New Scotland Yard, 12 June 1992
Strategy briefing, Cannon Row, 1 October 1992
Meeting with organizers, New Scotland Yard, 12 October 1992

Roghit Duggal Family Campaign, march and rally, 7 November 1992
Strategy meeting, Greenwich police station, 16 October 1992
Meeting with organizer, Greenwich police station, 29 October 1992
Strategy briefing, Maurice Drummond section house, 5 November 1992
Briefing, Maurice Drummond section house, 5 November 1992
March and rally, 7 November 1992

Remembrance Sunday, National Front march, 8 November 1992
Meeting with organizer, New Scotland Yard, 6 September 1992
Strategy meeting, Cannon Row, 19 October 1992
National Front march, 8 November 1992

National Union of Students (London Branch), march and rally, 10 November 1992
Meeting with organizer, New Scotland Yard, 18 August 1992
Meeting with organizers, New Scotland Yard, 3 November 1992

Ad Hoc Committee for Asylum Rights, 21 November 1992
Meeting with organizer, Cannon Row, 8 September 1992
Ad hoc strategy meeting, Cannon Row, 8 September 1992
Meeting with organizer, Cannon Row, 18 November 1992

Meeting with organizer, Cannon Row, 19 November 1992
Strategy meeting, New Scotland Yard, 20 November 1992
Briefing, New Scotland Yard, 20 November 1992
March and rally, 21 November 1992

Women Against Violence Against Women, march and rally, 28 November 1992
Meeting with organizer, Cannon Row, 26 November 1992
March and rally, 28 November 1992

Students of the College of Nursing and Midwifery, and St Bartholomew's Hospital, protest against proposed closure, march, 1 December 1992
Meeting with organizer, Cannon Row, 24 November 1992

New Year's Eve, 31 December 1992
Preliminary meeting, Cannon Row, 3 August 1992
Meeting with Westminster City Council, Department of National Heritage and other government department officials, Cannon Row, 12 August 1992
Strategy meeting, Cannon Row, 11 September 1992
Strategy meeting, Cannon Row, 29 September 1992
Meeting of support services, Cannon Row, 5 October 1992
Meeting with outside agencies, Cannon Row, 5 October 1992
Meeting with Westminster City Council and Department of National Heritage officials, Cannon Row, 10 November 1992
Strategy meeting, Cannon Row, 25 November 1992
Briefing, New Scotland Yard, 17 December 1992
Observations, Trafalgar Square, 31 December 1992/1 January 1993

222

References

Ackroyd, C., J. Rosenhead, T. Shallice 1977. *The technology of political control*. Harmondsworth, Middx: Penguin.

Atkinson, P. 1990. *The ethnographic imagination*. London: Routledge.

Benyon, J. 1984. The riots: perceptions and distortions. In *Scarman and after*, J. Benyon (ed.), 37–45. London: Pergamon.

Benyon, J. 1987. Interpretations of civil disorder. In *The roots of urban unrest*, J. Benyon & J. Solomos (eds), 23–41. Oxford: Pergamon.

Berk, R. A. 1972. The controversy surrounding analyses of collective violence: some methodological notes. See Short & Wolfgang (1972), 112–18.

Berkowitz, L. 1973. Studies of the contagion of violence. See Hirsch & Perry (1973), 41–51.

Bittner, E. 1951. Social movements. In *New outline of the principles of sociology*, A. M. Lee (ed.), 199–220. New York: Barnes & Noble.

Bittner, E. 1963. Radicalism and the organization of radical movements. *American Sociological Review* 28, 928–40.

Bittner, E. 1970. *The functions of the police in a modern society*. Washington, DC: US Government Printing Office.

Bittner, E. 1974. A theory of the police. In *Potential for reform of criminal justice*, H. Jacob (ed.), 17–44. Beverly Hills, Calif.: Sage.

Blain, M. 1989. Power and practice in peace movement discourse. See Kriesberg (1989), 197–218.

Blake, N. 1985. Picketing, justice and the law. See Fine & Millar (1985), 103–19.

Bréchon, P. & S. K. Mitra 1992. The National Front in France: the emergence of an extreme right protest movement. *Comparative Politics* 25, 63–82.

Brewer, J. D. 1990. *Inside the RUC*. Oxford: Clarendon.

Brewer, J. D., A. Guelke, I. Hume, E. Moxon-Browne, R. Wilford 1988. *The police, public order and the state*. London: Macmillan.

Brinton, C. 1965. *The anatomy of revolution*, rev. & exp. edn. New York: Vintage.

Brittan, P. 1987. Fighting fascism in Britain: the rôle of the Anti-Nazi League. *Social Alternatives* 6(4), 42–6.

REFERENCES

Brodeur, J. P. 1983. High policing and low policing: remarks about the policing of political activities. *Social Problems* 30(5), 507-20.

Brogden, M. 1983. *Autonomy and consent*. London: Academic.

Brogden, M. & C. Shearing 1993. *Policing for a new South Africa*. London: Routledge.

B.S.S.R.S. (British Society for Social Responsibility in Science) 1985. *Technocop*. London: Free Association.

Bunyan, T. 1976. *The political police in Britain*. London: Quartet.

Byrne, P. 1991. CND: the second phase. See Klandermans (1991b), 67-90.

Cain, M. 1973. *Society and the policeman's rôle*. London: Routledge & Kegan Paul.

Campbell, B. 1993. *Goliath: Britain's dangerous places*. London: Methuen.

Carter, V. 1992. Abseil makes the heart grow fonder: lesbian and gay campaigning tactics and Section 28. In *Modern homosexualities*, K. Plummer (ed.), 217-26. London: Routledge.

Cashmore, E. & E. McLaughlin (eds) 1991. *Out of order*. London: Routledge.

Chatterton, M. R. 1979. The supervision of patrol work under the fixed points system. In *The British police*, S. Holdaway (ed.), 83-101. London: Edward Arnold.

Chatterton, M. R. 1983. Police work and assault charges. In *Control in the police organization*, M. Punch (ed.), 194-221. Cambridge, Mass.: MIT Press.

Chibnall, S. 1977. *Law and order news*. London: Tavistock.

Chibnall, S. 1979. The Metropolitan Police and the news media. In *The British police*, S. Holdaway (ed.), 135-49. London: Edward Arnold.

Christian, L. 1985. Restriction without conviction. The rôle of the courts in legitimising police control in Nottinghamshire. See Fine & Millar (1985), 120-36.

Clutterbuck, R. 1973. *Protest and the urban guerrilla*. London: Cassell.

Cohen, A. 1980. Drama and politics in the development of a London carnival. *Man* 15, 65-87.

Cohen, A. 1982. A polyethnic London carnival as a contested cultural performance. *Ethnic and Racial Studies* 5, 23-41.

Cousin, G., T. Jones, R. Millar 1985. Conclusion: the politics of policing. See Fine & Millar (1985), 227-36.

Cowell, D., T. Jones, J. Young (eds) 1982. *Policing the riots*. London: Junction Books.

Critchley, T. 1970. *The conquest of violence*. London: Constable.

Cunningham, H. 1977. The Metropolitan fairs: a case study in the social control of leisure. In *Social control in nineteenth century Britain*, A. P. Donajgrodzki (ed.), 163-84. London: Croom Helm.

Currie, E. & J. H. Skolnick 1972. A critical note on conceptions of collective behaviour. See Short & Wolfgang (1972), 61-71.

Davies, J. C. 1962. Toward a theory of revolution. *American Sociological Review* 27, 5-18.

Davies, J. C. 1969. The J-curve of rising and declining satisfactions as a cause of some great revolutions and a contained rebellion. In *Violence in America. Vol. II. A report to the National Commission on the Causes and Prevention of Violence*, H. Davis Graham & T. R. Gurr (eds), 671-709. Washington, DC: US Government Printing Office.

Dear, G. J. 1986. *Report of the Chief Constable West Midlands Police, Handsworth/ Lozells - September 1985*. West Midlands: West Midlands Police.

Dixon, D. 1992. Legal regulation and policing practice. *Social and Legal Studies* 1, 515-41.

REFERENCES

Driscoll, J. 1987. Protest and public order: the Public Order Act 1986. *Journal of Social Welfare Law* (September), 280–99.

Driver, C. 1964. *The disarmers*. London: Hodder & Stoughton.

Dummett, M. 1980a. *Southall 23 April 1979*. London: National Council for Civil Liberties.

Dummett, M. 1980b. *The death of Blair Peach*. London: National Council for Civil Liberties.

East, R. & P. Thomas 1985. Road blocks: the experience in Wales. See Fine & Millar (1985), 137–44.

Edgar, D. 1988. Festivals of the oppressed. *Race and Class* 29(4), 61–76.

Eisinger, P. K. 1973. The conditions of protest behavior in American cities. *American Political Science Review* 67, 11–28.

Ekblom, P. & K. Heal 1982. *Police response to calls from the public*. RPU paper 9. London: Home Office.

Ericson, R. V. 1982. *Reproducing order*. Toronto: University of Toronto Press.

Ericson, R. V., P. M. Baranek, J. B. L. Chan 1987. *Visualizing deviance*. Milton Keynes: Open University.

Ericson, R. V., P. M. Baranek, J. B. L. Chan 1989. *Negotiating control*. Milton Keynes: Open University.

Ericson, R. V., P. M. Baranek, J. B. L. Chan 1991. *Representing order*. Milton Keynes: Open University.

Ewing, K. D. & C. A. Gearty 1990. *Freedom under Thatcher*. Oxford: Clarendon.

Feierabend, I. K. & R. L. Feierabend 1966. Systemic conditions of political aggression: an application of frustration–aggression theory. *Journal of Conflict Resolution* 10, 249–71.

Feierabend, I. K. & R. L. Feierabend 1969. Social change and political violence: cross-national patterns. In *Violence in America. Vol II. A report to the National Commission on the Causes and Prevention of Violence*, H. Davis Graham & T. R. Gurr (eds), 498–509. Washington, DC: US Government Printing Office.

Feierabend, I. K. & R. L. Feierabend 1973. Violent consequences of violence. See Hirsch & Perry (1973), 187–219.

Fielding, N. G. 1984. Police socialization and police competence. *British Journal of Sociology* 35(4), 568–90.

Fielding, N. G. 1991. *The police and social conflict*. London: Athlone.

Fine, B. & R. Millar (eds) 1985. *Policing the miners' strike*. London: Lawrence & Wishart.

Finer, S. E. 1966. *Anonymous empire*. London: Pall Mall.

Fisk, T. 1970. The nature and causes of student unrest. In *Protest and discontent*, B. Crick & W. A. Robson (eds), 78–85. Harmondsworth, Middx: Penguin.

Flanders, D. 1991. Poll tax demonstration, 20 October 1990. A review of policing arrangements. Unpublished paper, Metropolitan Police, London.

Fogelson, R. M. 1970. Violence and grievances: reflections on the 1960s riots. *Journal of Social Issues* 26, 141–63.

Fogelson, R. M. 1971. *Violence as protest*. Garden City, NY: Doubleday.

Frey, R. S., T. Dietz, L. Kalof 1992. Characteristics of successful American protest groups: another look at Gamson's *Strategy of Social Protest*. *American Journal of Sociology* 98, 368–87.

REFERENCES

Gamson, J. 1989. Silence, death and the invisible enemy: AIDS activism and social movement "newness". *Social Problems* **36**, 351–67.

Gamson, W. A. 1975. *The strategy of social protest*. Homewood, Ill.: Dorsey.

Garfield, S. 1991. The age of consent. *The Independent Magazine* (10 November), 2–6.

Geary, R. 1985. *Policing industrial disputes: 1893 to 1985*. Cambridge: Cambridge University Press.

Gerhards, J. & D. Rucht 1992. Mesomobilization: organizing and framing in two protest campaigns in West Germany. *American Journal of Sociology* **98**, 555–95.

Giddens, A. 1979. *Central problems in social theory*. London: Macmillan.

Goldstein, J. 1960. Police discretion not to invoke the criminal process. Low visibility decisions in the administration of justice. *Yale Law Journal* **69**, 543–94.

Gordon, P. 1985. "If they come in the morning ..." The police, the miners and black people. See Fine & Millar (1985), 161–76.

Greater London Council 1985. *Public order plans – the threat to democratic rights*. London: Greater London Council.

Greater London Council 1986. *The control of protest*. London: Greater London Council.

Gurr, T. R. 1968a. Urban disorder: perspectives from the comparative study of civil strife. In *Civil violence in the urban community*, L. H. Masotti & D. R. Bowen (eds), 51–67. Beverly Hills, Calif.: Sage.

Gurr, T. R. 1968b. Psychological factors in civil violence. *World Politics* **20**, 245–78.

Gurr, T. R. 1968c. A causal model of civil strife: a comparative analysis using new indices. *American Political Science Review* **62**, 1104–24.

Gurr, T. R. 1969. A comparative study of civil strife. In *Violence in America. Vol. II. A report to the National Commission on the Causes and Prevention of Violence*, H. Davis Graham & T. R. Gurr (eds), 544–99. Washington, DC: US Government Printing Office.

Gurr, T. R. 1970. *Why men rebel*. Princeton, NJ: Princeton University Press.

Gurr, T. R. 1979. Political protest and rebellion in the 1960s. In *Violence in America*, rev. edn, H. Davis Graham & T. R. Gurr (eds), 49–76. Beverly Hills, Calif.: Sage.

Gutzmore, C. 1982. The Notting Hill Carnival. *Marxism Today* (August), 31–3.

Hahn, H. & J. R. Feagin 1973. Perspectives on collective violence: a critical review. See Hirsch & Perry (1973), 125–55.

Hall, S. 1979. *Drifting into a law and order society*. London: Cobden Trust.

Hall, S., C. Chricher, T. Jefferson, J. Clarke, B. Roberts 1978. *Policing the crisis*. London: Macmillan.

Halloran, J. D., P. Elliott, G. Murdock 1970. *Demonstrations and communication: a case study*. Harmondsworth, Middx: Penguin.

Hanley, D. & P. Kerr (eds) 1989. *May '68: coming of age*. London: Macmillan.

Heirich, M. 1976. The spiral of conflict: Berkeley 1964. In *Readings in collective behavior*, R. Evans (ed.), 241–75. Chicago: Rand McNally.

Henriques, K. A. 1991. A case study and analysis of a nonviolent direct action campaign and coalition building. In *Research in social movements, conflict and change*, vol. 13 L. Kriesberg & M. Spencer (eds), 77–89. Greenwich, Conn.: JAI.

Hewitt, P. 1982. *The abuse of power: civil liberties in the UK*. Oxford: Robertson.

Heymann, P. 1992. *Towards peaceful protest in South Africa*. Pretoria: Human Sciences Research Council.

Hillyard, P. & J. Percy-Smith 1988. *The coercive state*. London: Fontana.

REFERENCES

Hirsch, H. & D. C. Perry (eds) 1973. *Violence as politics*. New York: Harper & Row.

Holdaway, S. 1983. *Inside the British police*. Oxford: Blackwell.

Home Affairs Committee 1980. *Fifth report: the law relating to public order*, HC 756. London: HMSO.

Home Affairs Committee 1985. *Fourth report: Special Branch*, HC 71. London: HMSO.

Home Office 1980. *Review of the Public Order Act 1936 and related legislation*, Cmnd 7891. London: HMSO.

Home Office/Scottish Office 1985. *Review of public order law*, Cmnd 9510. London: HMSO.

Home Office 1987. Circular No. 11/1987, Public Order Act 1986. London: Home Office.

Hutter, B. M. 1988. *The reasonable arm of the law*. Oxford: Clarendon Press.

Independent Inquiry Panel 1985. *Inquiry into Leon Brittan's visit to Manchester University Students' Union, 1 March 1985*. Manchester: Manchester City Council.

Jackson, B. (with T. Wardle) 1986. *The battle for Orgreave*. Brighton, Sussex: Vanson, Wardle.

Jefferson, T. 1987. Beyond paramilitarism. *British Journal of Criminology* 27(1), 47–53.

Jefferson, T. 1990. *The case against paramilitary policing*. Milton Keynes: Open University.

Jefferson, T. 1993. Pondering paramilitarism. *British Journal of Criminology* 33(3), 374–81.

Jeffery, A. J. 1991. *Riot policing in perspective*. Johannesburg: South African Institute of Race Relations.

Jenkins, J. C. & C. Perrow 1977. Insurgency of the powerless: farm worker movements (1946–1972). *American Sociological Review* 42, 249–68.

Johnson, L. 1992. *The rebirth of private policing*. London: Routledge.

Joshua, H. & T. Wallace (with the assistance of H. Booth) 1983. *To ride the storm*. London: Heinemann.

Jupp, J. 1970. The discontents of youth. In *Protest and discontent*, B. Crick & W. A. Robson (eds), 68–77. Harmondsworth, Middx: Penguin.

Kahn, P., N. Lewis, R. Livock, P. Wiles (with the assistance of J. Mesher) 1983. *Picketing: industrial disputes, tactics and the law*. London: Routledge & Kegan Paul.

Keith, M. 1993. *Race, riots and policing*. London: UCL Press.

Kemp, C. & R. Morgan 1990. *Lay visitors to police stations*. Bristol: Bristol Centre for Criminal Justice.

Kerner, O. 1968. *The report of the National Advisory Commission on Civil Disorders*. Washington, DC: US Government Printing Office.

Kettle, M. 1985. The National Reporting Centre and the 1984 miners' strike. See Fine & Millar (1985), 23–33.

Kettle, M. & L. Hodges 1982. *Uprising*. London: Pan.

Killian, L. M. 1984. Organization, rationality and spontaneity in the civil rights movement. *American Sociological Review* 49, 770–83.

Kitschelt, H. P. 1986. Political opportunity structures and political protest: anti-nuclear movements in four democracies. *British Journal of Political Science* 16, 57–85.

Klandermans, B. 1991a. The peace movement and social movement theory. See Klandermans (1991b), 1–39.

Klandermans, B. (ed.) 1991b. *International social movement research*, vol. 3. Green-

REFERENCES

wich, Conn.: JAI.

Kriesberg, L. (ed.) 1989. *Research in social movements, conflicts and change*, vol. 11. Greenwich, Conn.: JAI.

Lange, J. I. 1990. Refusal to compromise: the case of Earth First!. *Journal of Speech Communication* **54**, 473–94.

Law Commission 1982. *Offences against public order*, Working Paper No. 82. London: HMSO.

Law Commission 1983. *Offences relating to public order*, Law Com. No. 123. London: HMSO.

LeBon, G. 1896. *The crowd*. English translation, New York: Viking, 1960.

Leonard, T. 1985. Policing the miners. *Policing* **1**(2), 96–101.

Leopold, P. M. 1977. Incitement to hatred – the history of a controversial criminal offence. *Public Law* (Winter), 389–405.

Lewis, G. K. 1970. Protest among the immigrants. In *Protest and discontent*, B. Crick & W. A. Robson (eds), 86–97. Harmondsworth, Middx: Penguin.

Lewis, J. M. 1972. A study of the Kent State incident using Smelser's Theory of Collective Behaviour. *Sociological Inquiry* **42**, 87–96.

Lipsky, M. 1968. Protest as a political resource. *American Political Science Review* **62**, 1144–58.

Lipsky, M. 1970. *Protest in city politics*. Chicago: Rand McNally.

Lipsky, M. & D. J. Olson 1973. Civil disorders and the American political process: the meaning of recent urban riots. See Hirsch & Perry (1973), 161–86.

Lofland, J. 1985. *Protest*. New Brunswick, NJ: Transaction.

Loveday, B. 1984. The rôle of the police committee. *Local Government Studies* **10**(1), 39–52.

Lukes, S. 1972. *Power: a radical view*. London: Macmillan.

Lustgarten, L. 1986. *The governance of police*. London: Sweet & Maxwell.

McAdam, D. 1982. *Political process and the development of black insurgency*. Chicago: University of Chicago Press.

McCabe, S. & P. Wallington (with J. Alderson, L. Gostin, C. Mason) 1988. *The police, public order and civil liberties: legacies of the miners' strike*. London: Routledge.

McCarthy, J. D. & M. N. Zald 1977. Resource mobilization and social movements: a partial theory. *American Journal of Sociology* **82**, 1212–41.

McCarthy, J. D., D. W. Britt, M. Wolfson 1991. The institutional channelling of social movements by the state in the United States. In *Research in social movements, conflicts and change*, vol. 13 L. Kriesberg & M. Spencer (eds), 45–76. Greenwich, Conn.: JAI.

McCone, J. A. 1965. *Violence in the city – an end or a beginning? A report by the Governor's Commission on the Los Angeles riots*. Los Angeles, Calif.: Governor's Commission on the Los Angeles Riots.

MacDougall, J. 1991. The freeze movement, Congress, and the M–X missile: processes of citizen influence. See Klandermans (1991b), 263–82.

McEvoy, J. 1971. *Radicals or conservatives: the contemporary American right*. Chicago: Rand McNally.

McIlroy, J. 1985. "The law struck dumb"? – Labour law and the miners' strike. See Fine & Millar (1985), 79–102.

McPhail, C. 1971. Civil disorder participation: a critical examination of recent research. *American Sociological Review* **36**, 1058–73.

REFERENCES

McPhail, C. 1991. *The myth of the madding crowd*. Hawthorne, NY: Aldine de Gruyter.

McPhail, C. & D. Miller 1973. The assembling process: a theoretical and empirical examination. *American Sociological Review* 38, 721–35.

Manning, P. K. 1977. *Police work*. Cambridge, Mass.: MIT Press.

Manning, P. K. 1988. *Symbolic communication: signifying calls and the police response*. Cambridge, Mass.: MIT Press.

Manwaring-White, S. 1983. *The policing revolution*. Brighton, Sussex: Harvester.

Marullo, S. 1991. US grass-roots opposition to the Euromissile deployment. See Klandermans (1991b), 283–310.

Marx, G. T. 1972. Issueless riots. See Short & Wolfgang (1972), 47–59.

Marx, G. T. 1974. Thoughts on a neglected category of social movement participant: the agent provocateur and the informant. *American Journal of Sociology* 80(1), 402–42.

Mattausch, J. 1991. CND: The first phase, 1958 to 1967. See Klandermans (1991b), 43–66.

Metcalfe, J. 1991. Public order debriefing: Trafalgar Square riot. Unpublished paper, Metropolitan Police, London.

Meyer, D. S. & R. Kleidman 1991. The nuclear freeze movement in the United States. See Klandermans (1991b), 1–39.

Morgan, J. 1987. *Conflict and order: the police and labour disputes in England and Wales 1900–1939*. Oxford: Clarendon.

Morgan, R. 1987. Police accountability: developing the local infrastructure. *British Journal of Criminology* 33(3), 87–96.

Morgan, R. 1989. "Policing by consent": legitimating the doctrine. In *Coming to terms with policing*, R. Morgan & D. J. Smith (eds), 217–34. London: Routledge.

Morgan, R. & C. Maggs 1984. *Following Scarman*. Bath: Centre for the Analysis of Social Policy.

Morgan, R. & C. Maggs 1985a. *Setting the P.A.C.E.* Bath: Centre for the Analysis of Social Policy.

Morgan, R. & C. Maggs 1985b. Consultative group. *Policing* 1(2), 87–95.

National Council for Civil Liberties 1986. *Stonehenge: a report into the civil liberties implications of the events relating to the convoys of summer 1985 and 1986*. London: National Council for Civil Liberties.

Northam, G. 1988. *Shooting in the dark*. London: Faber & Faber.

Oberschall, A. 1989. The 1960 sit-ins: protest diffusion and movement take-off. See Kriesberg (1989), 31–53.

Parkin, F. 1968. *Middle class radicalism*. Manchester: Manchester University Press.

Pettigrew, T. F. 1979. The ultimate attribution error: extending Allport's cognitive analysis of prejudice. *Personality & Social Psychology Bulletin* 5(4), 461–76.

Pinard, M. & R. Hamilton 1989. Intellectuals and the leadership of social movements. See Kriesberg (1989), 73–107. Greenwich, Conn.: JAI.

Piven, F. F. & R. A. Cloward 1977. *Poor people's movements*. New York: Random House.

Policy Studies Institute 1983. *Police and people in London: vol. 4. The police in action*. London: Policy Studies Institute.

Polsby, N. W. 1960. Toward an explanation of McCarthyism. *Political Studies* 8, 250–71.

Pryce, E. A. 1985. The Notting Hill Carnival – black politics, resistance, and leadership

REFERENCES

1976–1978. *Caribbean Quarterly* **31**(2), 35–52.

Punch, M. 1979. *Policing the inner city*. London: Macmillan.

Punch, M. 1985. *Conduct unbecoming: the social construction of police deviance and control*. London: Tavistock.

Rabel, R. G. 1992. The Vietnam antiwar movement in New Zealand. *Peace and Change* **17**, 3–33.

Reiner, R. 1985. *The politics of the police*. Brighton: Harvester.

Reiner, R. 1990. *Chief constables*. Oxford: Oxford University Press.

Reuss-Ianni, E. & F. A. Ianni 1983. Street cops and management cops: the two cultures of policing. In *Control in police organizations*, M. Punch (ed.), 251–74. Cambridge, Mass.: MIT Press.

Robertson, G. 1989. *Freedom, the individual and the law*. London: Penguin.

Rogin, M. P. 1967. *The intellectuals and McCarthy: the radical specter*. Cambridge, Mass.: MIT.

Sanders, A., L. Bridges, A. Mulvaney, G. Crozier 1989. *Advice and assistance at police stations and the 24 hour duty solicitor scheme. A report to the Lord Chancellor*. London: Lord Chancellor's Department.

Scarman, Rt Hon. The Lord 1975. *The Red Lion Square disorders of 15 June 1974*. Cmnd. 5915, London: HMSO.

Scarman, Rt Hon. The Lord 1981. *The Brixton disorders 10–12 April 1981: report of an inquiry by the Rt. Hon. The Lord Scarman, O.B.E.* Cmnd 8427, London: HMSO.

Scraton, P. 1985. From Saltley gates to Orgreave: a history of the policing of recent industrial disputes. See Fine & Millar (1985), 145–60.

Scraton, P. (ed.) 1987a. *Law, order and the authoritarian state*. Milton Keynes, England: Open University.

Scraton, P. 1987b. Unreasonable force: policing, punishment and marginalization. In *Law, order and the authoritarian state*, P. Scraton (ed.), 145–89. Milton Keynes, England: Open University.

Sherman, D. & M. Wallace 1991. Why do strikes turn violent? *American Journal of Sociology* **96**, 1117–50.

Shipman, M. 1988. *The limitations of social research* 3rd edn. London: Longman.

Short, B. 1991. Earth First! and the rhetoric of moral confrontation. *Communication Studies* **42**, 172–88.

Short, J. F. & M. E. Wolfgang (eds) 1972. *Collective violence*. Chicago: Aldine-Atherton.

Silverman, J. 1986. *Independent inquiry into the Handsworth disturbances, September 1985*. Birmingham: City of Birmingham District Council.

Skolnick, J. H. 1966. *Justice without trial*. New York: Wiley.

Skolnick, J. H. 1969. *The politics of protest: a task force report to the National Commission on the Causes and Prevention of Violence*. New York: Simon & Schuster.

Smelser, N. J. 1962. *Theory of collective behaviour*. London: Routledge.

Smelser, N. J. 1972. Two critics in search of a bias: a response to Currie and Skolnick. See Short & Wolfgang (1972), 73–81.

Smith, A. T. H. 1987a. *Offences against public order*. London: Sweet & Maxwell.

Smith, A. T. H. 1987b. Free speech, public order and the law. Unpublished inaugural lecture, University of Reading.

Smith, R. B. 1972. Campus protests and the Vietnam War. See Short & Wolfgang

REFERENCES

(1972), 250–77.

Snyder, D. & C. Tilly 1972. Hardship and collective violence in France, 1830 to 1960. *American Sociological Review* 37, 520–32.

Spiegel, J. P. 1972. Cultural value orientations and student protest. See Short & Wolfgang (1972), 236–49.

Staunton, M. 1985. *Free to walk together*. London: National Council for Civil Liberties.

Stephens, M. 1988. *Policing: the critical issues*. Hemel Hempstead: Harvester Wheatsheaf.

Strauss, A. 1966. Coaching. In *Role theory*, B. Biddle & E. Thomas (eds), 350–53. New York: Wiley.

Sykes, R. E. & E. E. Brent 1983. *Policing: a social behaviorist perspective*. New Brunswick, NJ: Rutgers University Press.

Taft, P. & P. Ross 1979. American labor violence: its causes, character, and outcome. In *Violence in America*, rev. edn. H. Davis Graham & T. R. Gurr (eds), 187–241. Beverly Hills, Calif.: Sage.

Tarrow, S. 1989. *Democracy and disorder*. Oxford: Clarendon.

Tarrow, S. 1993. Social protest and policy reform: May 1968 and the *Loi d'Orientation* in France. *Comparative Political Studies* 25, 579–607.

Tatchell, P. 1990. Time for civil disobedience. *Rouge* (Autumn), 24–5.

Tatchell, P. 1992a. Equal rights for all: strategies for lesbian and gay equality in Britain. In *Modern homosexualities*, K. Plummer (ed.), 237–47. London: Routledge.

Tatchell, P. 1992b. Outrageous campaigners show size isn't everything. *Socialist* (May), 2.

Tatchell, P. 1994. Making waves for freedom. *Gay and Lesbian Humanist* (Spring), in press.

Taylor, Rt Hon. Lord Justice, 1989. *The Hillsborough stadium disaster, 15 April 1989: Interim Report*, Cm. 765. London: HMSO.

Thomas, J. E. 1972. *The English prison officer since 1850*. London: Routledge & Kegan Paul.

Thornton, P. 1985. *We protest*. London: National Council for Civil Liberties.

Tilly, C. 1973. The chaos of the living city. See Hirsch & Perry (1973), 98–124.

Trow, M. 1970. Small businessmen, political tolerance, and support for McCarthy. In *Protest, reform, and revolt*, J. R. Gusfield (ed.), 403–18. New York: Wiley.

Turner, R. H. 1969. The public perception of protest. *American Sociological Review* 34, 815–31.

Turner, R. H. & L. Killian 1972. *Collective behavior*, 2nd edn. Englewood Cliffs, NJ: Prentice-Hall.

Uglow, S. 1988. *Policing liberal society*. Oxford: Oxford University Press.

Van Maanen, J. 1978. The asshole. In *Policing: a view from the street*, P. K. Manning & J. Van Maanen (eds), 221–38. New York: Random House.

Voirst, M. 1979. *Fire in the streets*. New York: Simon & Schuster.

Waddington, D. 1992. *Contemporary issues in public disorder*. London: Routledge.

Waddington, D., K. Jones, C. Critcher 1987. Flashpoints of public disorder. In *The crowd in contemporary Britain*, G. Gaskell & R. Benewick (eds), 155–99. London: Sage.

Waddington, D., K. Jones, C. Critcher 1989. *Flashpoints: studies in public disorder*. London: Routledge.

REFERENCES

Waddington, D., M. Wykes, C. Critcher (with S. Hebron) 1991. *Split at the seams*. Milton Keynes, England: Open University.

Waddington, P. A. J. 1991. *The strong arm of the law*. Oxford: Clarendon.

Waddington, P. A. J. 1992. Problems of ethnography: the case of the police. *Reviewing Sociology* 8(2), 26–32.

Waddington, P. A. J. 1993a. *Calling the police*. Aldershot: Avebury.

Waddington, P. A. J. 1993b. "The case against paramilitary policing" considered. *British Journal of Criminology* 33(3), 353–73.

Waddington, P. A. J. 1994. Coercion and accommodation: policing public order after the Public Order Act. *British Journal of Sociology* 45(3), 367–85.

Walker, D. 1968. *Rights in conflict: the violent confrontation of demonstrators and police during the week of the Democratic National Convention*. New York: Bantam.

Wallington, P. T. 1976. Injunctions and the "right to demonstrate". *Cambridge Law Journal* 35(1), 82–111.

Wallington, P. T. (ed.) 1984. *Civil liberties 1984*. Oxford: Martin Robertson/Cobden Trust.

Watney, S. 1990. Practices of freedom: "citizenship" and the politics of identity in the age of aids. In *Identity: community, culture, difference*, J. Rutherford (ed.), 157–87. London: Lawrence & Wishart.

Weinberger, B. 1991. *Keeping the peace? Policing strikes in Britain, 1906–1926*. Oxford: Berg.

Wiles, P. 1985. The policing of industrial disputes. In *Industrial relations and the law in the 1980s*, P. Fosh & C. R. Littler (eds), 151–75. Farnborough: Gower.

Wilson, J. Q. 1968. Dilemmas of police administration. *Public Administration Review* 29, 407–17.

Wright, P. 1985. *Policing the coal industry dispute in South Yorkshire*. Sheffield: South Yorkshire Police.

Zimbardo, P. G. 1970. The human choice: individuation, reason, and order versus deindividuation, impulse and chaos. In *Nebraska Symposium on Motivation, vol. 17*, W. J. Arnold & D. Levine (eds), 237–307. Lincoln, Nebraska: University of Nebraska.

Table of cases

Index

INDEX

For Product Safety Concerns and Information please contact our EU
representative GPSR@taylorandfrancis.com
Taylor & Francis Verlag GmbH, Kaufingerstraße 24, 80331 München, Germany